JOURNEY THROUGH THE WETLANDS

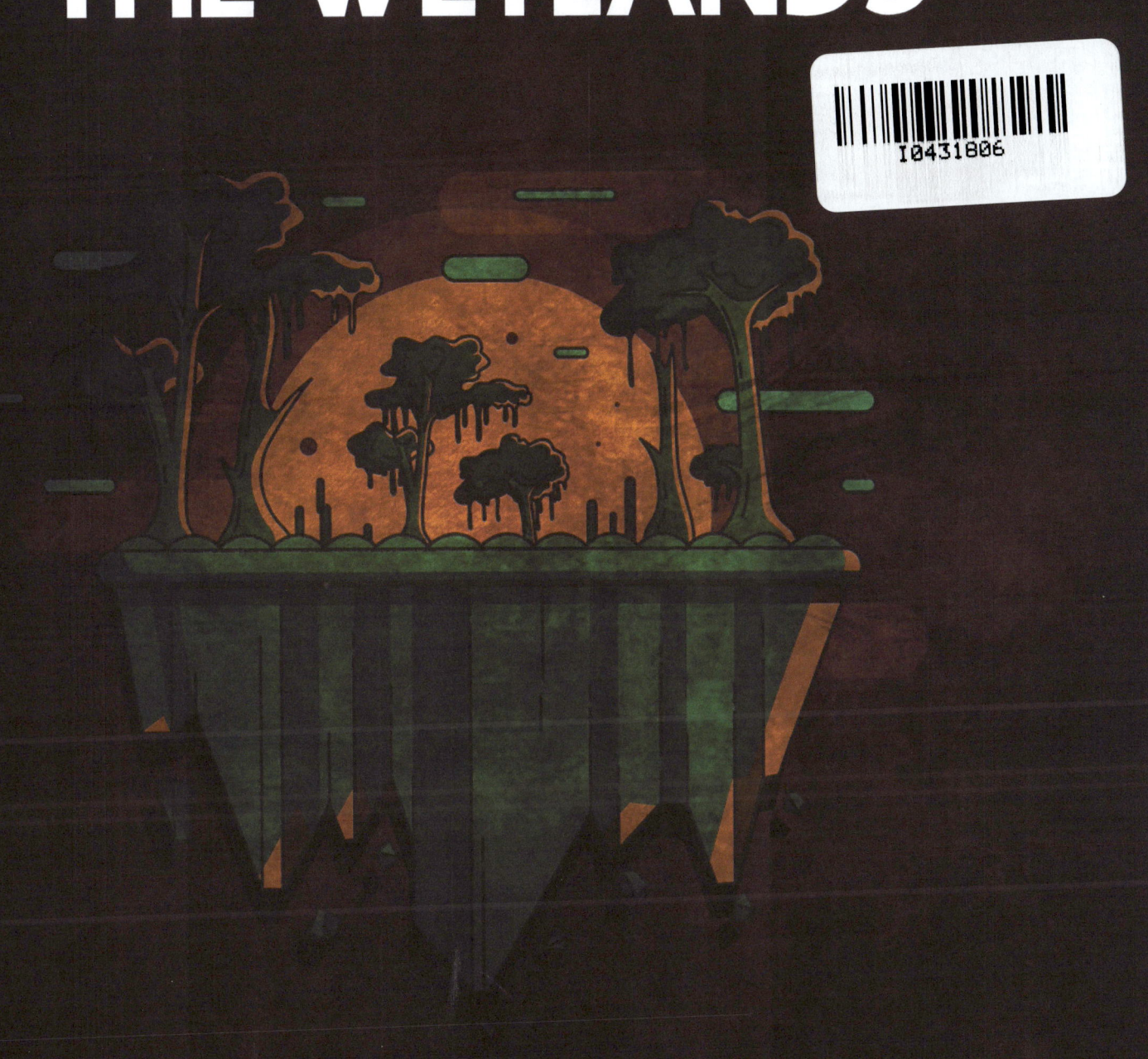

J. A. DUNBAR

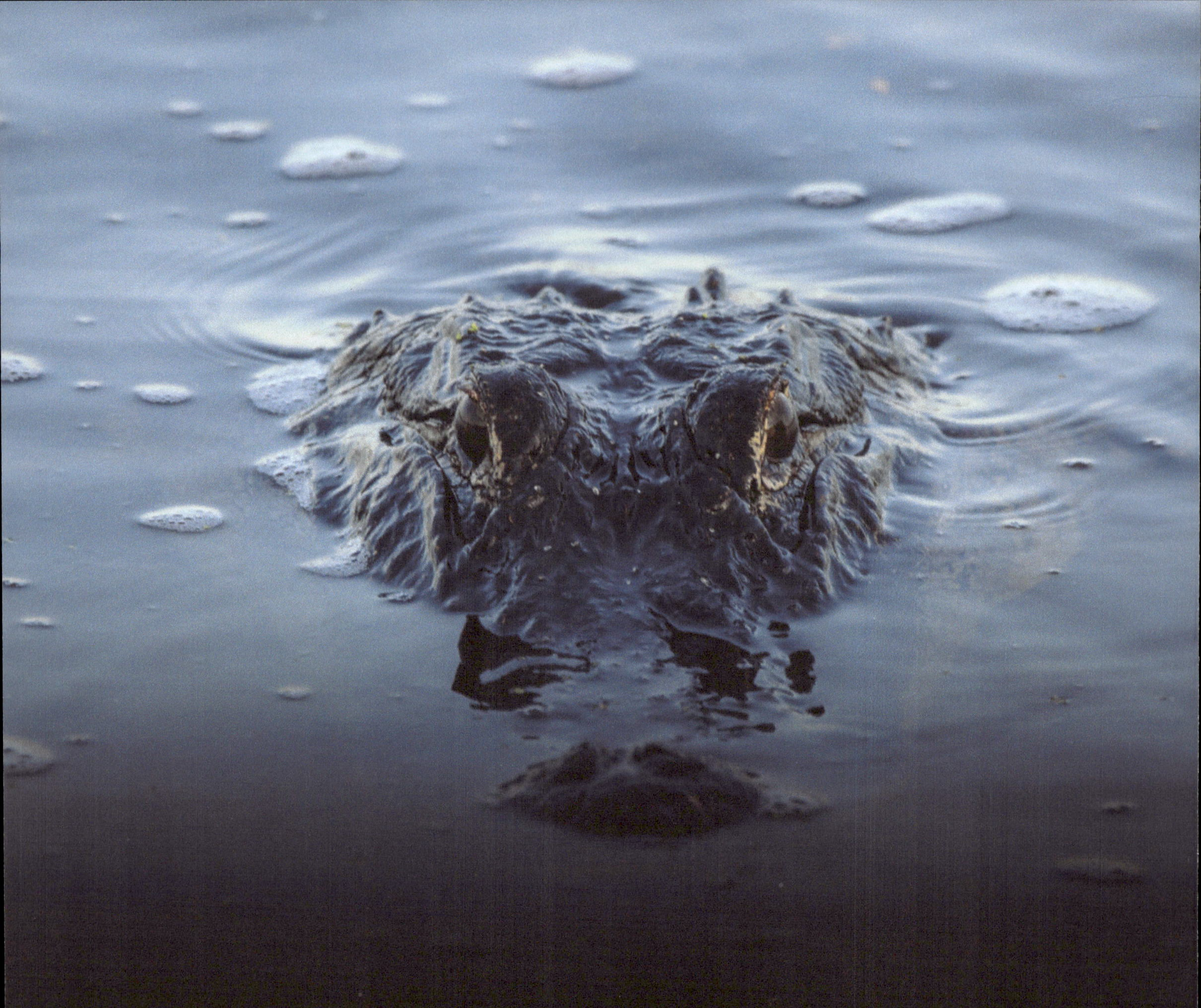

WRITTEN AND PHOTOGRAPHED BY J.A. DUNBAR
EDITED BY JOSHUA WERNER & PAUL BURKE
DESIGNED BY JOSHUA WERNER

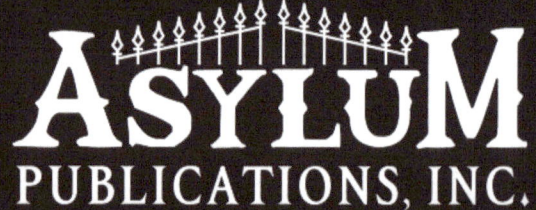

Distributed by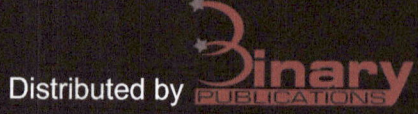

CEO AND EDITOR IN CHIEF PAUL BURKE
CREATIVE DIRECTOR JOSHUA WERNER

ISBN:
Journey Through the Wetlands™. Published by Asylum Publications, Inc.™ All photos are © by J.A. Dunbar. Asylum Pulications, Inc.™ is TM 2019. All rights reserved. No portion of this publication may be reproduced or transmitted, in any form by any means, without written consent from the Publisher, except for any small excerpts for the purpose of review.
For further information regarding custom photo/art books, ordering wholesale, or other inquiries, please write to asylumpublications75@gmail.com.

ABOUT THE AUTHOR

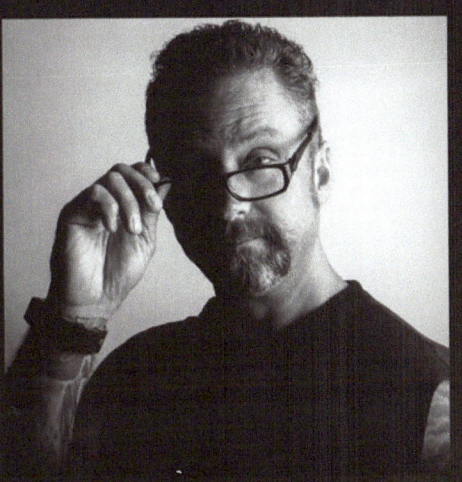

Photography was something passed on to me at a very young age… age 8 to be exact. My grandfather gifted me a late 60's Honeywell Pentax camera body, and a few lenses. At such a young age, there were no rules, no mistakes, (and most of the time…no film!) Just the pure excitement of pressing the shutter button and getting that satisfying "ka-chunk." I was occasionally given a roll or two of film (with some instruction on settings that I would not understand for another decade.) As time passed, and numerous trips to the "Phot-Mat," my hit/miss ratio began to improve. Fortunately for me, both my father and grandfather were excellent and experienced photographers, whom insisted on learning the basics, technique, and most of all the ancient art of "Manual" photography. This would pay dividends years later, as these skills would directly apply to all cameras regardless of brand and media type. My first photo gig was the school newspaper, in 8th grade. I covered social and sporting events, as well as community happenings.

After high school and attending college, I transitioned into a career in law enforcement. I was fortunate to receive specialized training in crime scene and critical incident photography and videography. 2005, I opened my own detective agency, and found photograph and videography had no become the center focus of my career. I am still an active investigator, as well as a studio, commercial and stock photographer for several agencies and national publications.

ABOUT THE JOURNEY

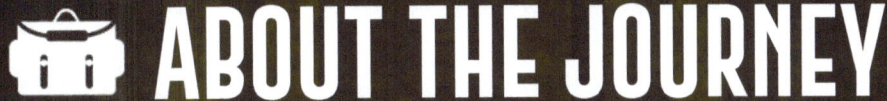

In the early part of 2017 I decided to dedicate full-time efforts to Wilderness photography. I had recently relocated to the state of Florida and had yet to set up a physical Studio. I found this to be a fantastic opportunity to immerse myself into the wild life scene, expand my portfolio, as well as have some once in a lifetime experiences. Given the general Wildlife population and species in Florida, many adventures could be had within close proximity, so I began to map out locations that were within a close driving distance from my home (east coast of Florida near Cape Canaveral.) I began to explore the Florida wetlands within about 4-6 hour radius of driving. This gave me many choices for my daily expeditions. This quickly became an 18 month/ 40 plus hours a week dedication, that produced thousands upon thousands of images. At the time, I was also shooting concert journalism in the evenings. Many days I would go from 95-degree hiking trails in the Florida Sun, photographing alligators, snakes and Raptors directly to a concert venue to photograph your favorite bands. The book that you hold before you is a miniature highlight reel of this expedition. Pictures just don't do what the in-person experience does, but I'm hopeful that I'll be able to get you part of the way there with the images I captured. During the course of this journey, I met numerous photographers (professional/hobbyist) hikers, tourists from around the world, reptiles, birds and various assorted other members of the Florida Everglades and wetlands ecosystem. Every encounter was a humbling and learning experience, and these memories serve as a daily reminder of just how right it feels to step away from society, technology, and the everyday grind to experience nature in its most simple and basic form.

📷 ABOUT THE GEAR

As a 70's child, I grew up in an exciting time for photographers and witnessed the evolution of technology from the dark room to current digital media. I owned a bit of all formats over the years... 35mm, "Polaroids," 110 cartridges, floppy disks, mini-dv, SD, compact CF and on. Currently, as of 2019, I have settled into a combination of Canon full-frame DSLR and Sony mirrorless camera bodies. Both systems have some nice features to offer to this type of shooting. As a result, it was hard for me to make a final decision to cut one system loose, so yeah, I try and stay current with both systems and they are both used frequently. If I am headed into the elements and expect to encounter rain or ocean waves, I take my Canon gear. If I'm going to be later into the evening hours and in more lowlights scenarios, I will bring my Sony system. I am using Canon L glass and some Sigma lenses as well. The sigma mc-11 adapter for my Sony has tested quite well for me. My Canon mount Sigma lenses actually perform faster on the Sony bodies with a Sigma mc-11 adapter. Early on, I came into the Wilderness field with a Canon 5D Mark 3, and a 70 to 200 mm 2.8 L Series lens. This was an excellent combination that provided me with some spectacular results. This rig did have significant limitations for distance and certain high-speed action. I ended up adding a Canon 5DSR to my fleet, although not a better AF system, under perfect conditions it does provide some of the most detailed images I have ever seen. Both of these camera bodies we're somewhat limited by the AF points they offered, and the 5DSR was useless with ISO above 3200, and very noticeable above 1600. I also found the fact that the AF points did not extend far enough to the sides of the view finder to be problematic when photographing wildlife. Wildlife scenarios can be very sporadic and fast-moving, and you may only have a milli-second to frame a shot. Extra AF points with wide coverage is a big help … enter the Sony. Another issue is visible noise when wanting to make prints or publish your work oh, here again the Sony noise in grain I found to be a little more desirable even as far as 6400 ISO. The last point to make regarding the camera systems, is the blue hour and low light shooting. These images can sometimes be very dramatic also very dark as your ambient life decays. Again, I give Sony the win here as it is much more tolerable to the low-light scenarios. Even when using adapted lenses, it seems they would acquire focus quicker with a wider AF point field of coverage. In defense of my Canon bodies, the 5DSR shot at high noon with a relatively docile subject will produce an incredible image, and in my opinion is still the king of the perfect storm. Wanting more out of my AF system in low light systems prompted me to pick up a Sony A7R II.

I was not impressed with this edition and for many reasons it was returned. I've then picked up a Canon 5D Mark 4 oh, and I found the live view shooting to be quite amazing. Autofocus acquisition in low-light was a bit better than the Mark 3 and the 5DSR, and it produced a more tolerable noise at higher ISO's. This new Canon body offered 30 megapixels that would still allow me to crop and utilize all my Canon glass without jumping ship to Sony. Shortly after I brought the Mark 4 home, the Mark 3 went up for sale, and now lives a happy life in the big island of Hawaii. A few months past oh, and I was still looking to get some more beef in my auto focus. Of course, I happen to notice all the hype for the Sony A7R III and decided that I would pre-order it. I also ordered the sigma MC 11 to accommodate my Canon glass collection. After much anticipation, my new Sony arrived, and it quickly became my go-to body. They had overcome all of the obstacles from version 2 and made this a very powerful camera body for all genres of photography. I'm not sponsored, and I don't get free gear, and in the end, it really matters what you want to use and what you can afford. I did find some issues with a Sony, namely rolling shutter as well as horizontal banding in certain lighting situations. Those issues don't exist for my Canon system, and the antiquated CF card of the Canon is hands-down faster than the SD card system for my Sony. Here we are nearly a year-and-a-half later, and I still own the Mark 4 and the 5DSR… as well as the A7RIII. The Sony does get the most use, but they usually travel together. In the lens category as I stated earlier, I use mainly Canon L Series glass. Of course, the 24 to 70 mm 2.8, the 70 to 200mm 2.8, the 100 mm macro, as well as the 1.4 extender. I also have a 150 to 600 mm that does a very good job with a Sony AF system. Another nice feature is that I am able to use the crop mode on the Sony and take that 600 mm to a crop of x 1.6 which comes in to be a little bit less than a thousand millimeters. I normally don't take much with me, except for my glass, and an occasional extension tube. I do make sure to bring along a small first aid kit, a charged cell phone, bug spray and waterproof garbage bags and of course plenty of water. Those are my ingredients for the images that you see here, hopefully will answer some questions for you or at the very least stir up some motivation to get out there and get shooting.

My trusty #1 Canon 5DSR and 70-200mm Lens.

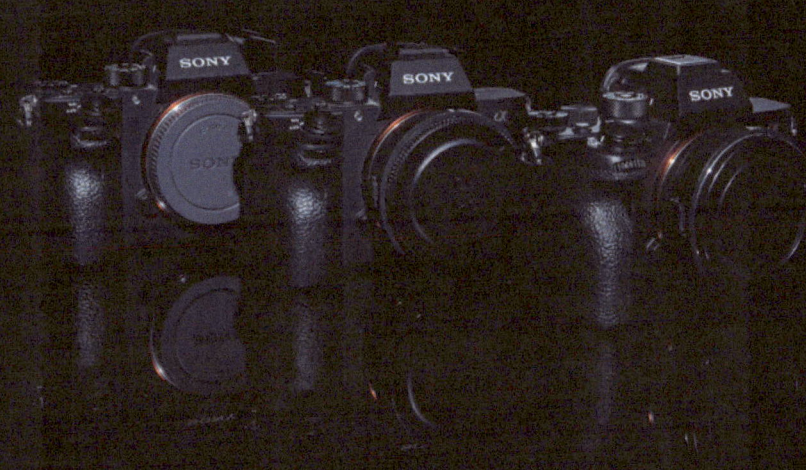

Sony a7 III, Sony a7R III, and sony a7R IV.

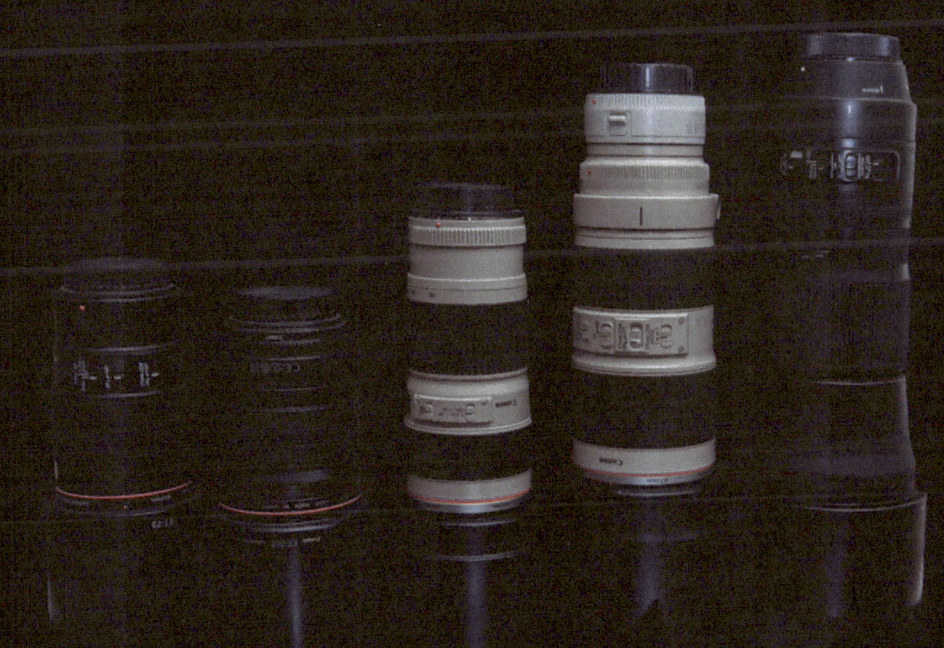

Canon 100mm macro, Canon 135mm, Canon 70-200 f4, Canon 70-200 f2.8 x1.4x, Sigma 150-600mm.

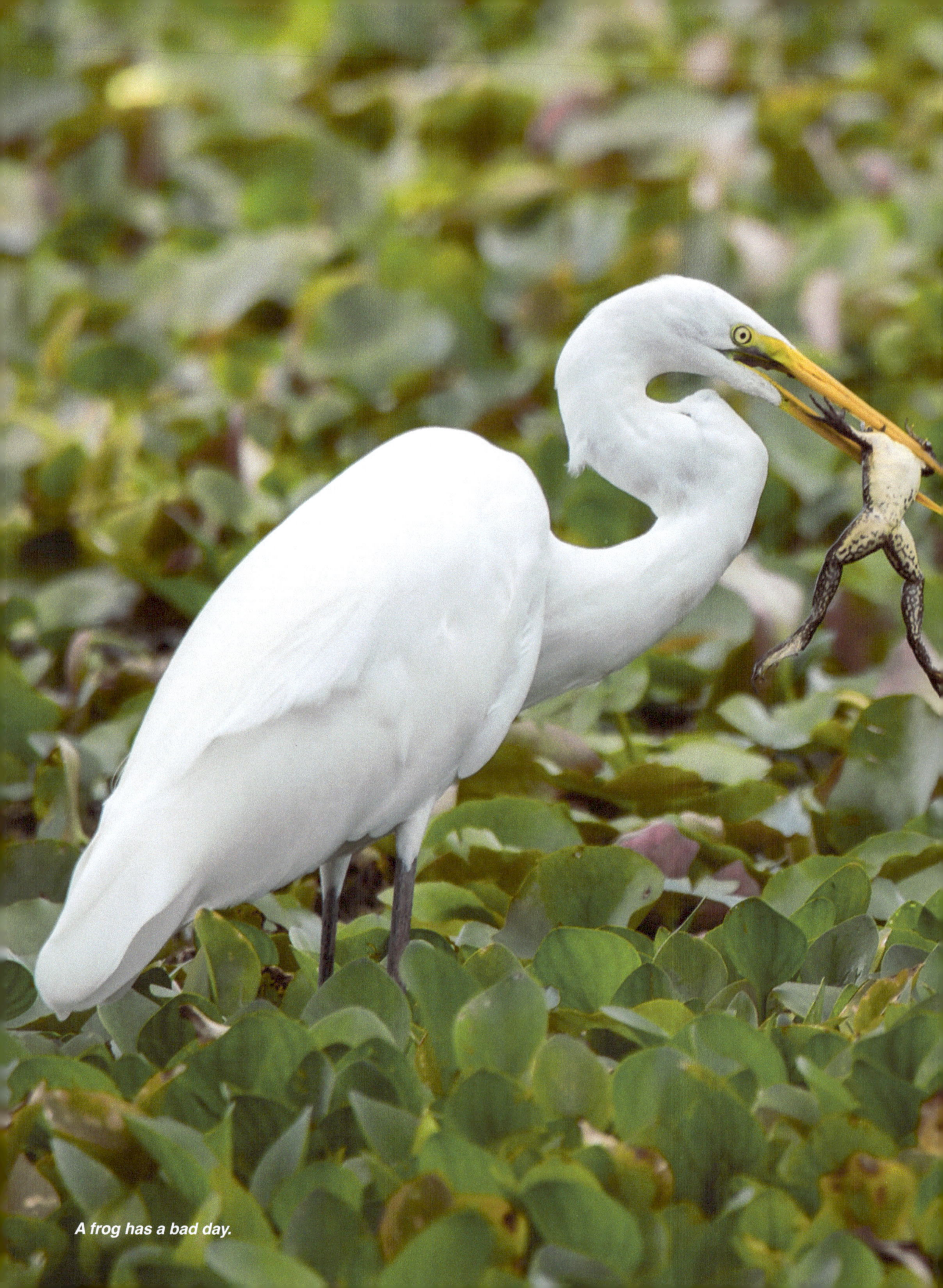
A frog has a bad day.

ABOUT THE HERONS AND EGRETS

The great blue heron and the great snowy egret are by far the most available cast members to the wetlands. I do have to give an honorable shout out to the anhinga, the sandhill crane, the black bellied whistling duck and an occasional grackle. The great blue heron is pretty common in the wetlands, as is the egret. But to have an opportunity to photograph a mated pair and watch their eggs hatch in the nest and their young grow into unruly teenagers is pretty awesome. Eventually "Pops" moves out to leave "Mum" with the kids, in a nest that they don't fit in… (ironically paradoxical to reality.)

I had been in the wetlands six months, before I saw a blue heron spearfish a snack with its beak. I had no idea this was a method to use to hunt for their food. They strike hard and come up with a fish pierced between upper and lower beak and then somehow get it down. I had watched a large adult great blue heron use this method with a large eel. This encounter ended with the Heron flying off with the eel halfway out of the mouth looking much like a large black tongue. It seems that all of the larger birds, herons, egrets and cranes, also showed some pretty intense battle scars. I would imagine most of these are close calls with alligators.

The sandhill crane offered the greatest avian challenge to my presence. Many of them stand almost 5 ft tall and have zero fear of a human being. There were a handful of times when a male and female would land in close proximity to me, and just kind of hang out. Interestingly enough, they mate for life, so the pairs you see season after season are lifelong partners. One particular afternoon my wife accompanied me on a hike, and ten minutes in we had an unscheduled encounter with a trio of cranes. This would have been Mom, Dad and their teenager. We politely walked past them snapping photos while mutually observing one another's comfort barrier. I received a cell phone call at this point and my ring jingle elicited quite the response. One of the adult cranes stood upright, looked directly at me and proceeded to make Jurassic Park noises. As you might expect, we mutually parted ways and went about our business. We did meet again, months later… and with my cell phone on vibrate.

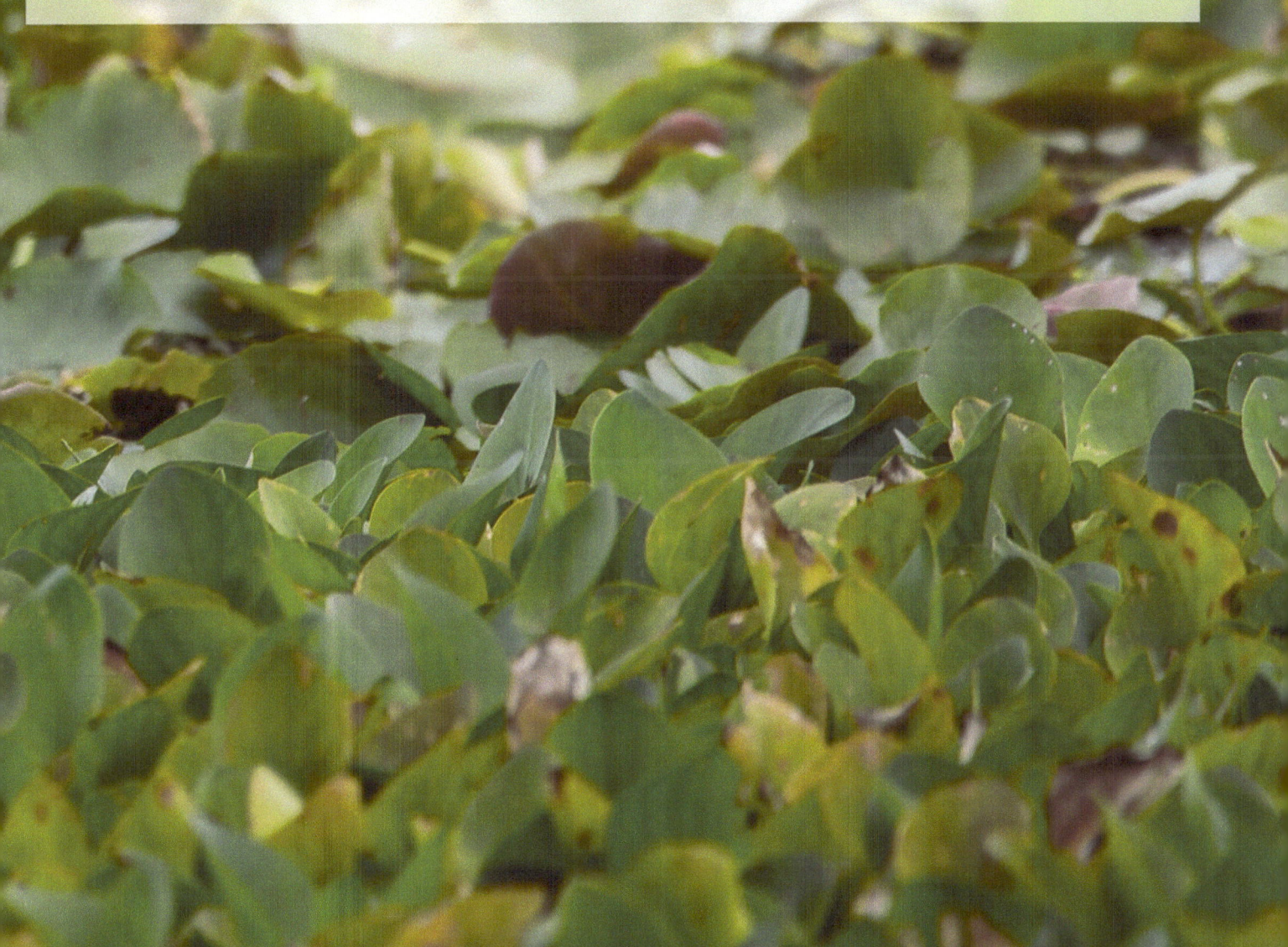

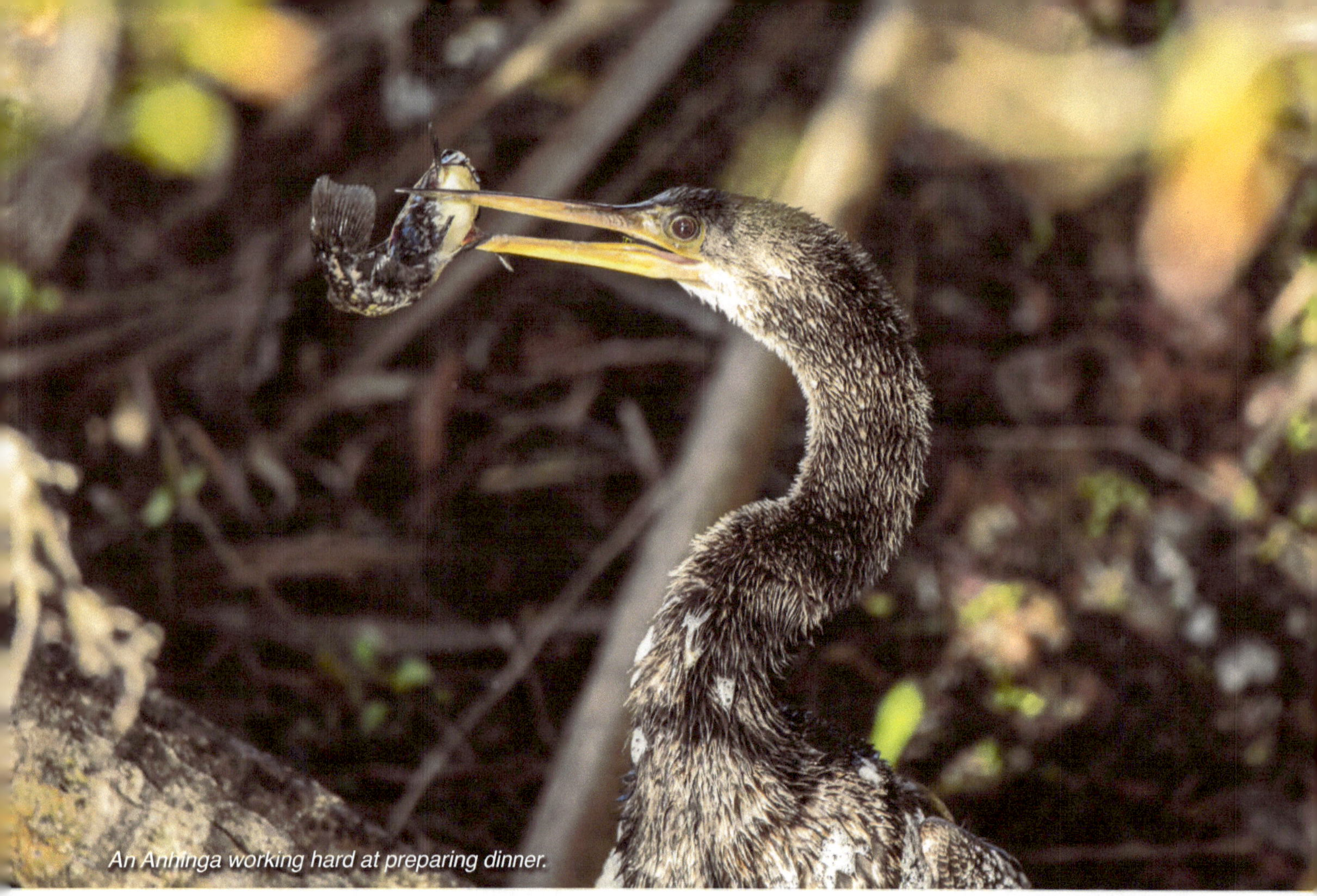

An Anhinga working hard at preparing dinner.

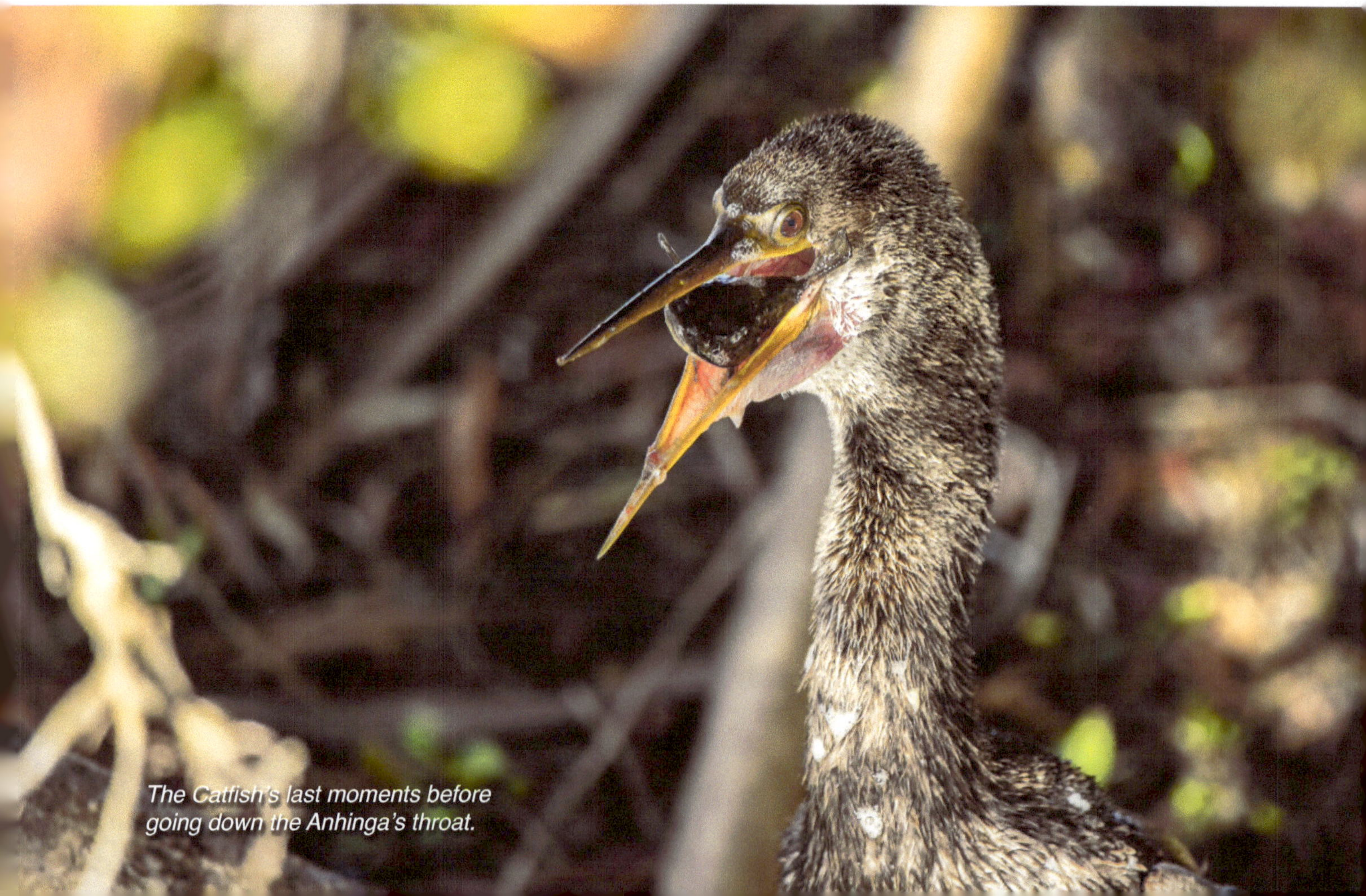

The Catfish's last moments before going down the Anhinga's throat.

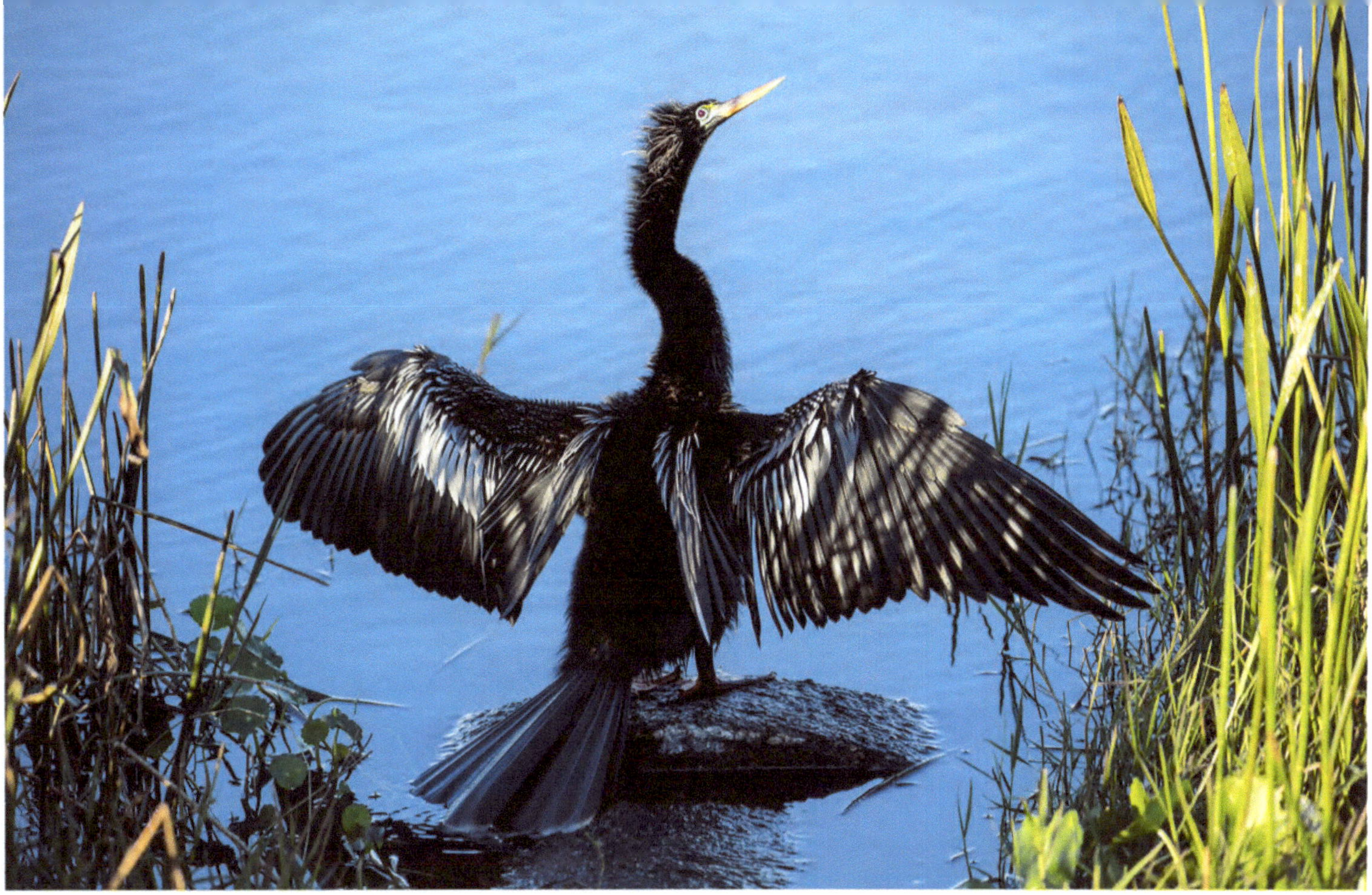

Above: An Anhinga posturing in the mating season.
Bottom left: A juvenile Heron waits for mother. Bottom right: A Tricolored Heron calls to its mate.

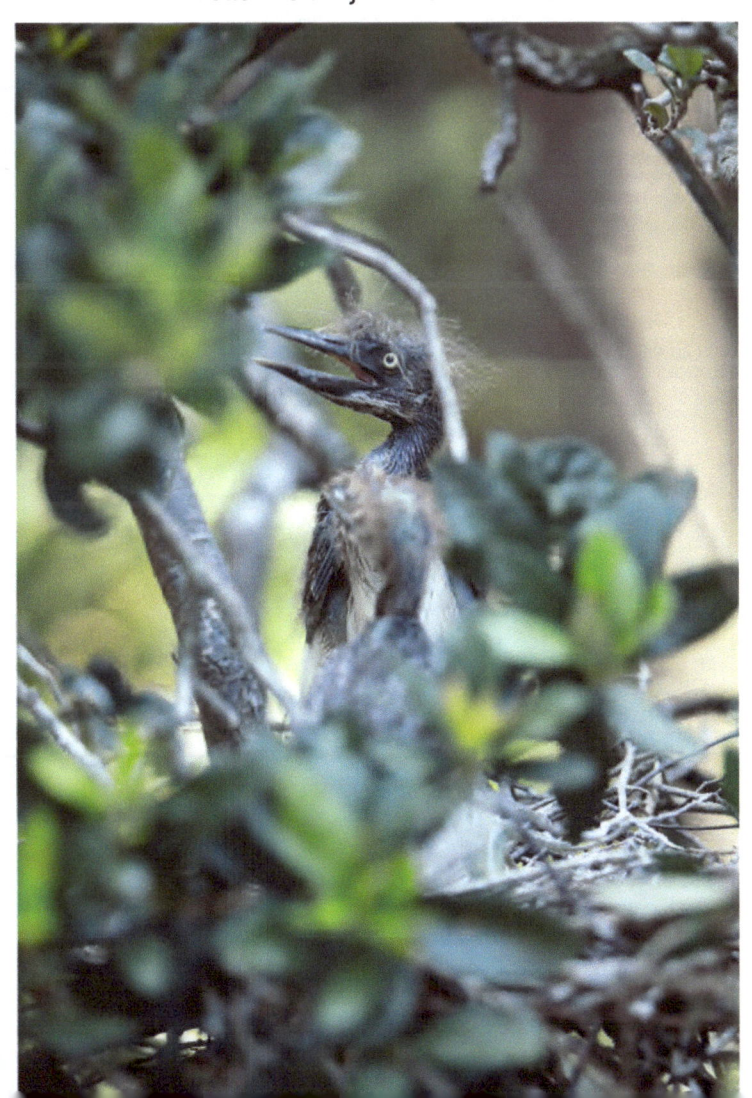
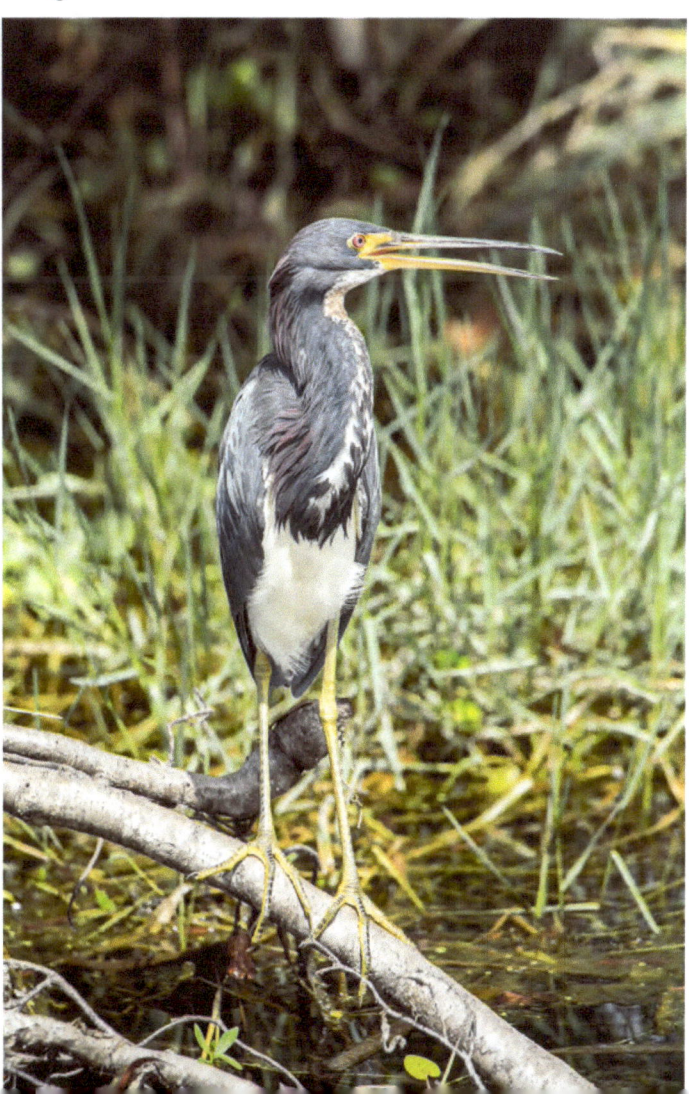

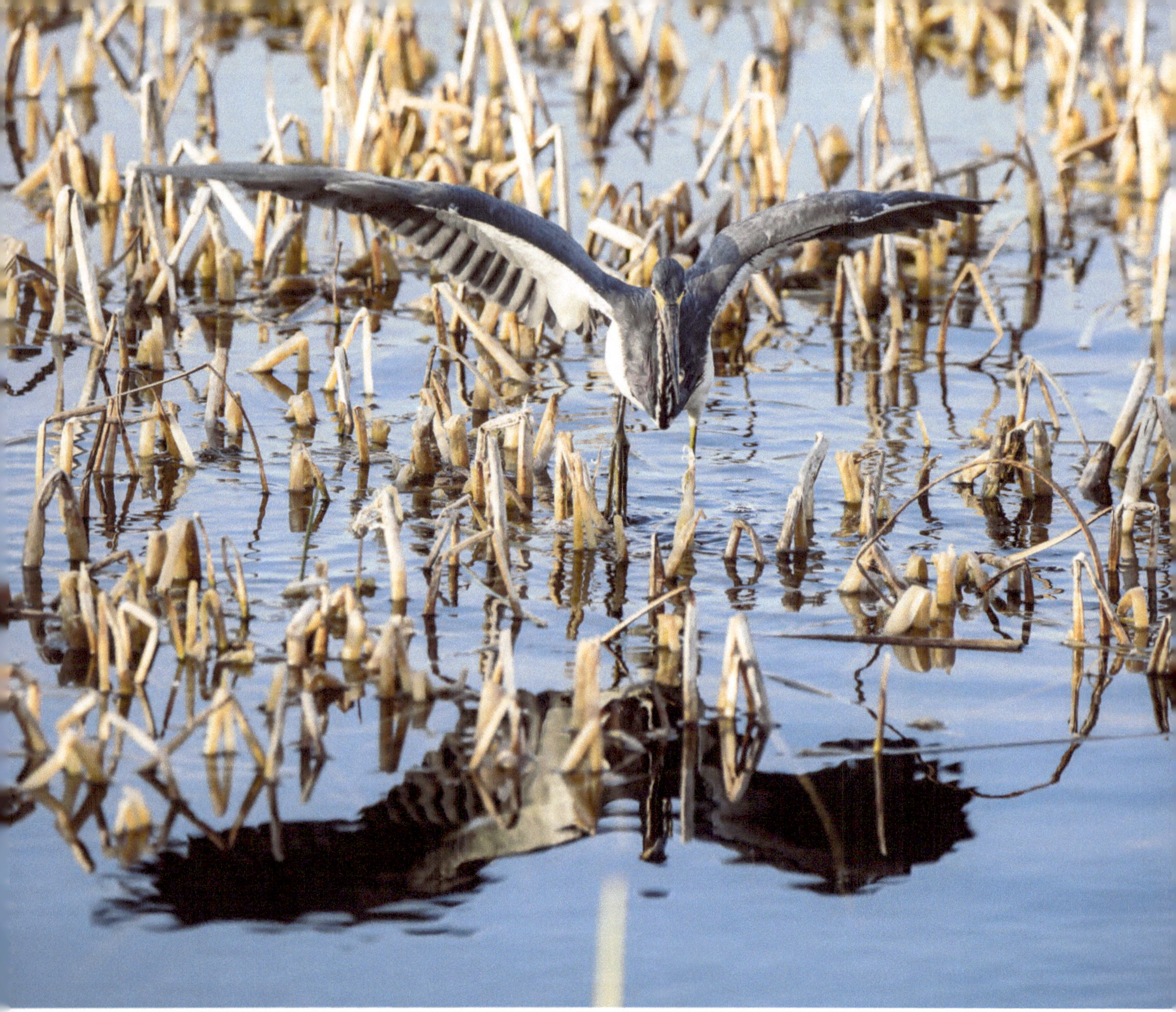

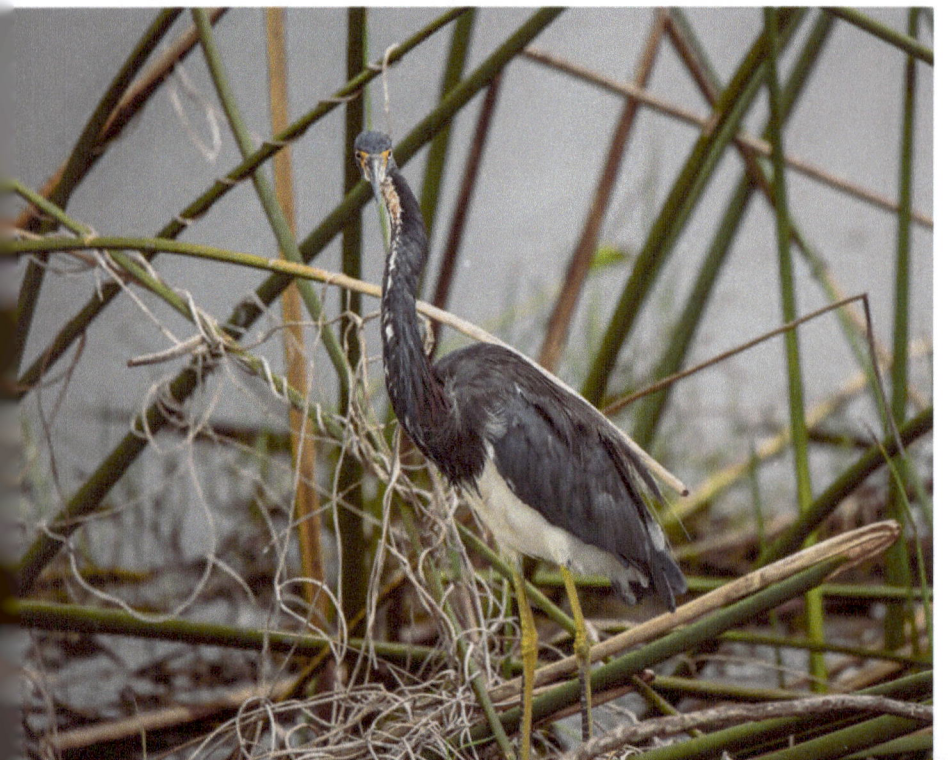

Above: A Tricolored Heron takes flight.

Left: A Tricolored Heron cautiously watches your approach.

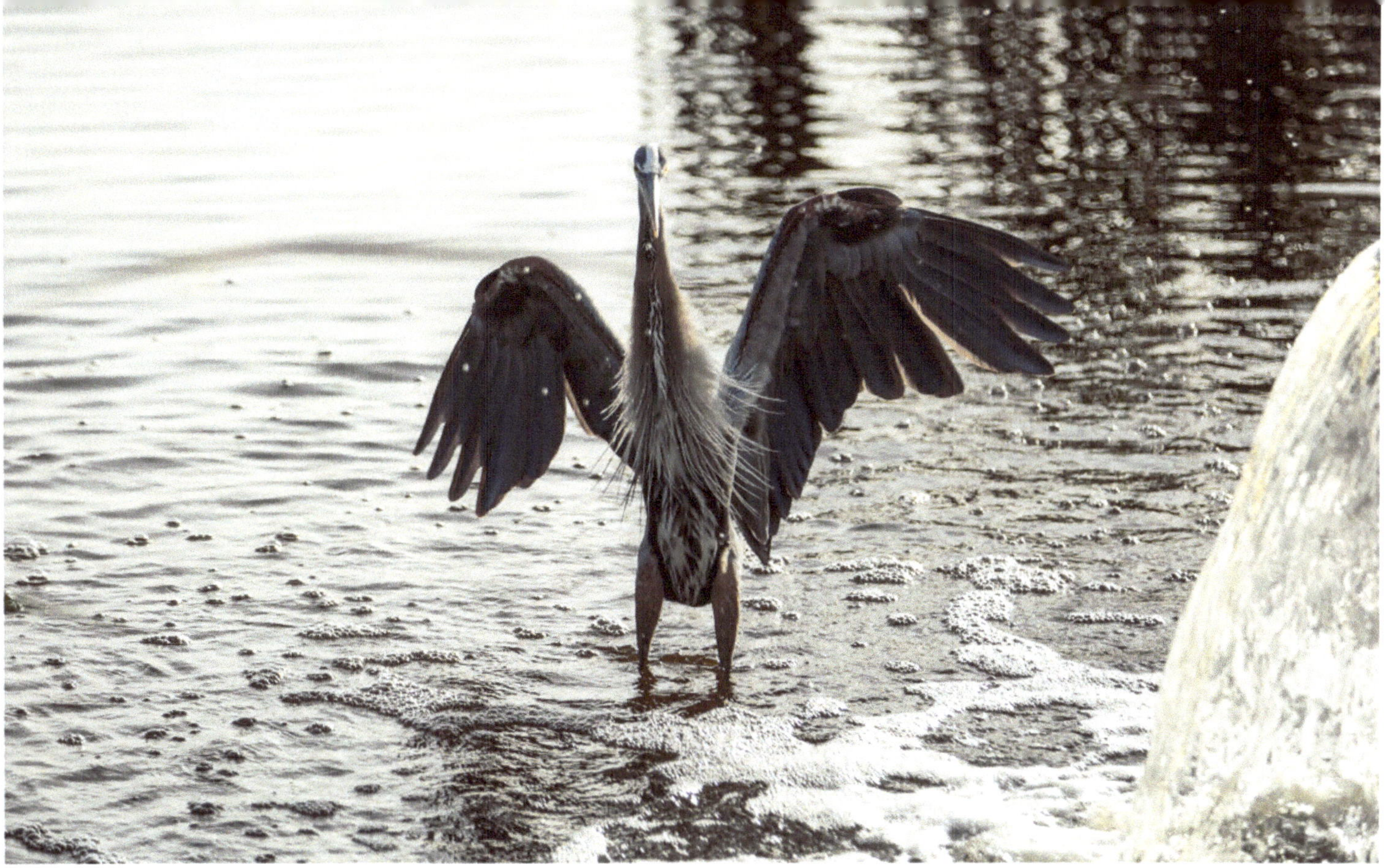

Above: A Great Blue Heron sends a warning.
Below: A Great Blue Heron takes flight.

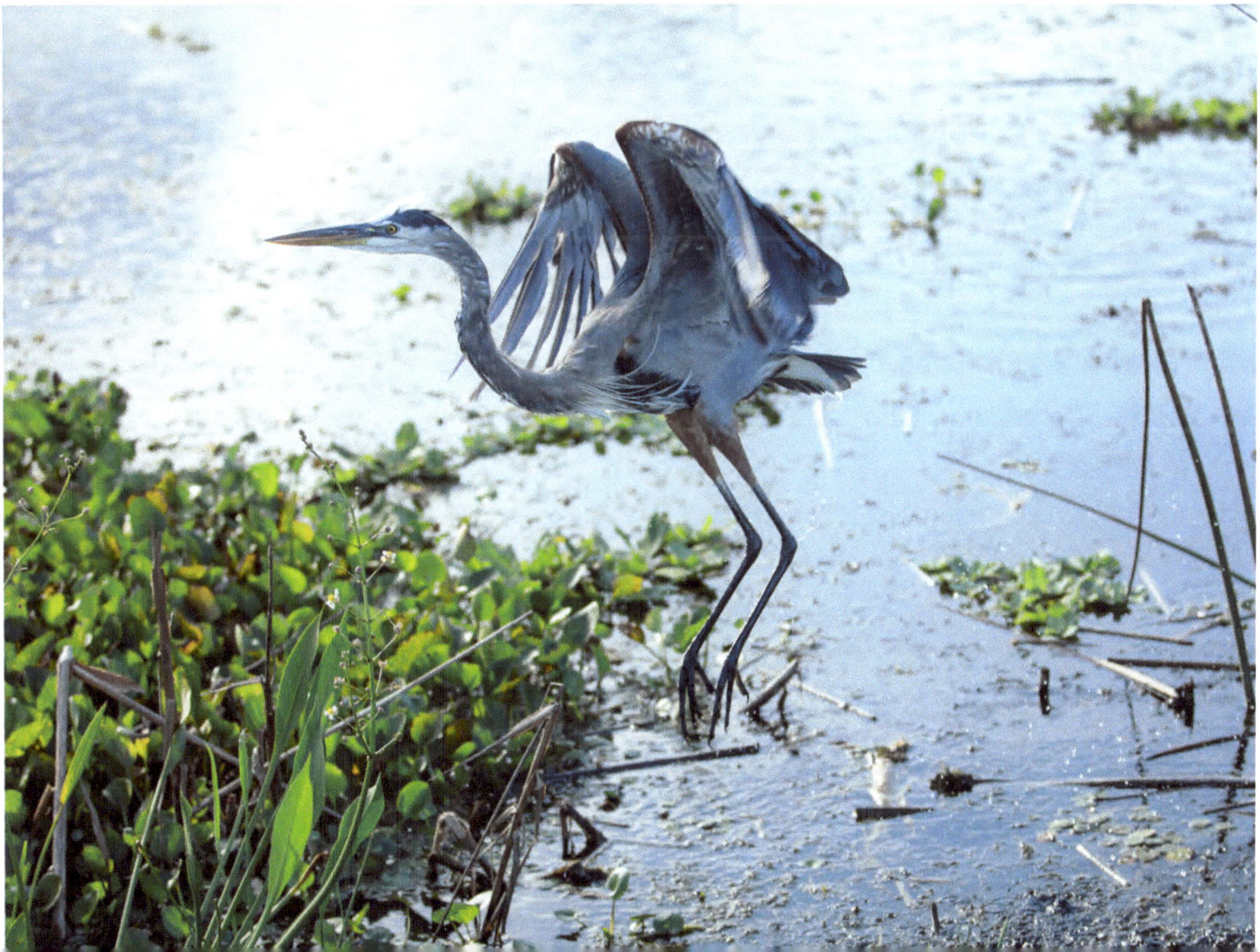

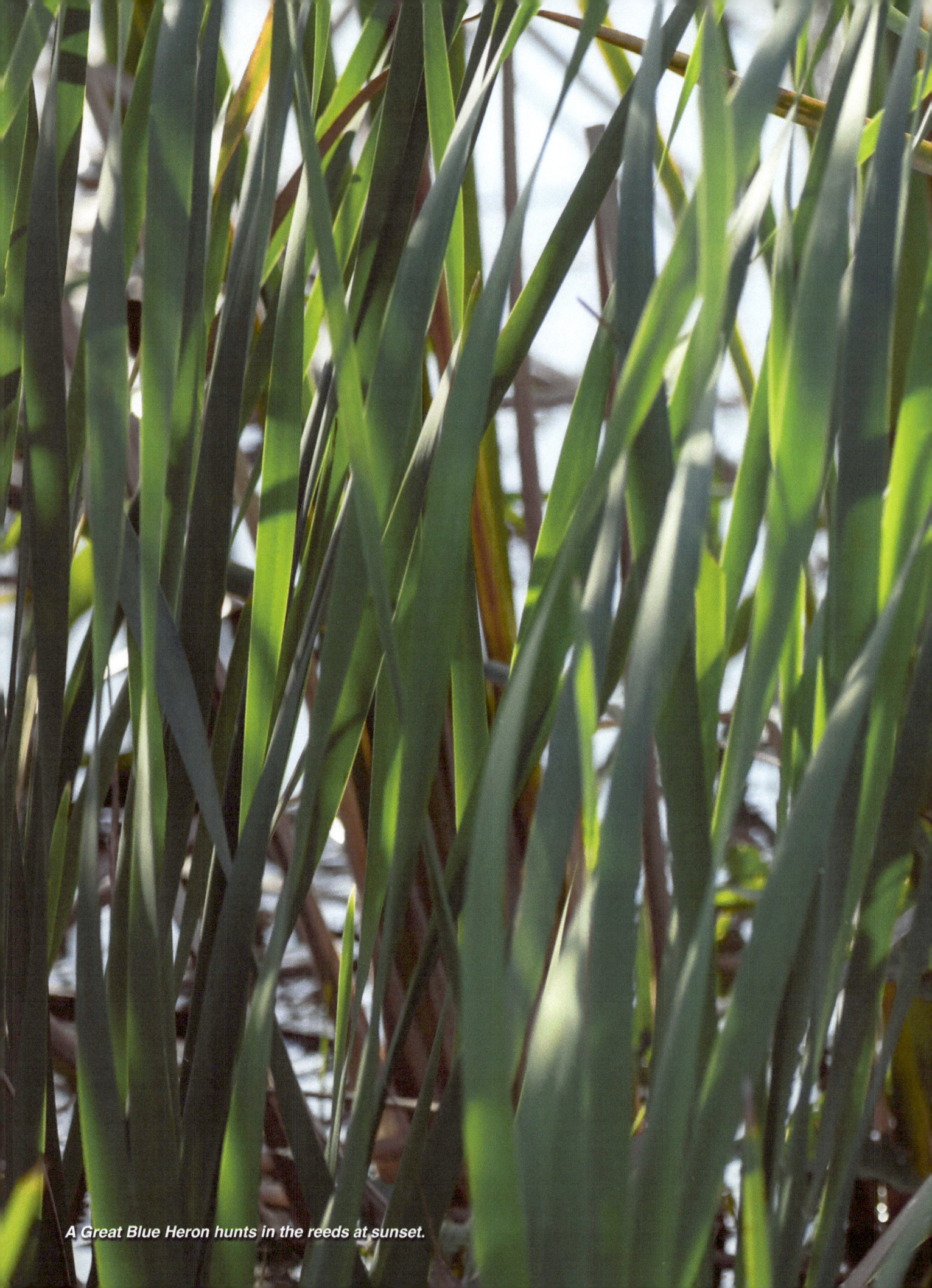
A Great Blue Heron hunts in the reeds at sunset.

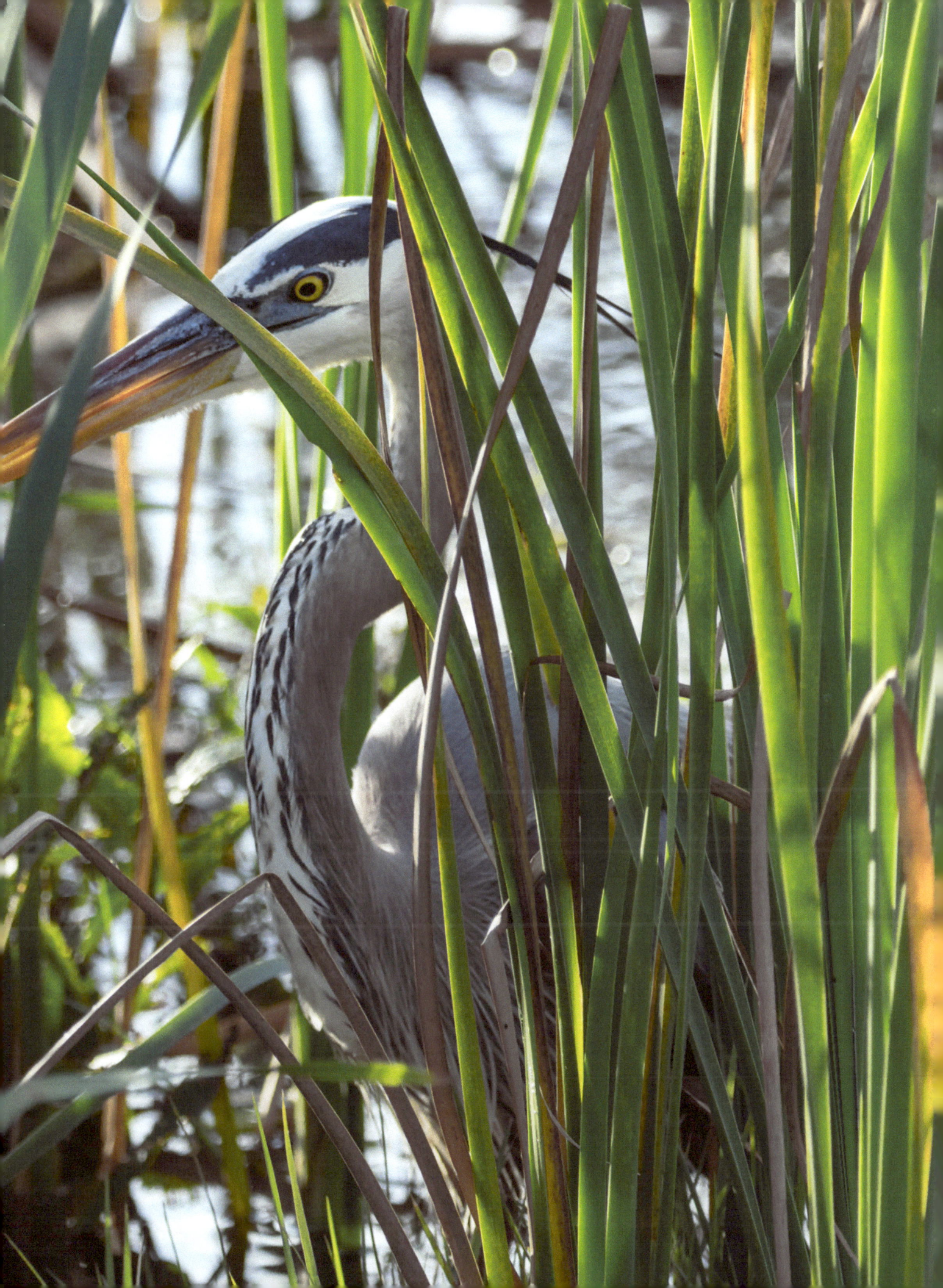

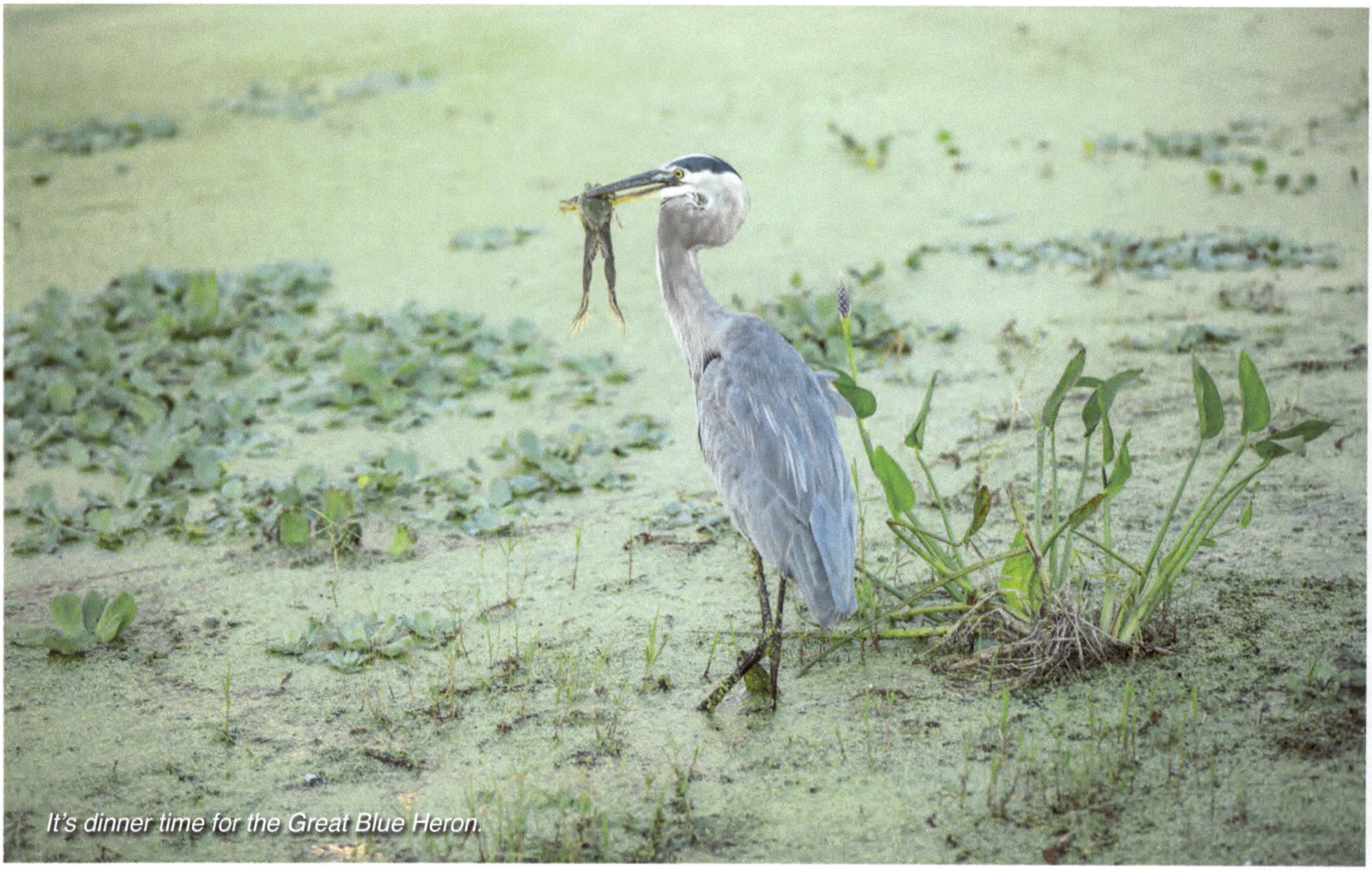

It's dinner time for the Great Blue Heron.

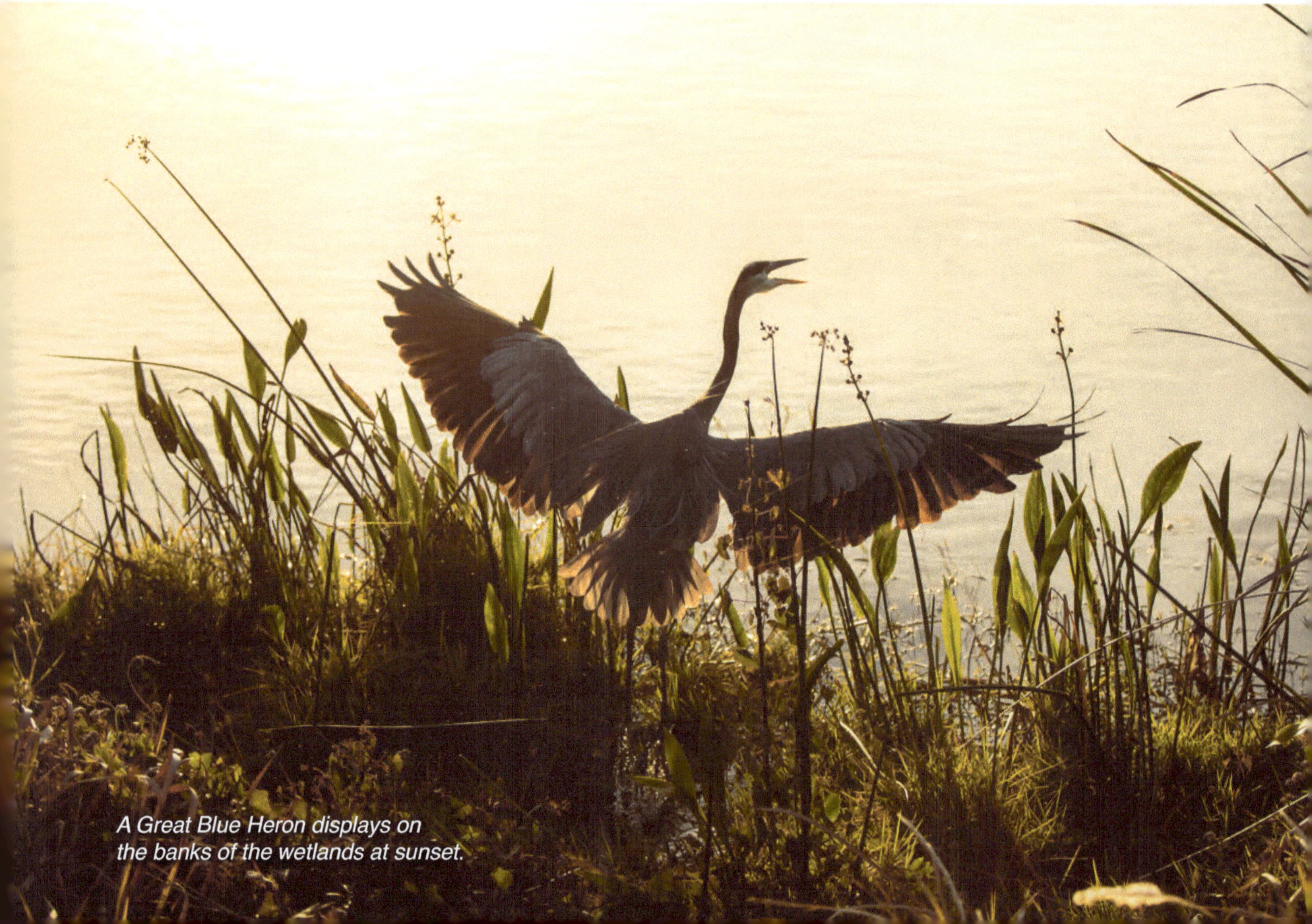

A Great Blue Heron displays on the banks of the wetlands at sunset.

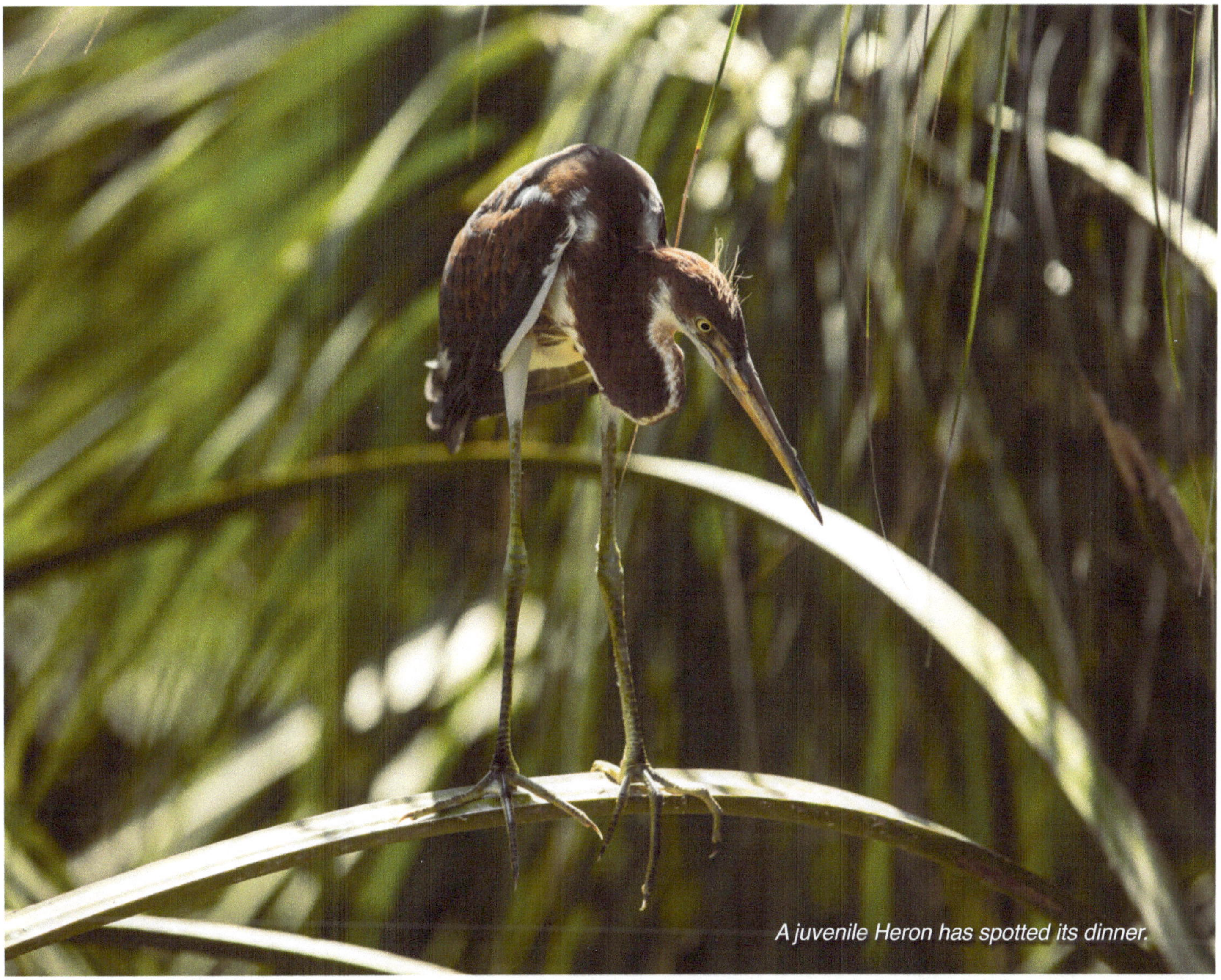

A juvenile Heron has spotted its dinner.

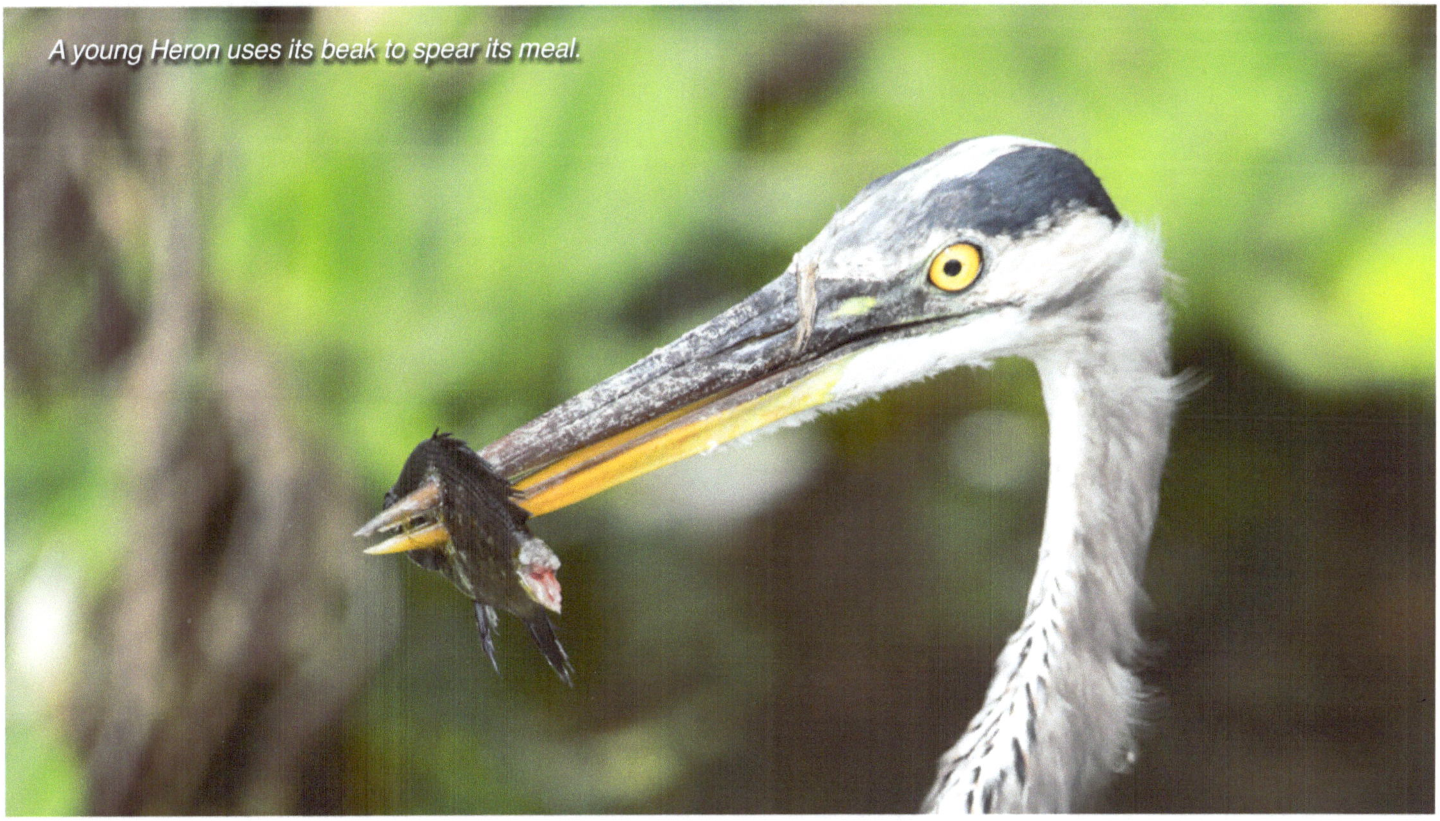

A young Heron uses its beak to spear its meal.

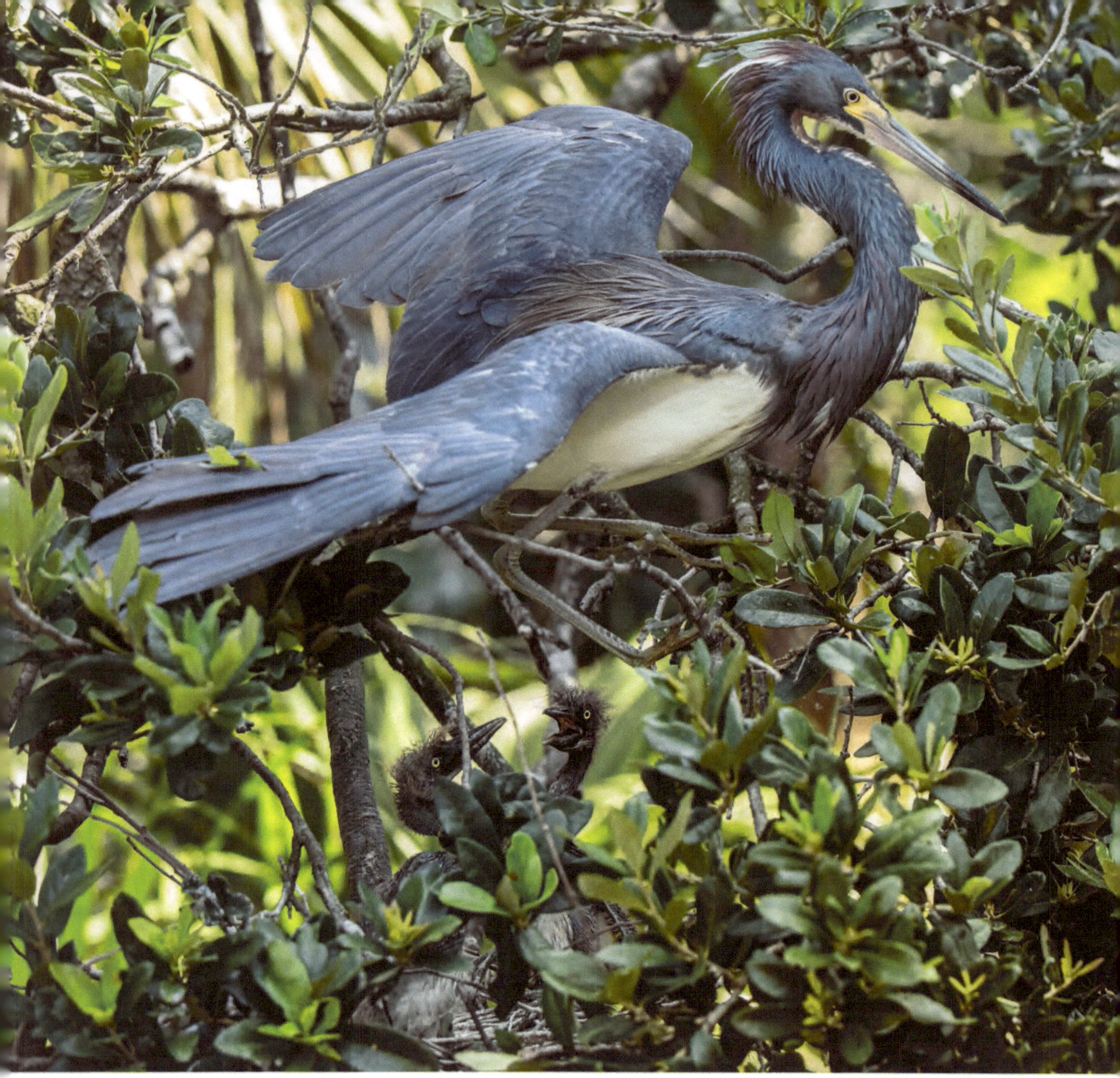

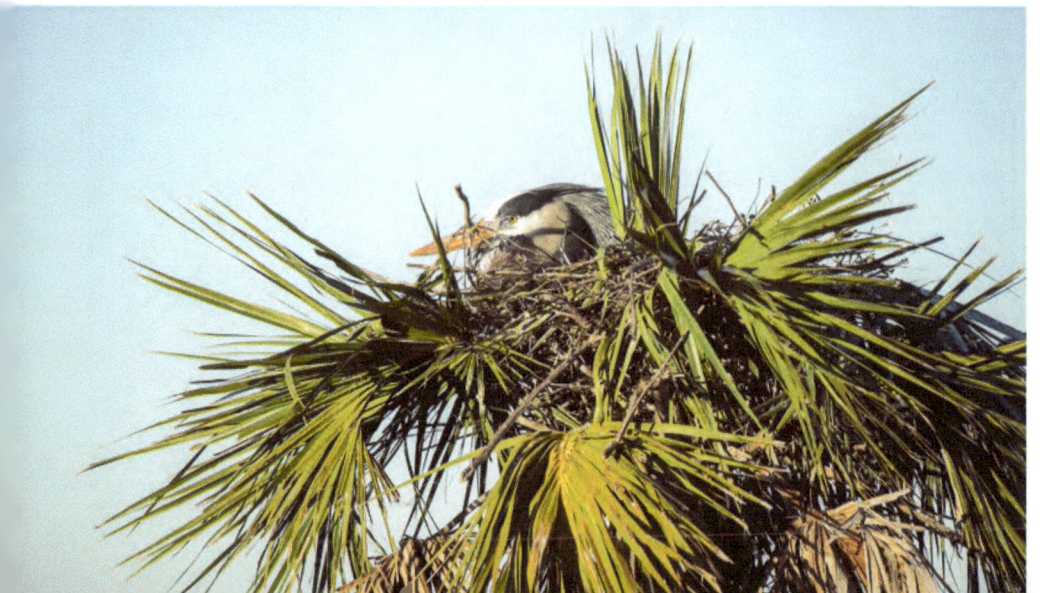

Above: A mother Heron and her chicks.

Left: A mother Heron awakens to a bright sunrise..

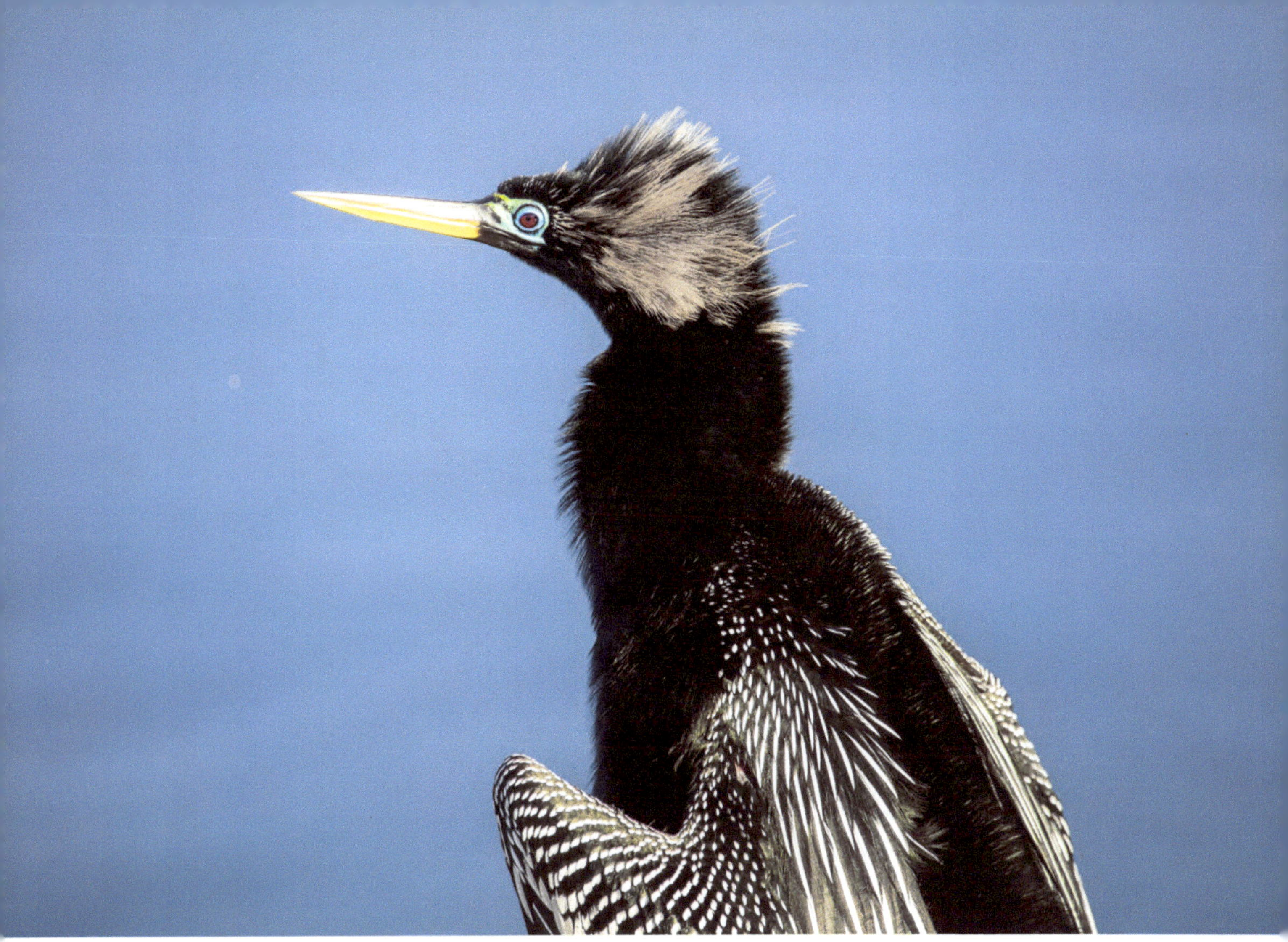

Above: A male Piano Bird gets a close-up.   Below: A little Snowy Egret has spotted something tasty.

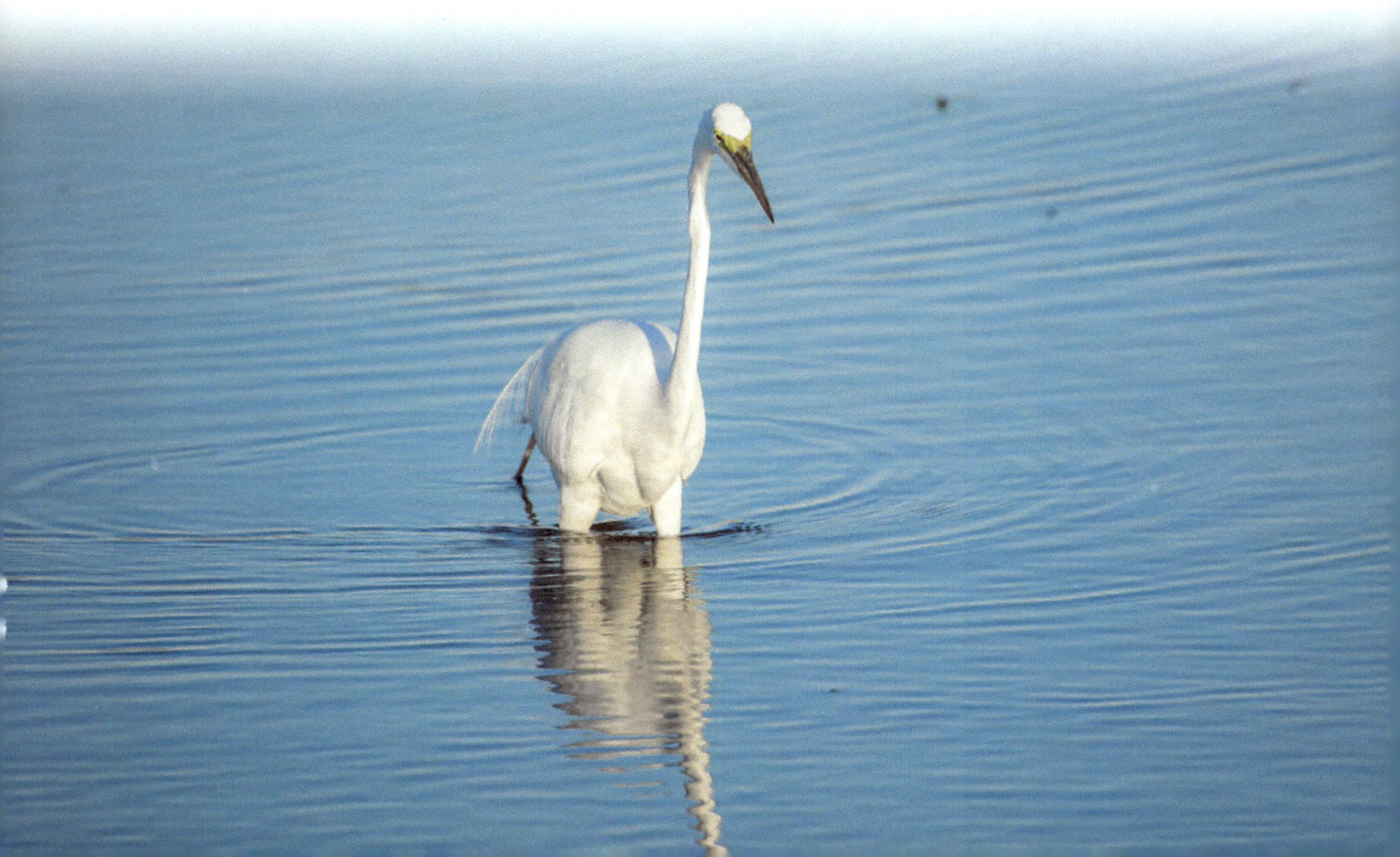

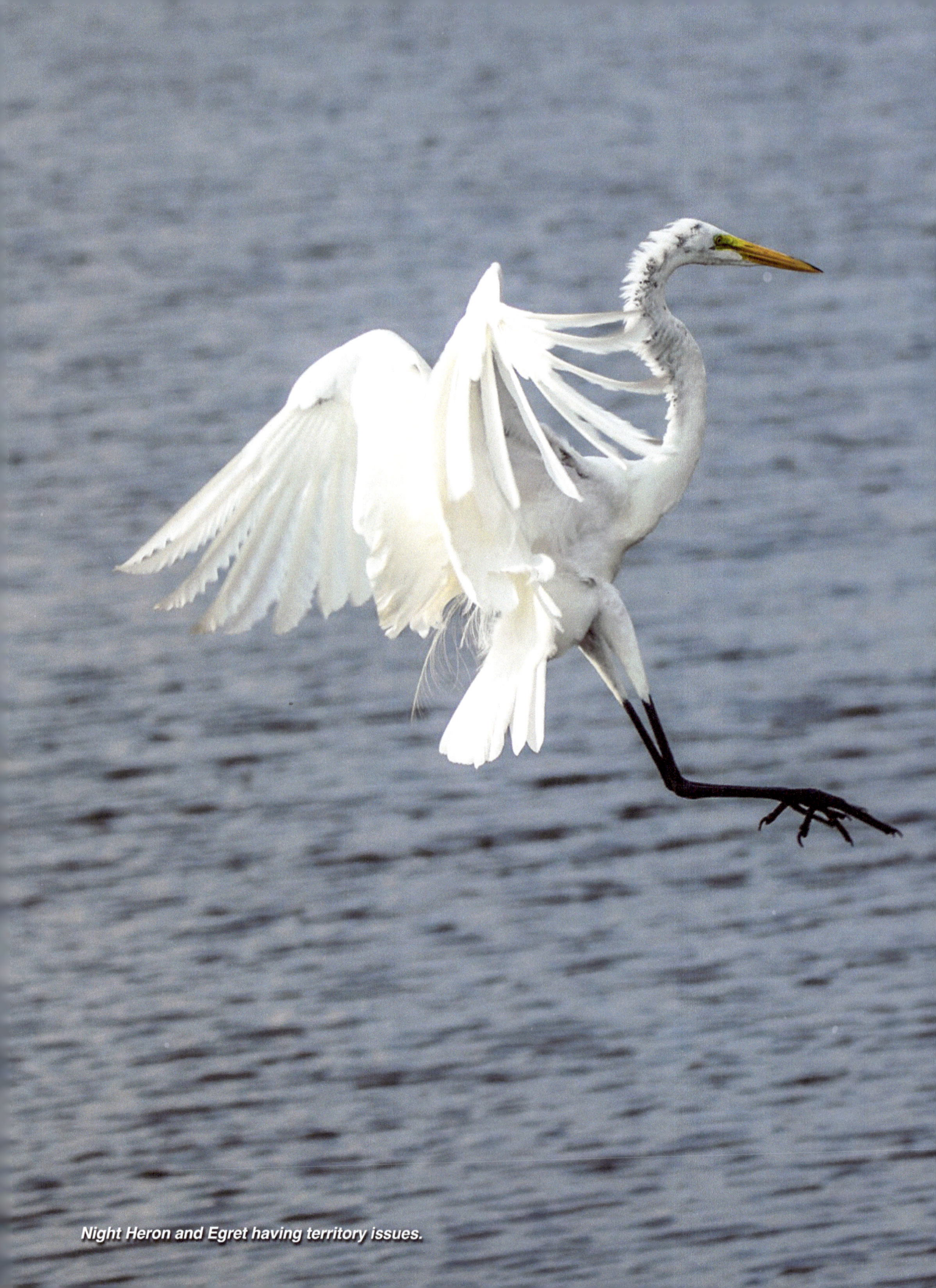
Night Heron and Egret having territory issues.

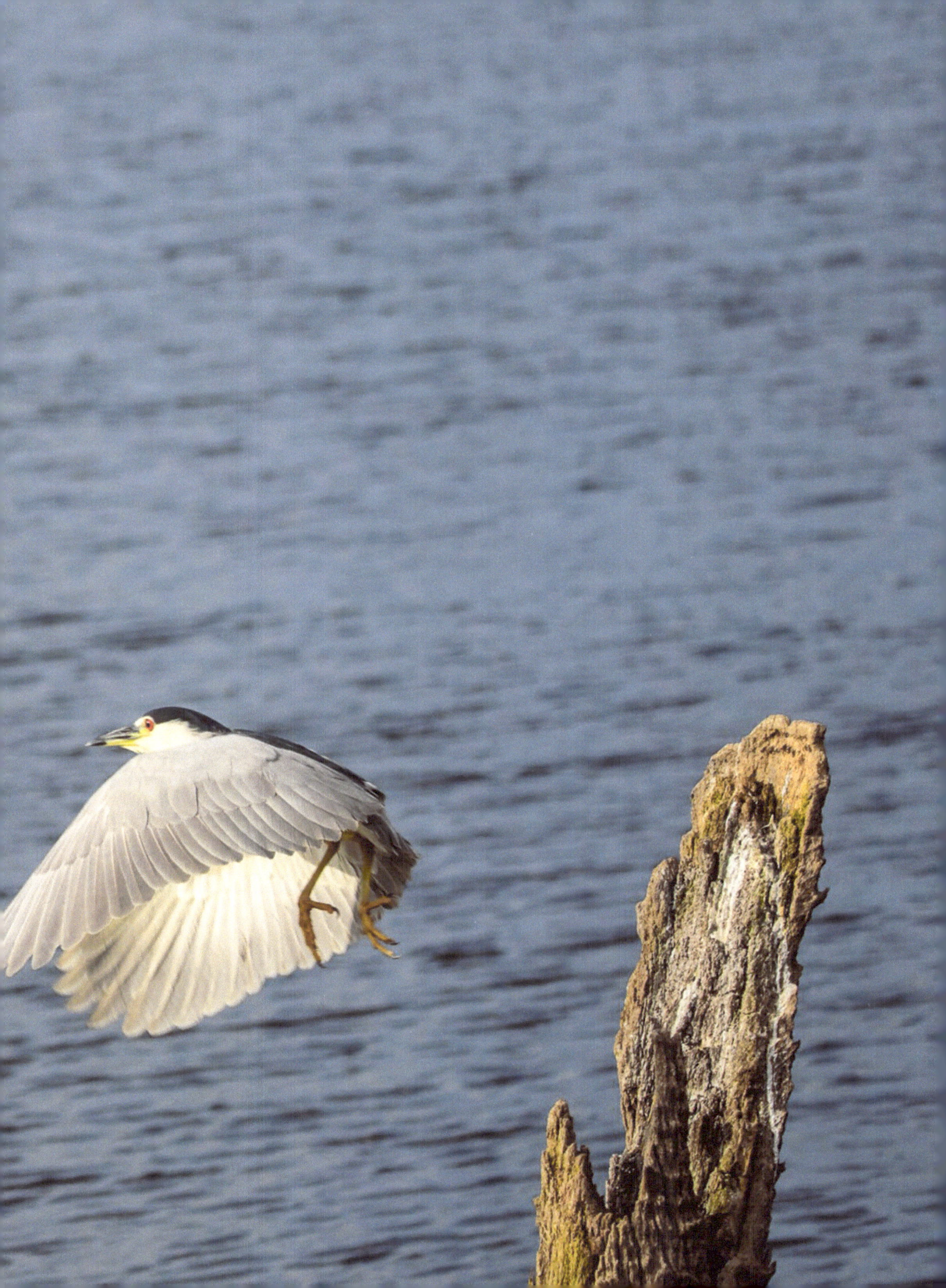

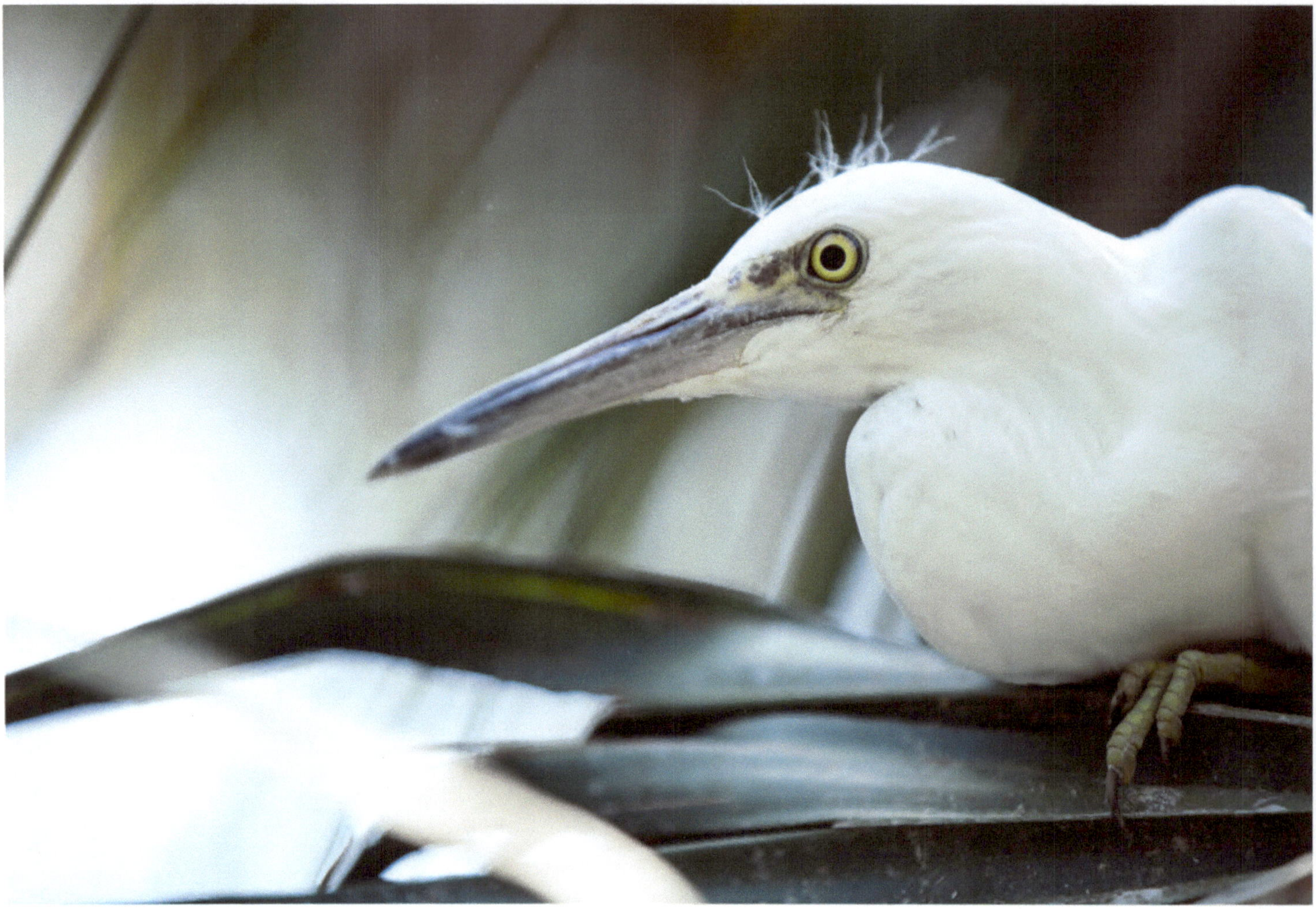

Above: A juvenile Snowy Egret waits for mother.

Left: A Grackle perched high at sunset.

Below: An Emerald Ibis spreads its colorful wings.

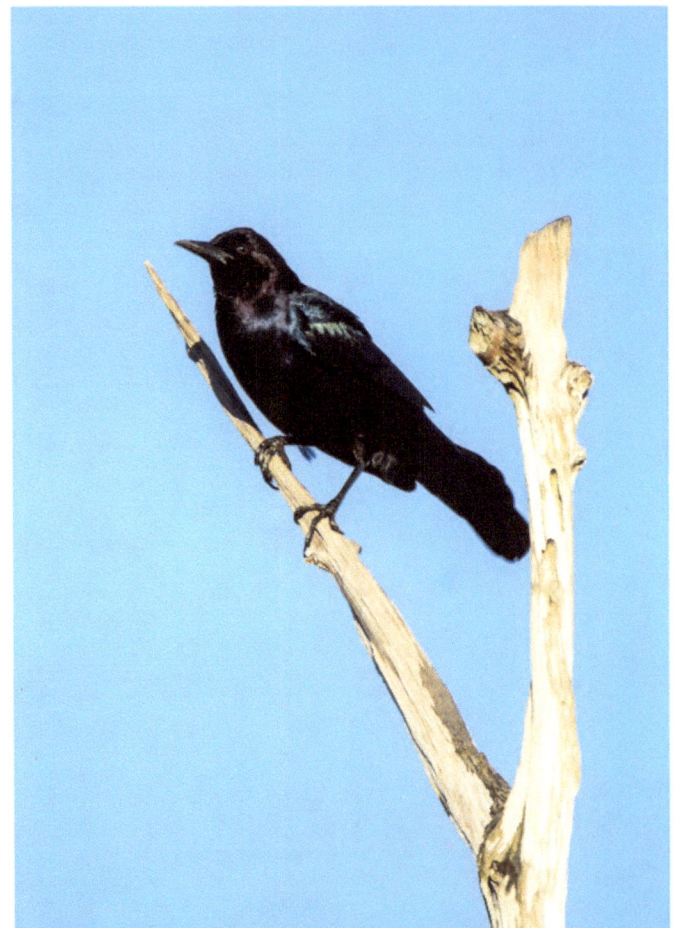

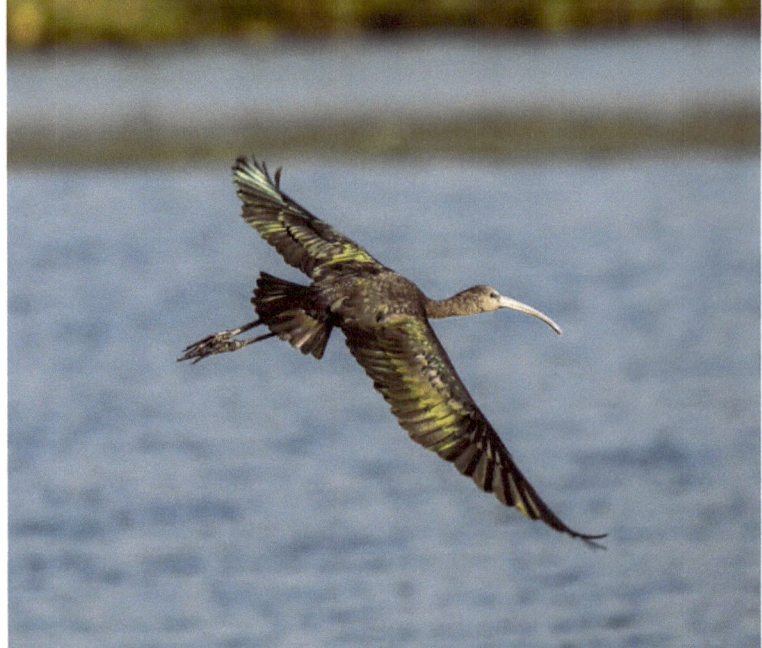

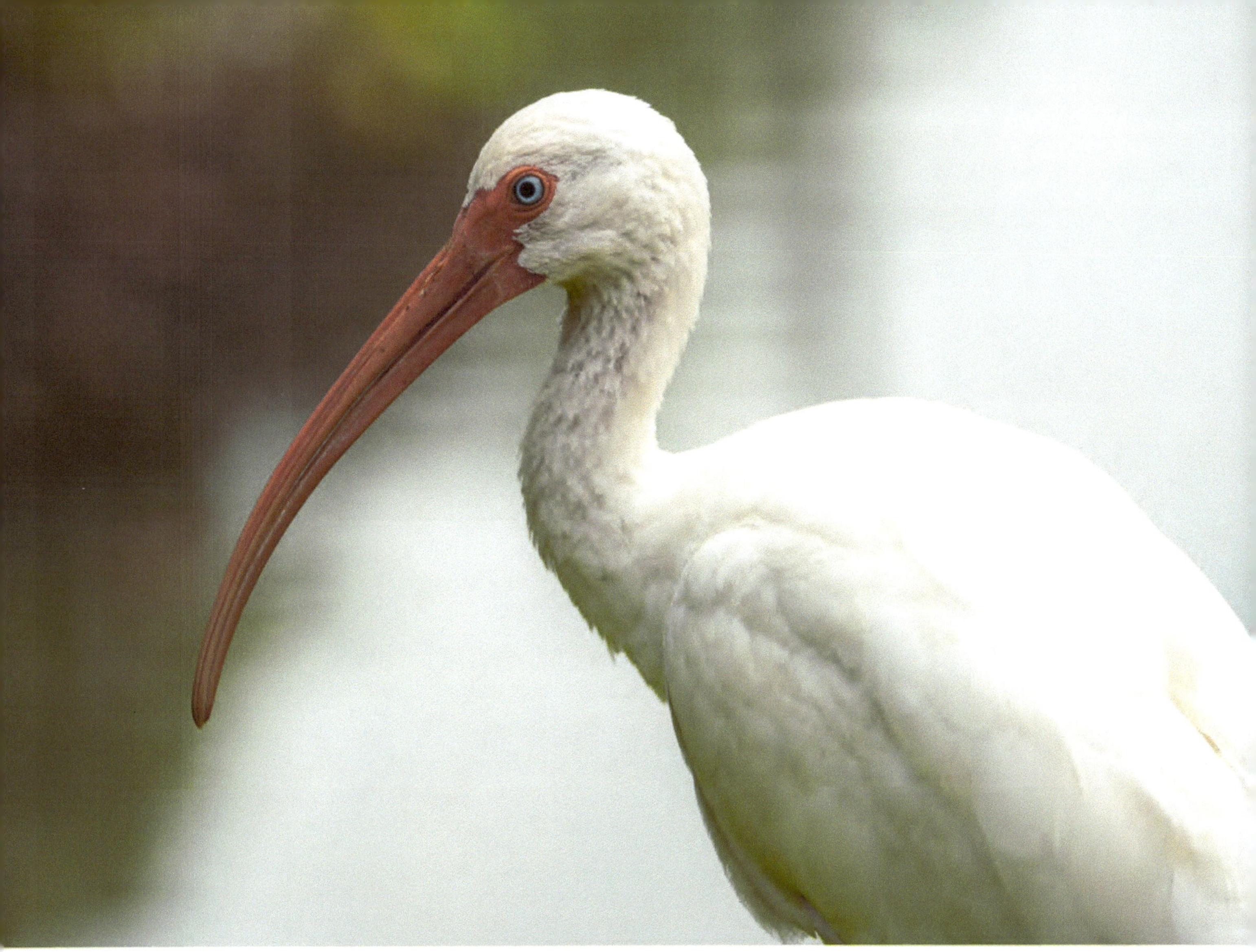

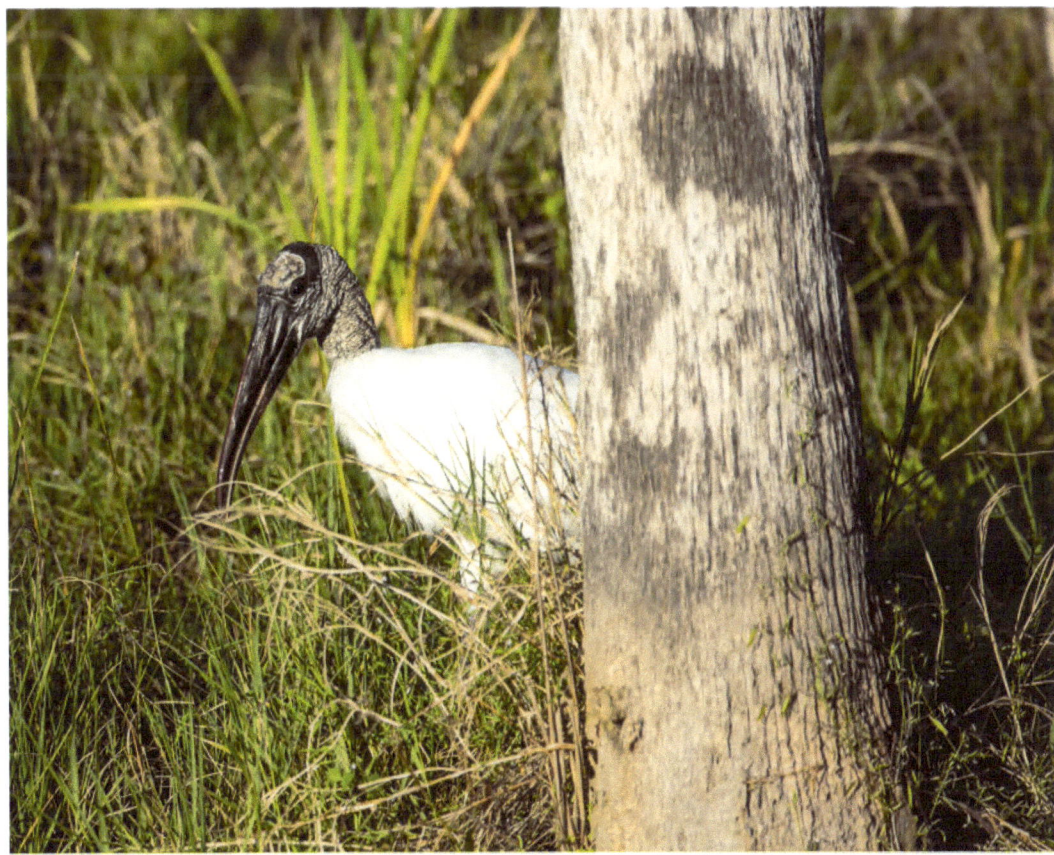

Above: A White Ibis gets a headshot.

Right: A Wood Stork is watching you approach.

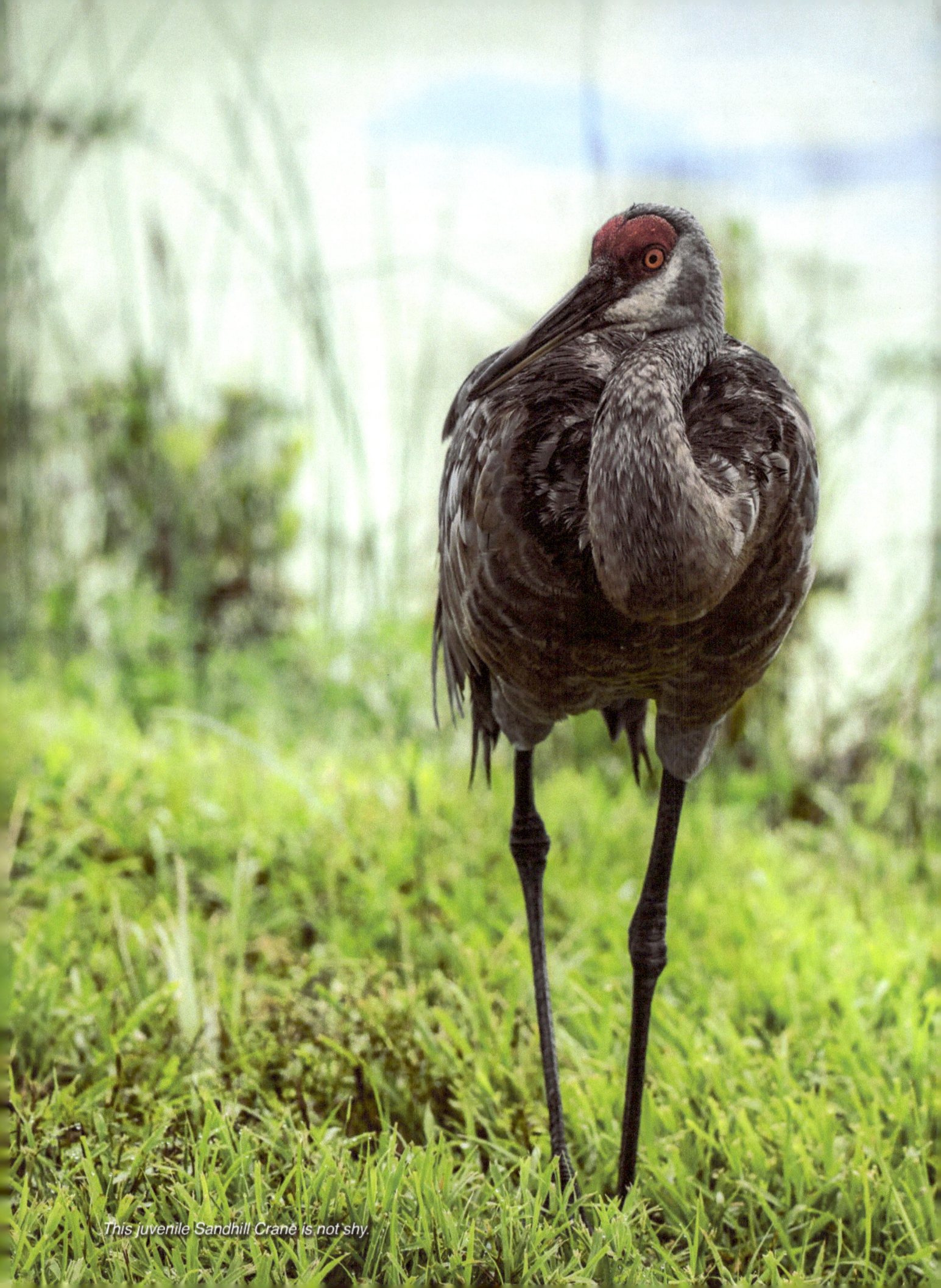
This juvenile Sandhill Crane is not shy.

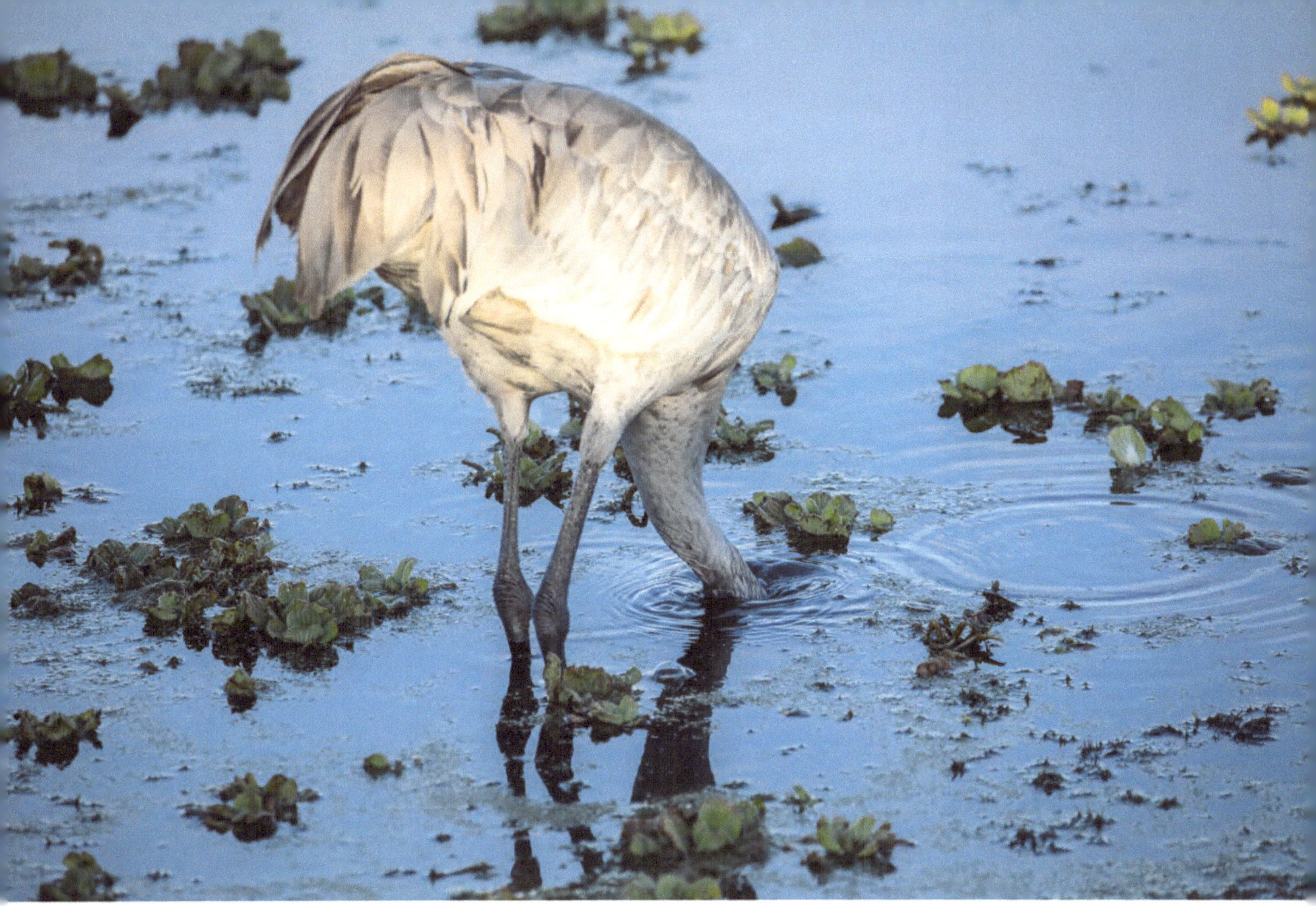

Above: Sandhill Crane has its head in deep, looking for goodies. Below: A young Sandhill Crane in side profile.

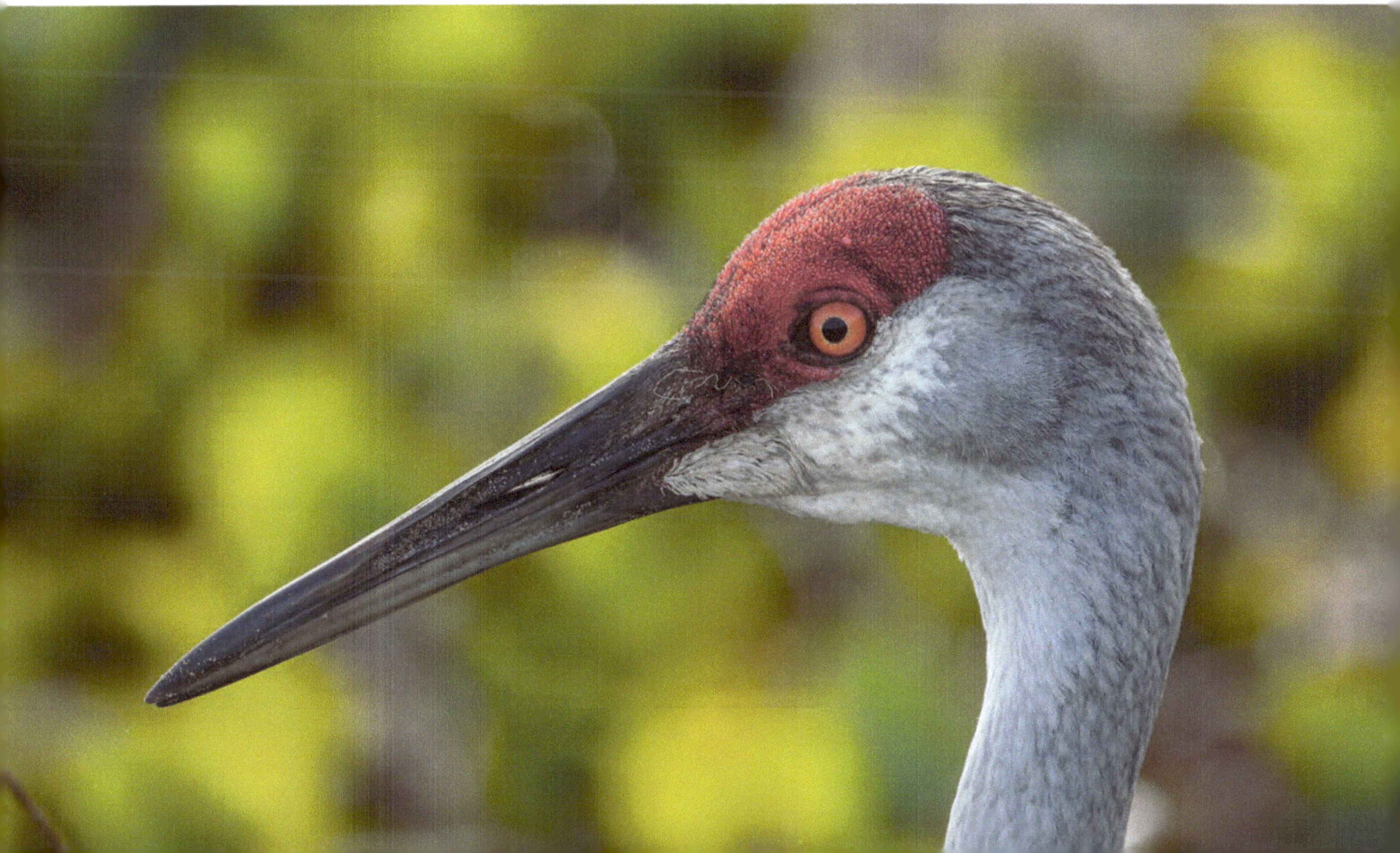

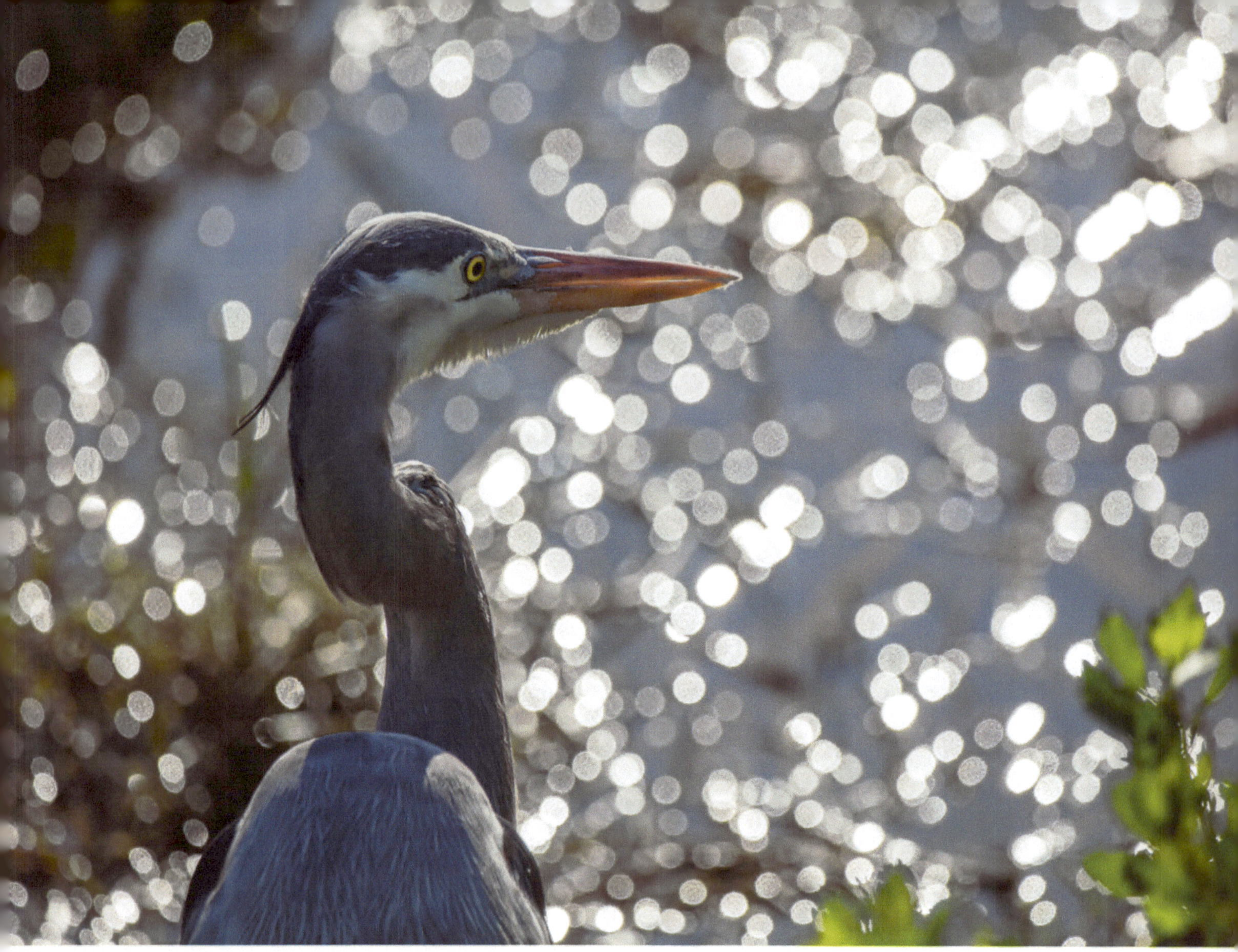

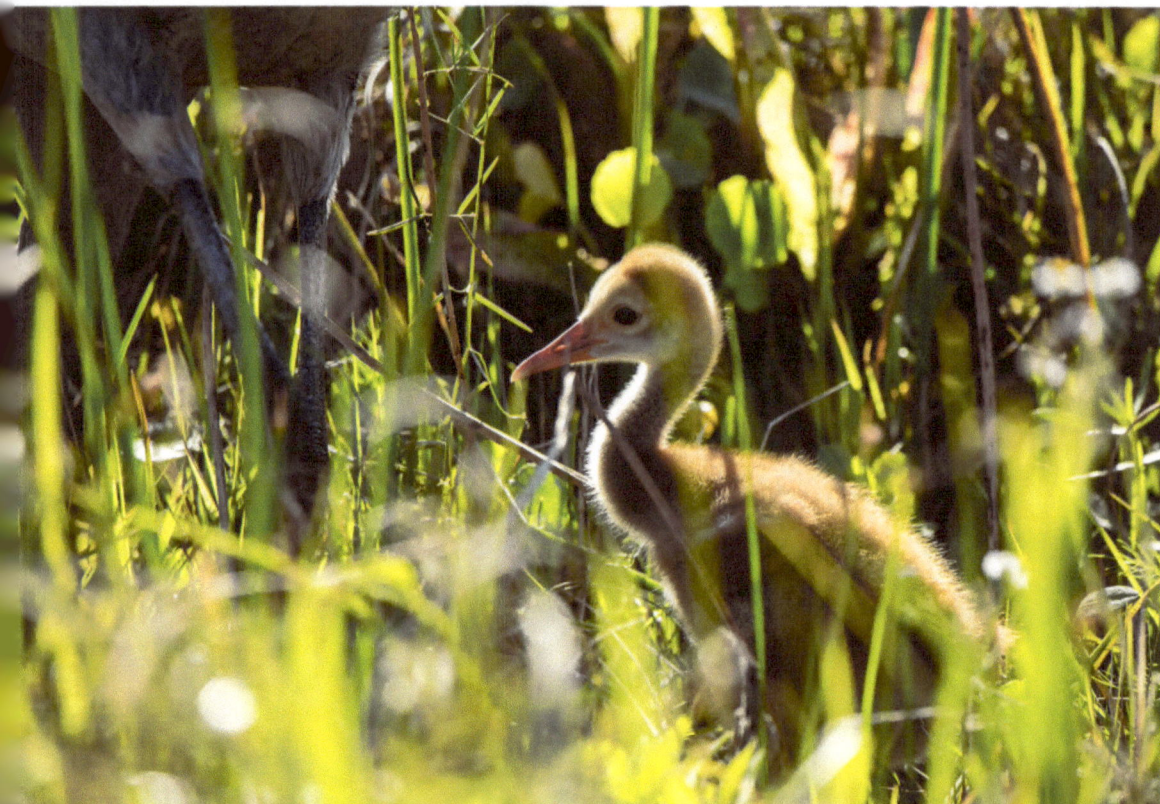

Above: Great Blue Heron reflects on a shimmering lake.

Left: Baby Crane follows Mom.

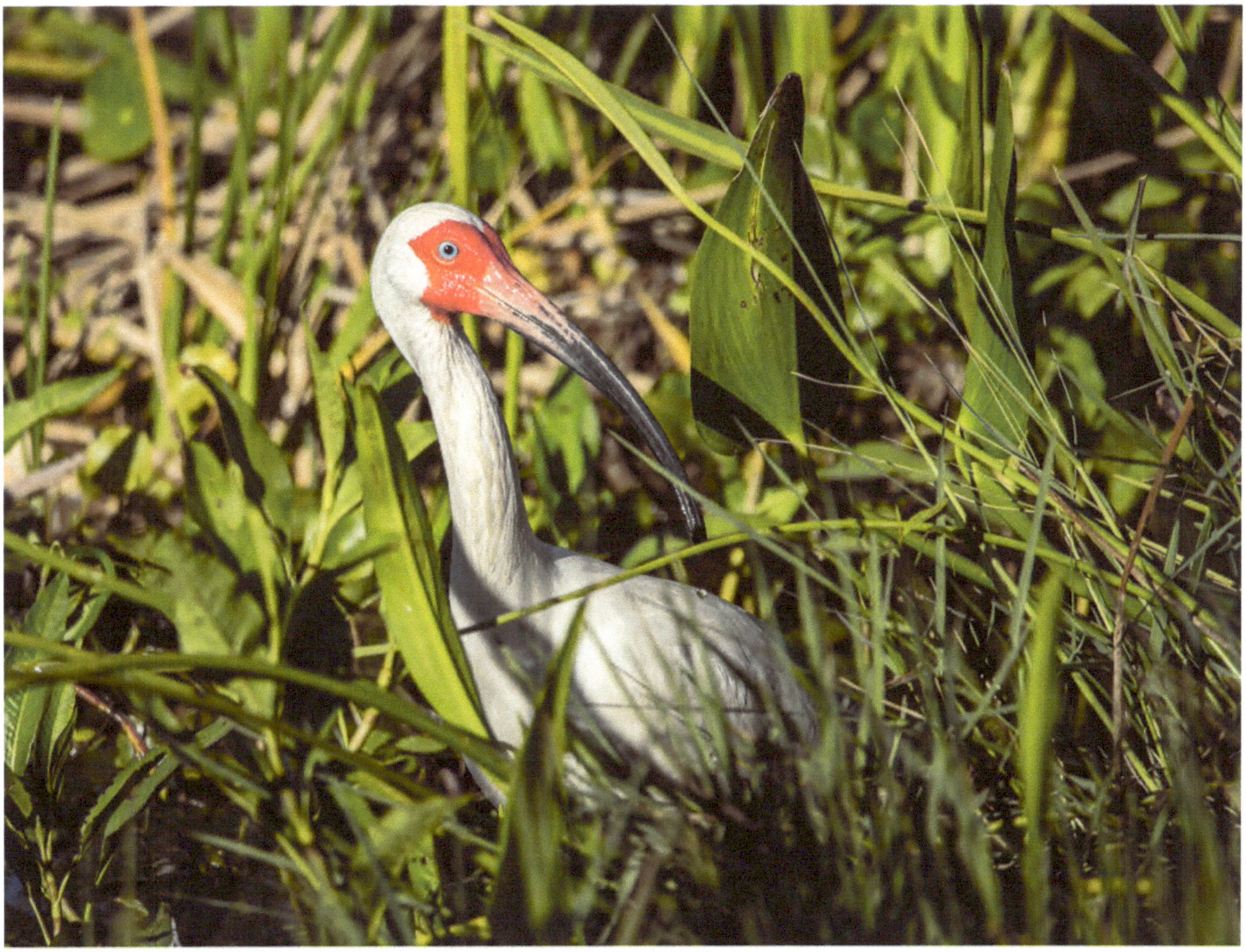

Ibis is on alert.

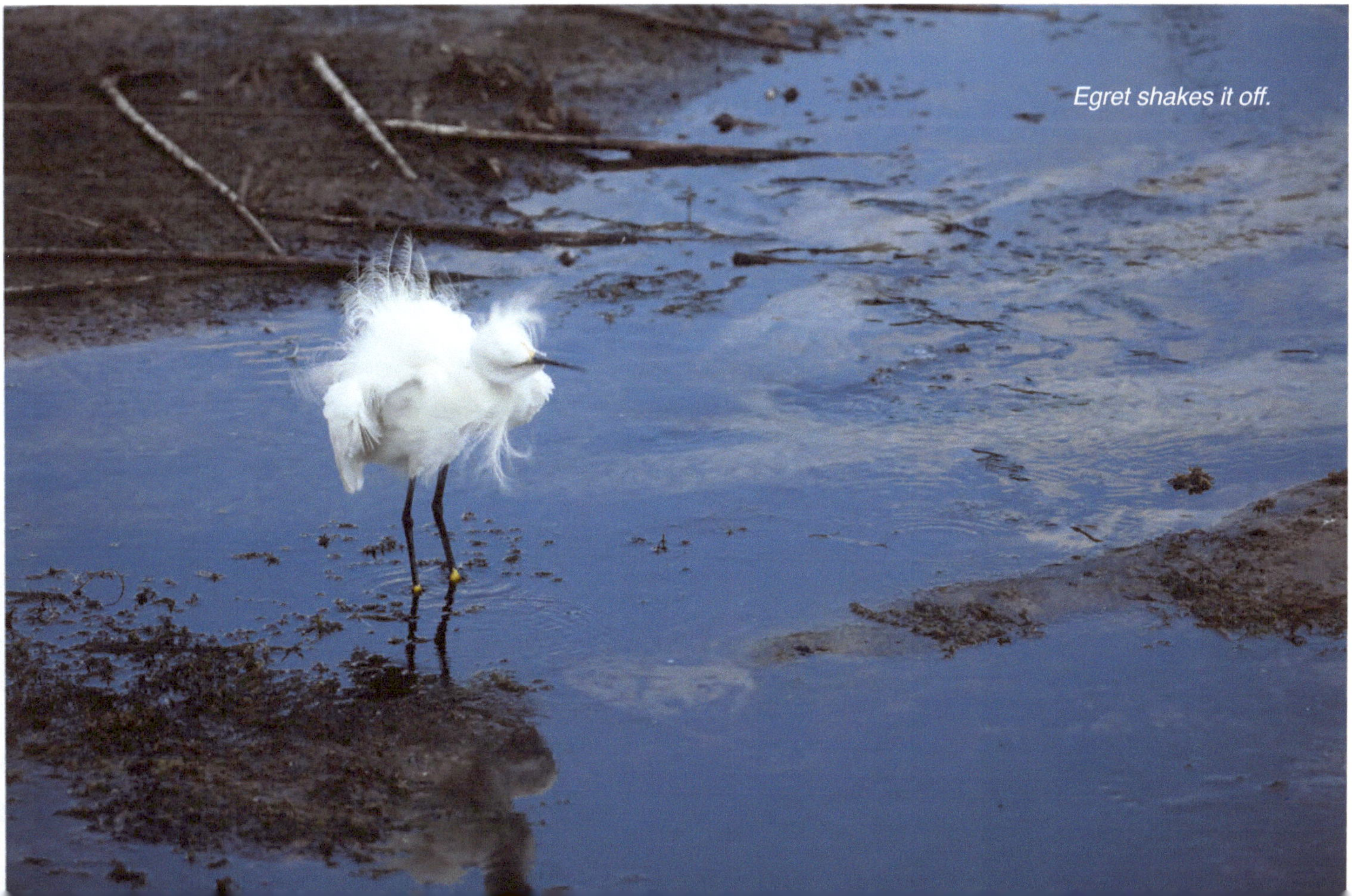

Egret shakes it off.

ABOUT THE RAPTORS

Having an opportunity to see the raptors in their natural environment is nothing short of awesome. It seems would go for weeks where I would only see Osprey, or hawks, but when the Eagles would come to town (late October or November,) the hierarchy in the hood would change drastically. There are some turf wars going on when this happens. Normally the Osprey is the big dog on the block, but when the American Bald Eagle slides into town, they move to the outskirts of their hunting territories. The Ospreys can be seen pretty much year around and are known for their dramatic and frequent dive-bombs for fish. Having the patience to wait for that as well as getting your camera settings right is an art all to its own. Crank that shutter speed up so you get the action. The Eagles do a lot of perching and watching. They migrate south from the northern states mid to late October. I would spend considerable time watching them, and it was a rarity that I would get them out on the prowl. I would frequently run across other photographers, dressed in camouflage who had set for hours to get eagle activity. I recall one afternoon the whistling ducks or grouping in the lake in two masses. 30 to 40 or more at a time or huddle together floating on the water. Not sure if this was done as a defense mechanism against the alligators from below, or from the Eagles above. This particular day, I witnessed a large bald eagle make three attempts at snatching one of these ducks off the water… and it actually failed. I never considered the duck a food source for the eagle, but I guess a little variety from time to time is good. It seems that the hawk is readily available, and almost in all scenarios in the wetlands. You just stand still long enough, and watch the tree lines, they're there I promise. The osprey is as well, and they are year-round. All raptors have distinct high-pitched bird calls, that you eventually realize they're announcing themselves as they come toward you. Of all the raptors that are in the wetlands, I spent the most time with the osprey. On two occasions, I recall coming across a copperhead snake that had met his doom in the talons of an osprey but had been dropped onto the trail just a short distance in front of me. The second occasion I ran across a fish that had fallen from the talons of an osprey. Just minutes before I had photographed this bird snatching the fish out of the water, little did I know that I'd walk up on him minutes later, on my trail, out of water, still alive and with a hole in its side (I threw him back to see if he would make something of himself with a second chance).

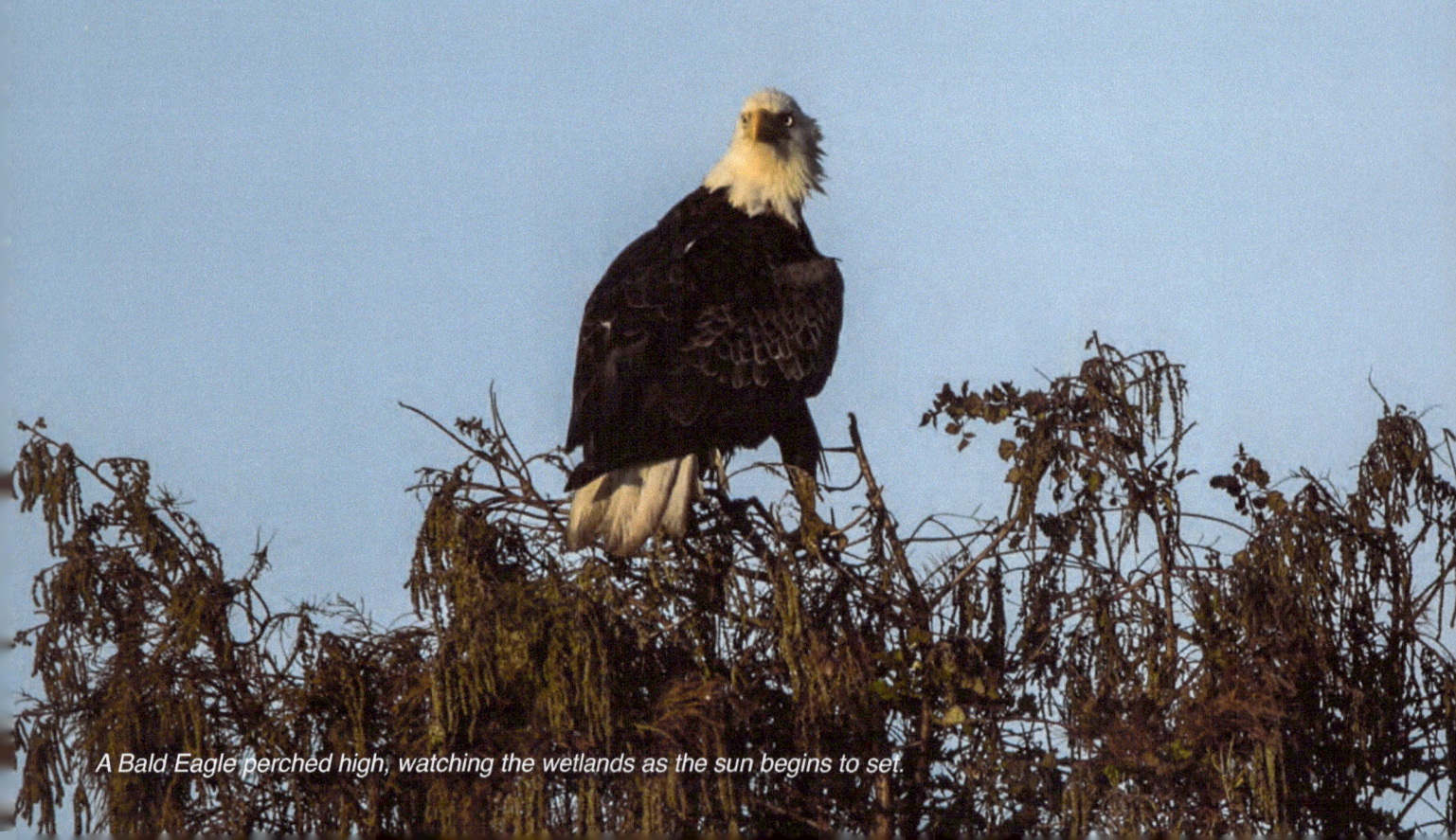

A Bald Eagle perched high, watching the wetlands as the sun begins to set.

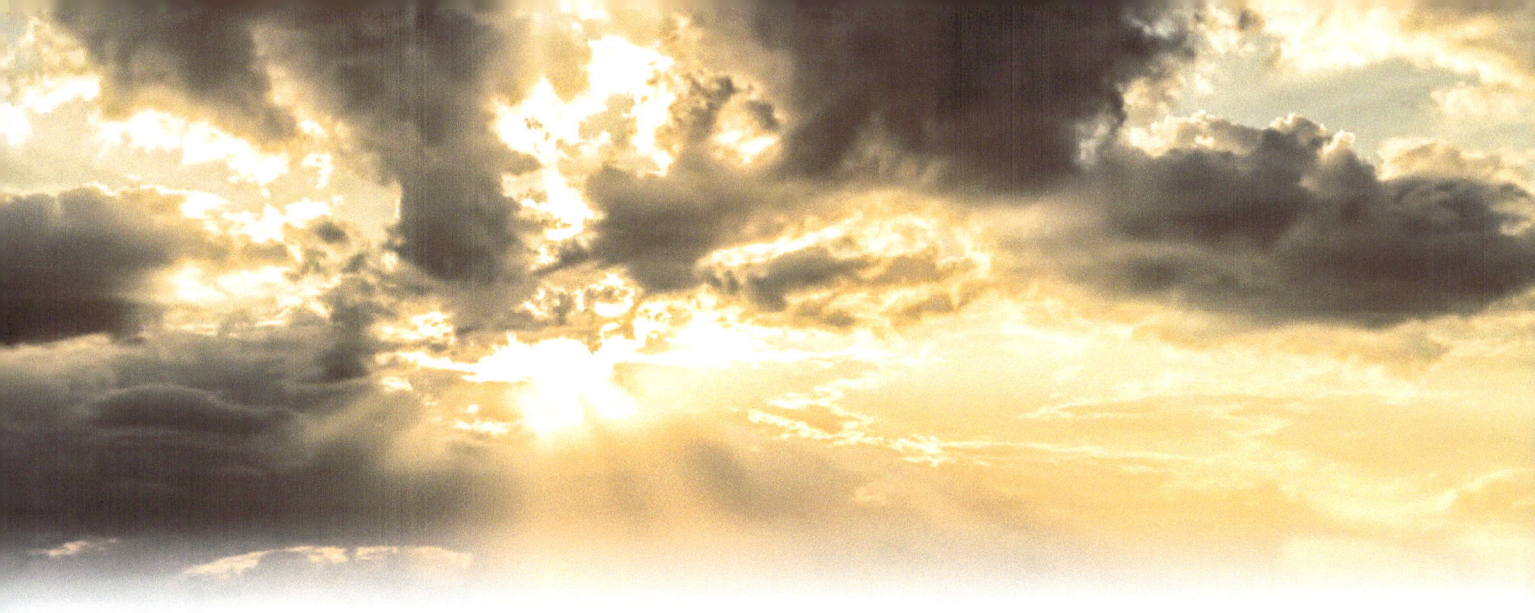

Hawk is well disguised while perched.

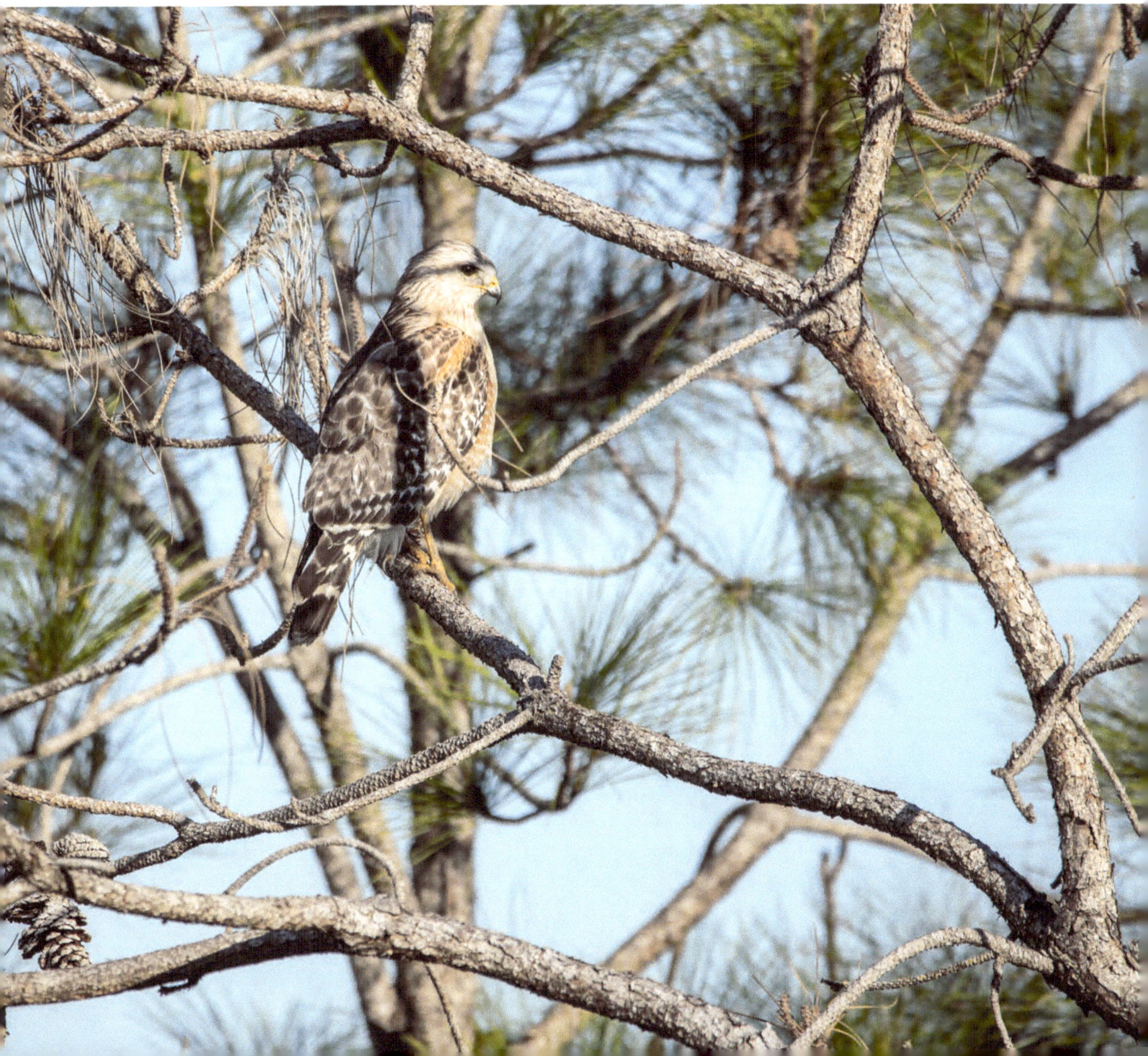

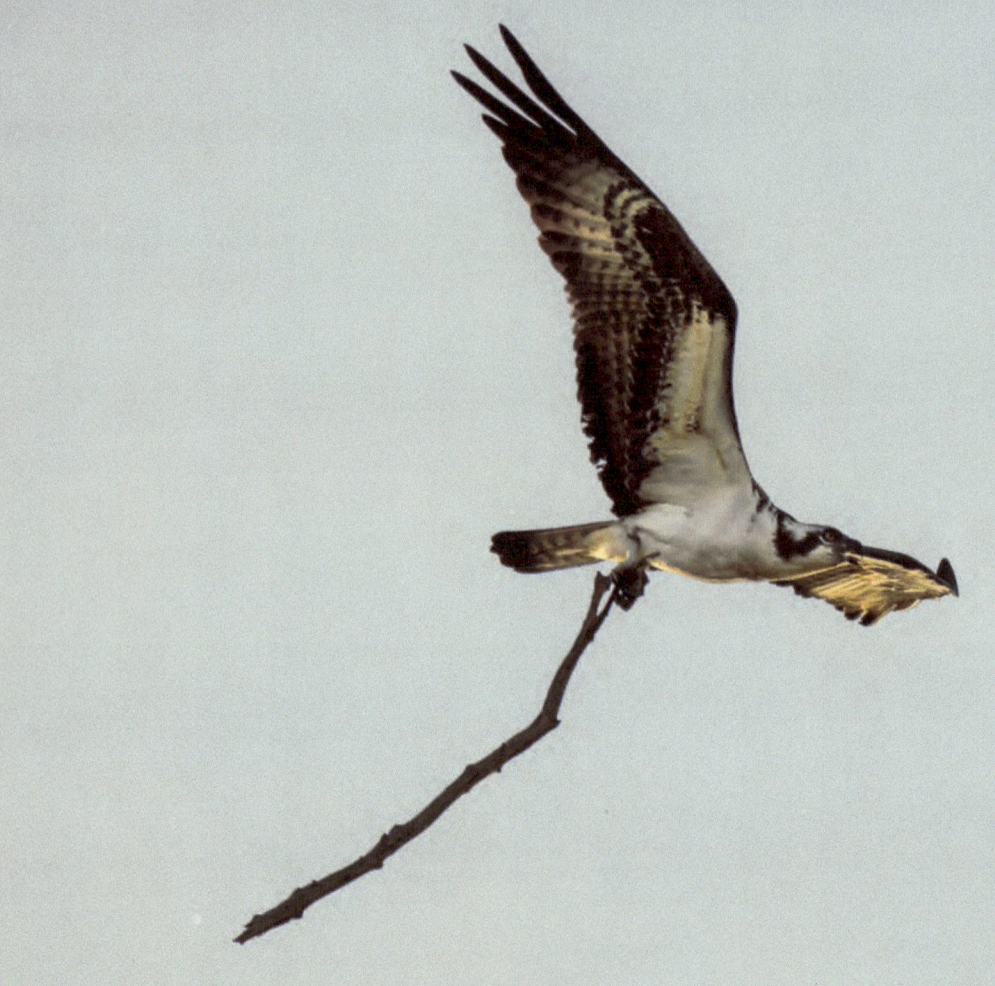

Above: An adult Osprey gathers branches to build his very large nest. Below: An Osprey poses for you at sunset.

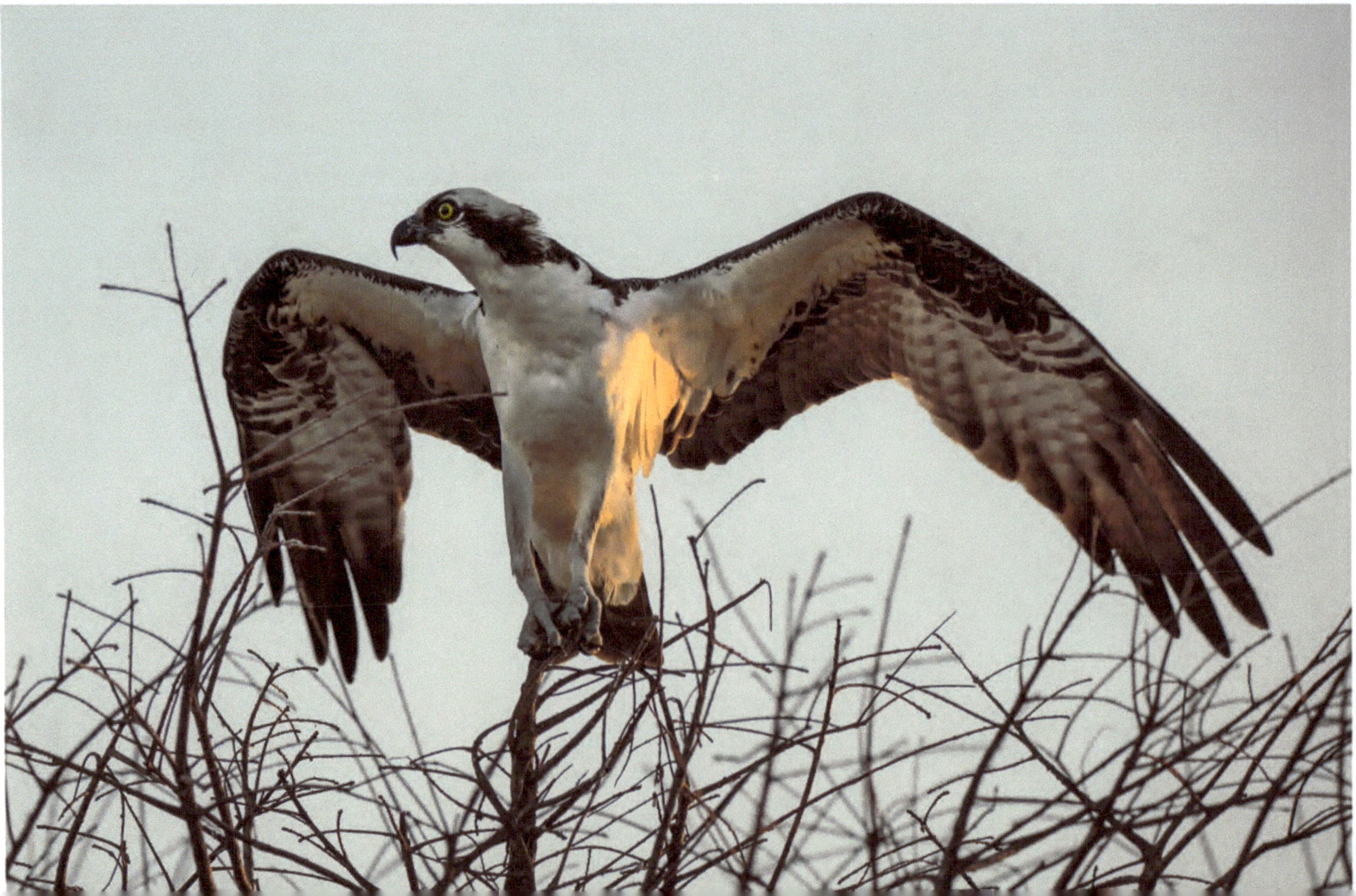

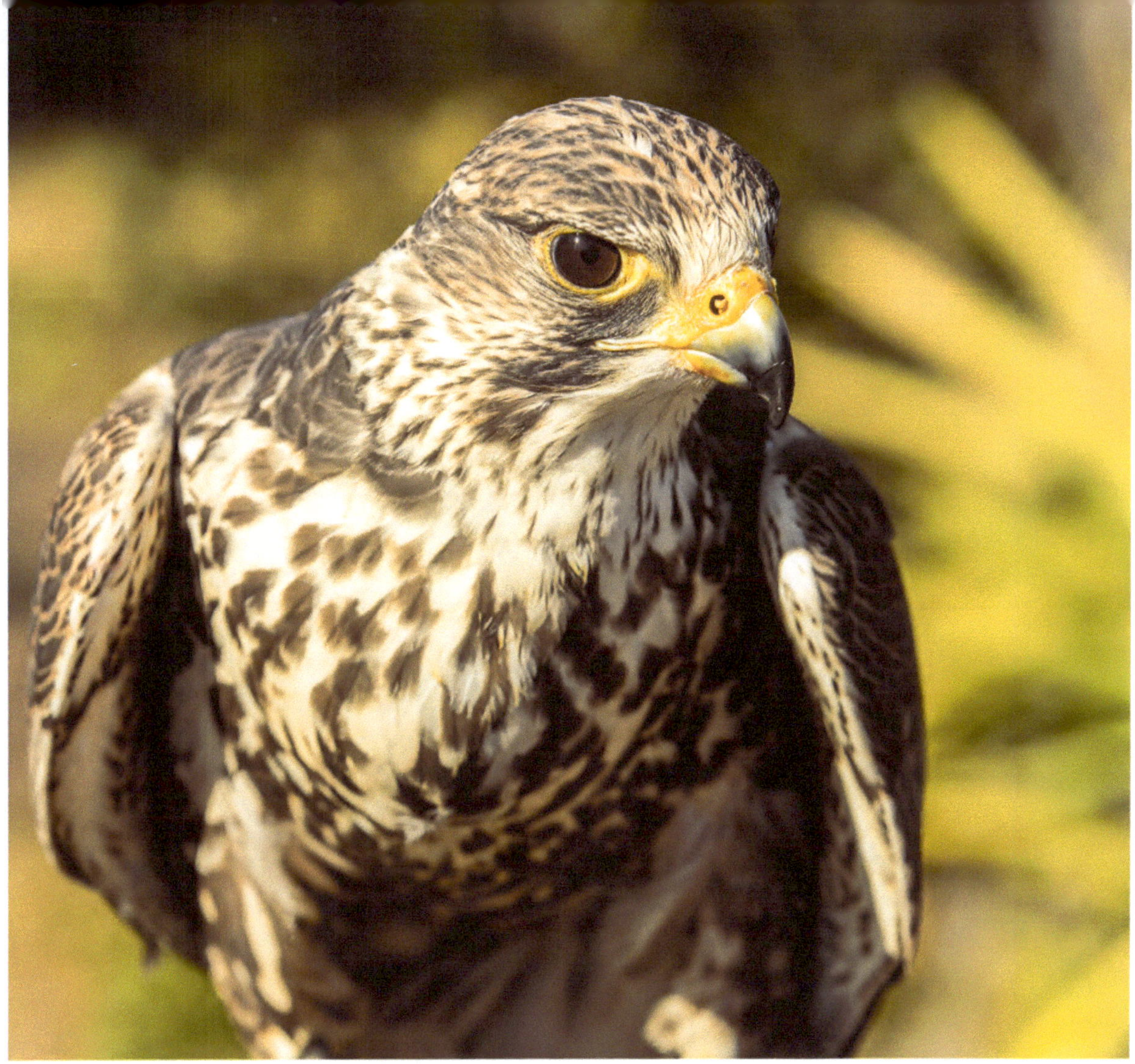

Above: A Hawk has spotted something of interest...

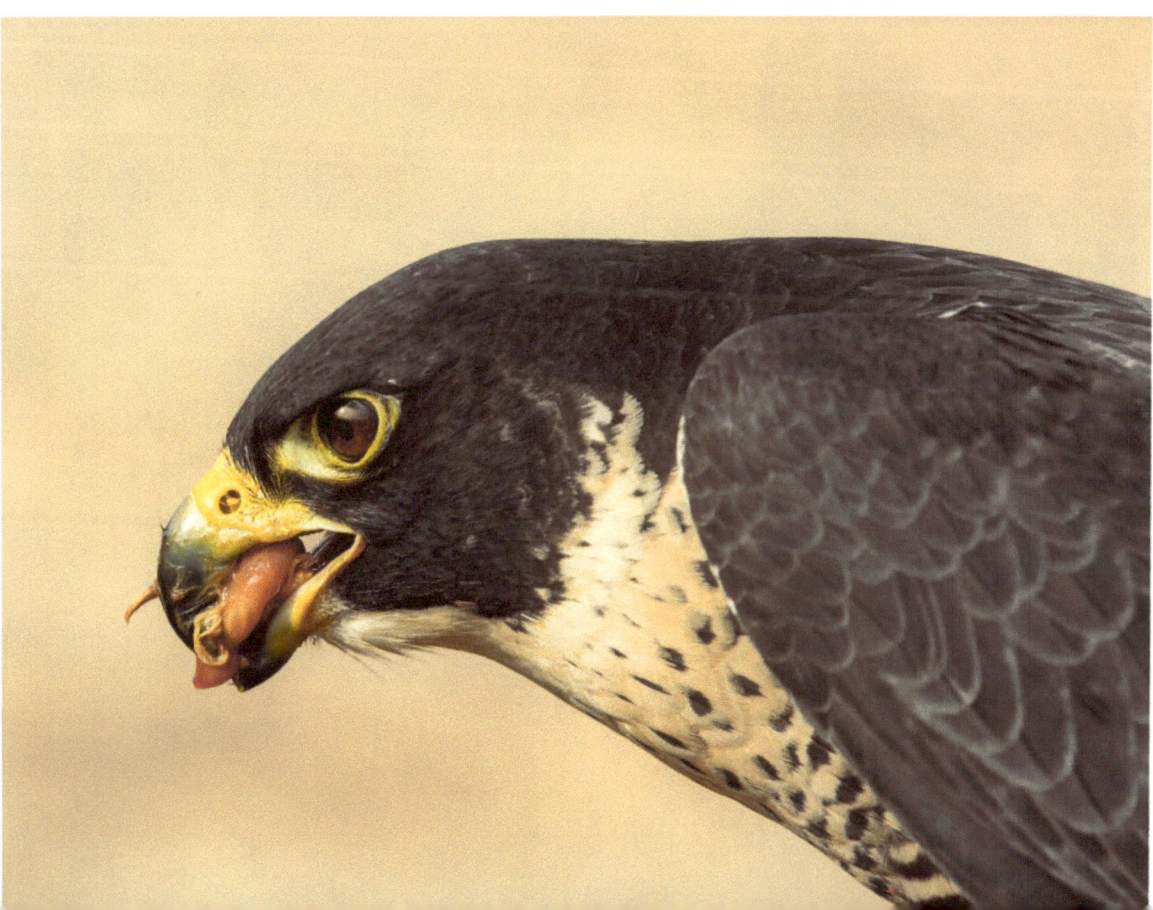

Right: A Hawk enjoys a juicey lunch.

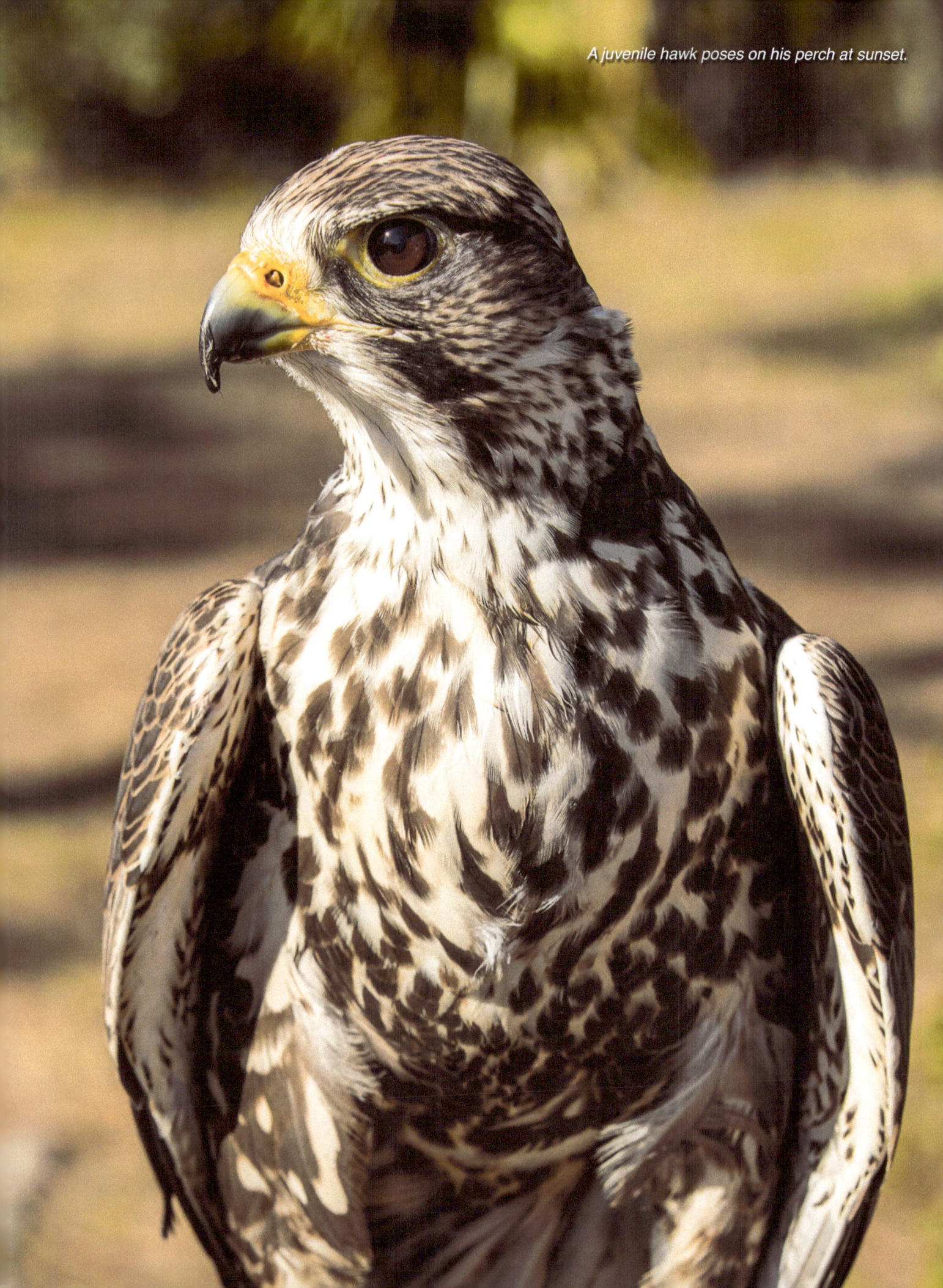

A juvenile hawk poses on his perch at sunset.

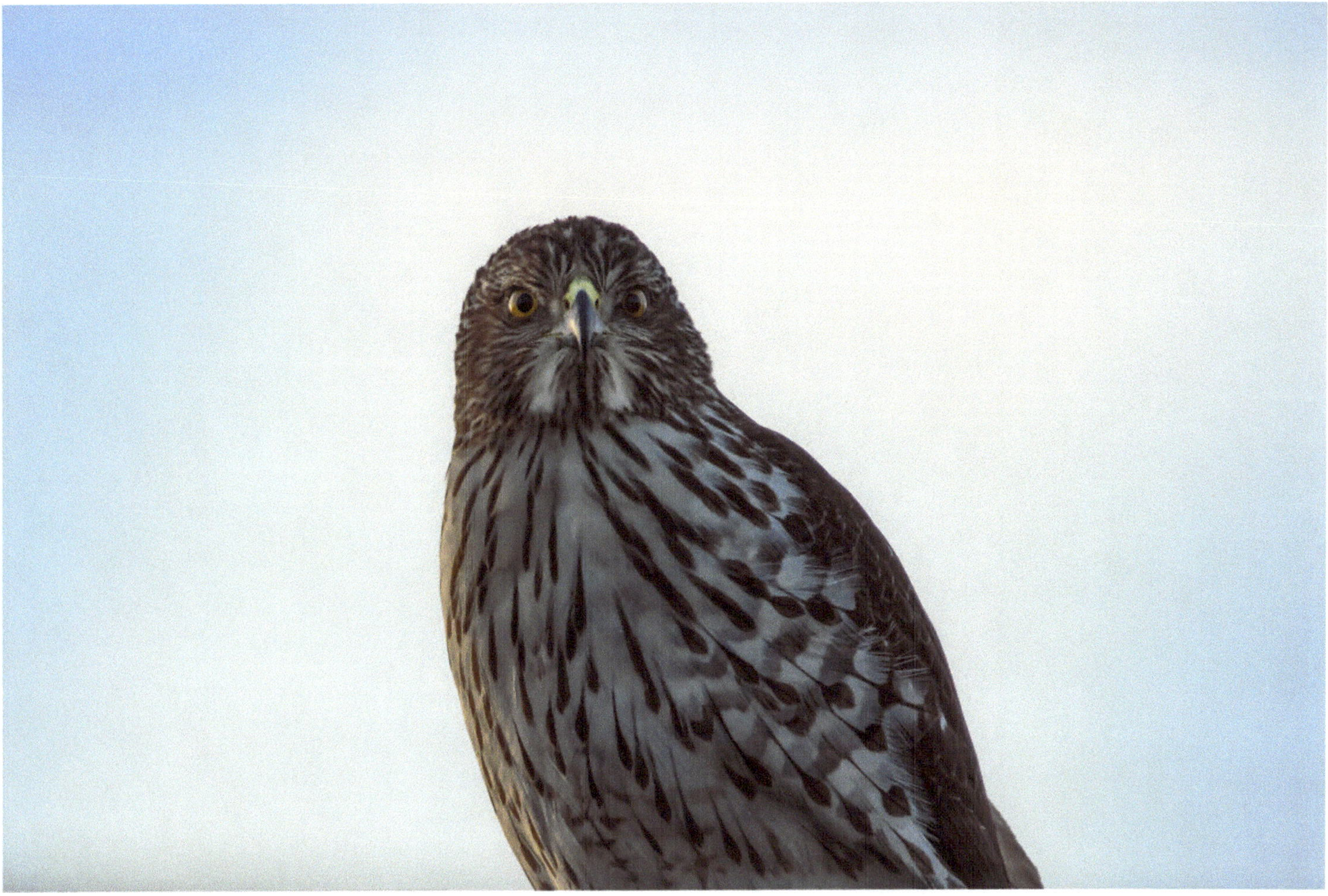

Above: A juvenile hawk is watching you at sunset.

Right: A hawk's eyes catch the light of the sunset.

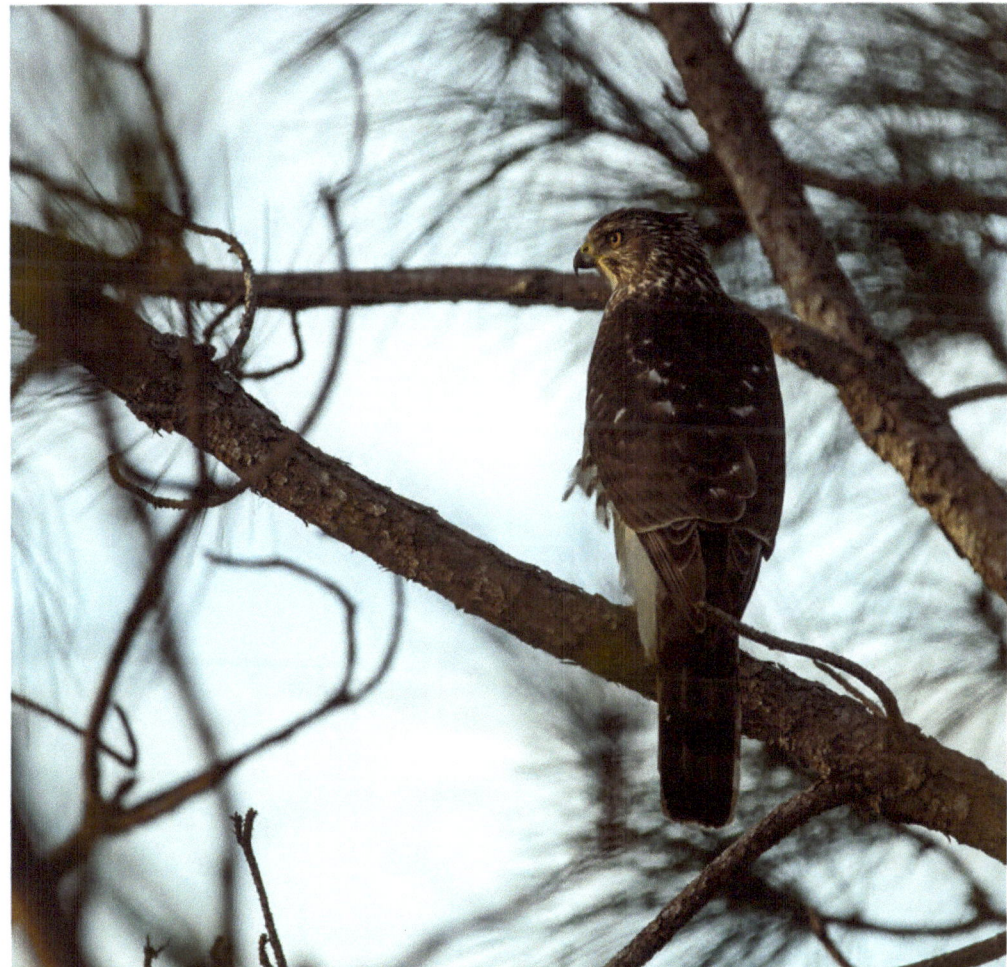

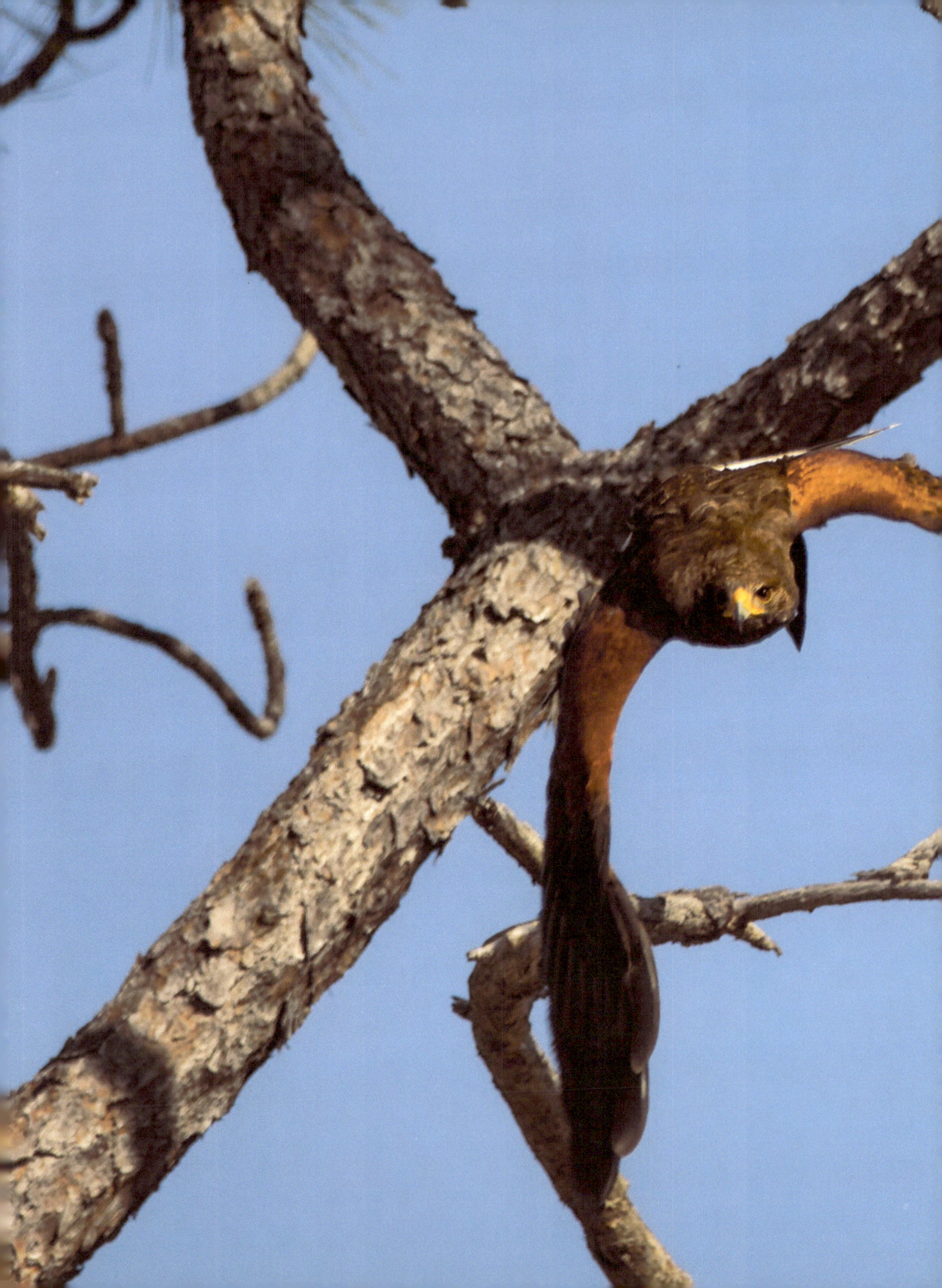

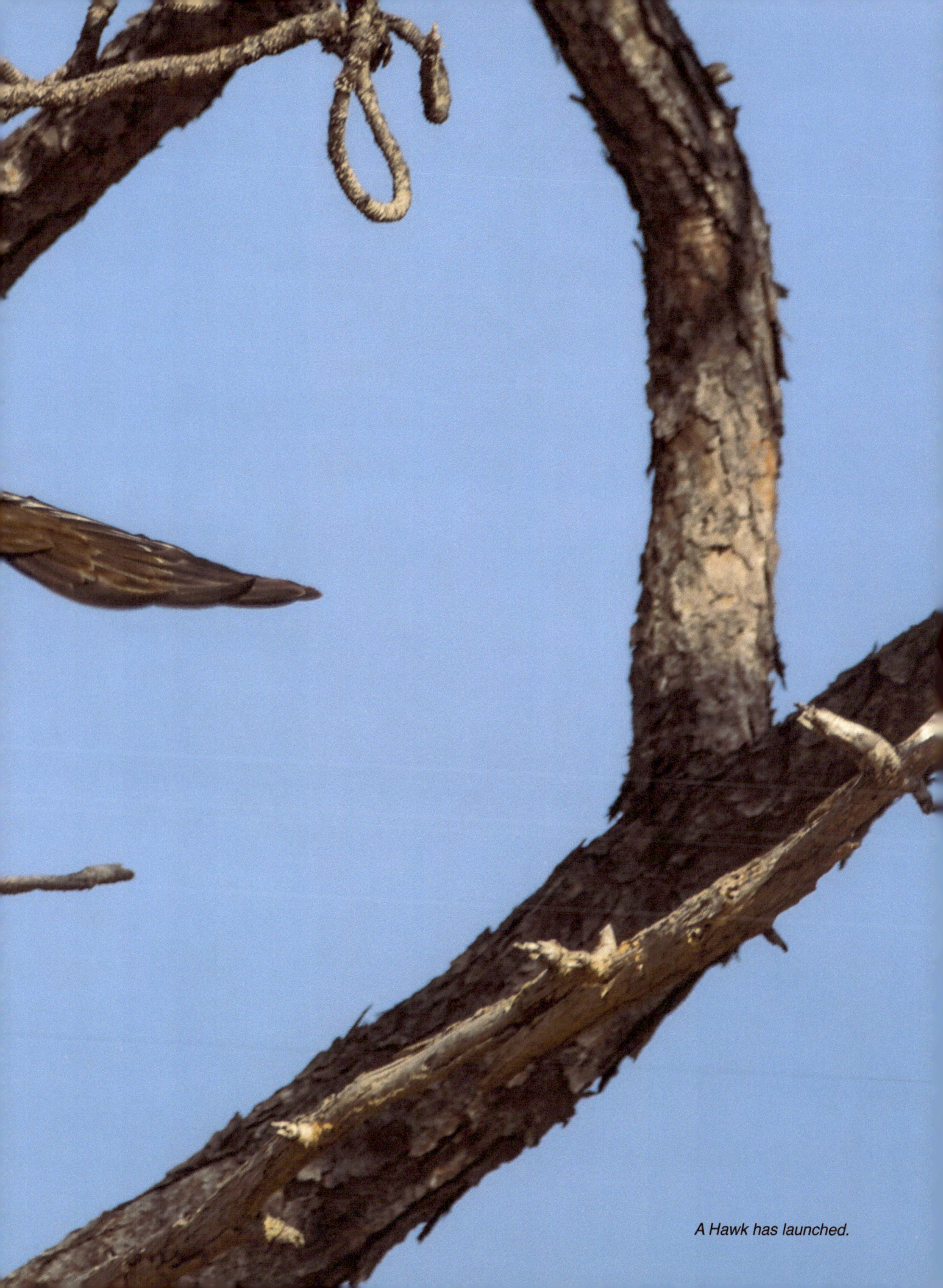

A Hawk has launched.

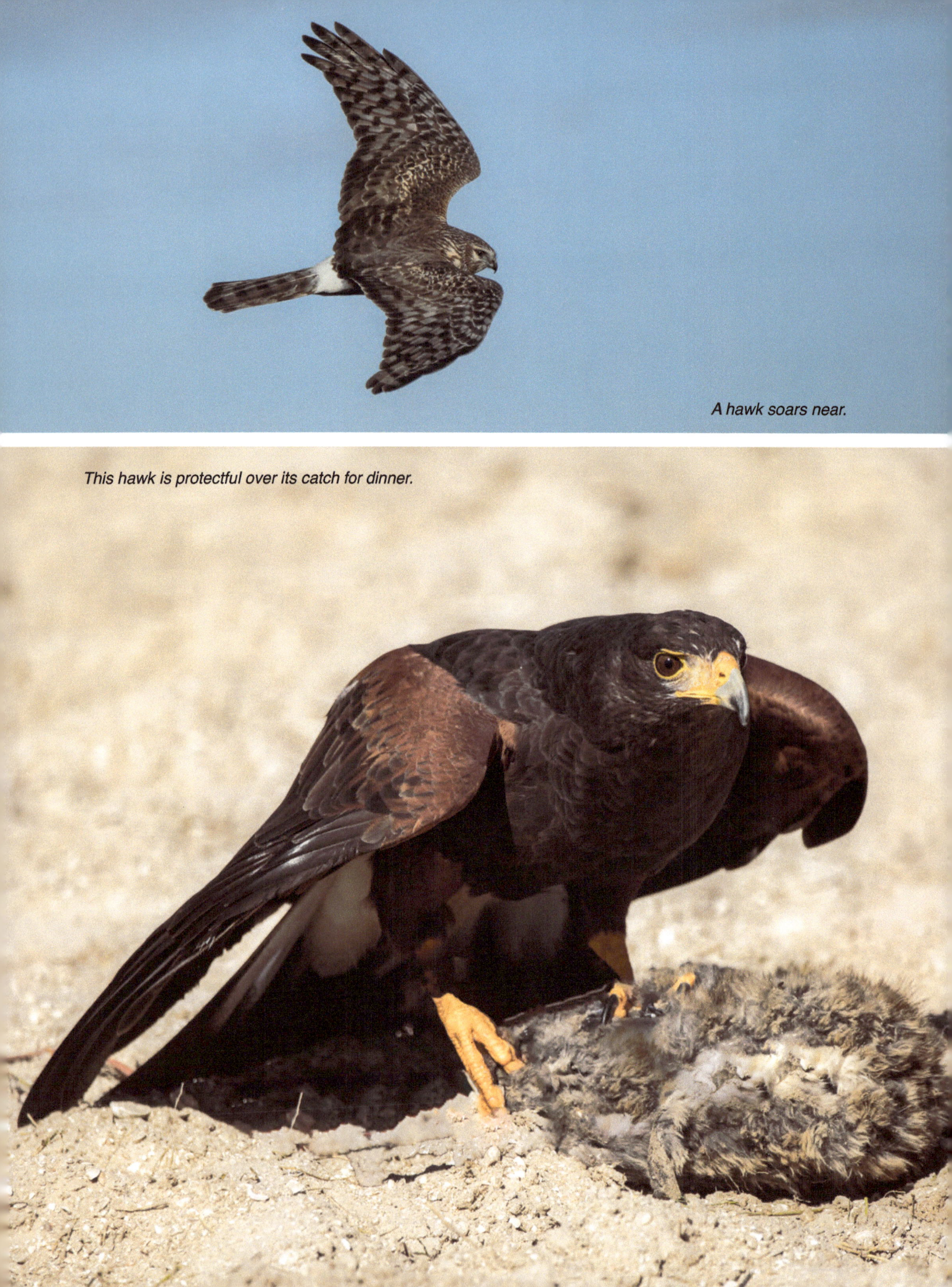

A hawk soars near.

This hawk is protectful over its catch for dinner.

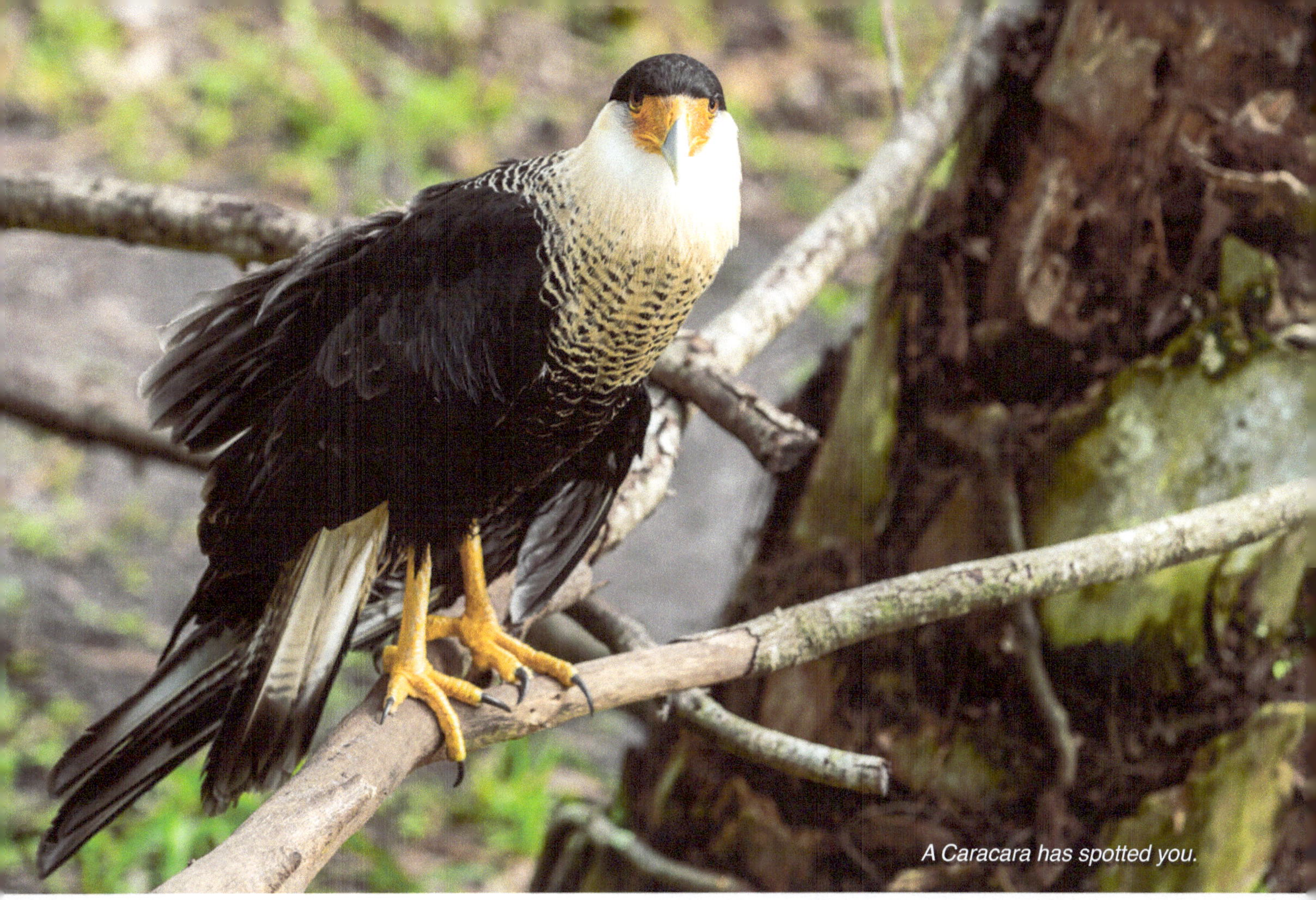

A Caracara has spotted you.

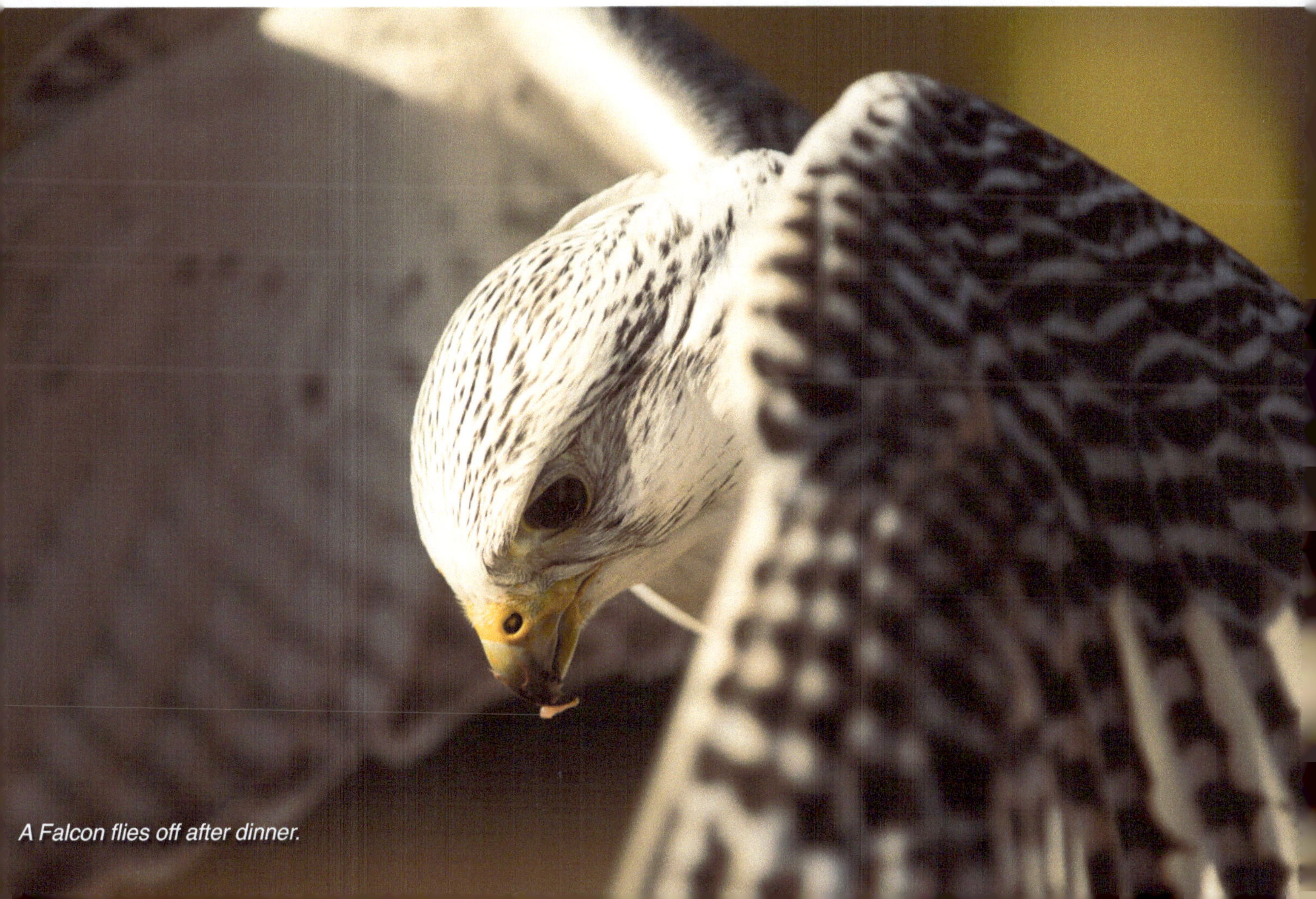

A Falcon flies off after dinner.

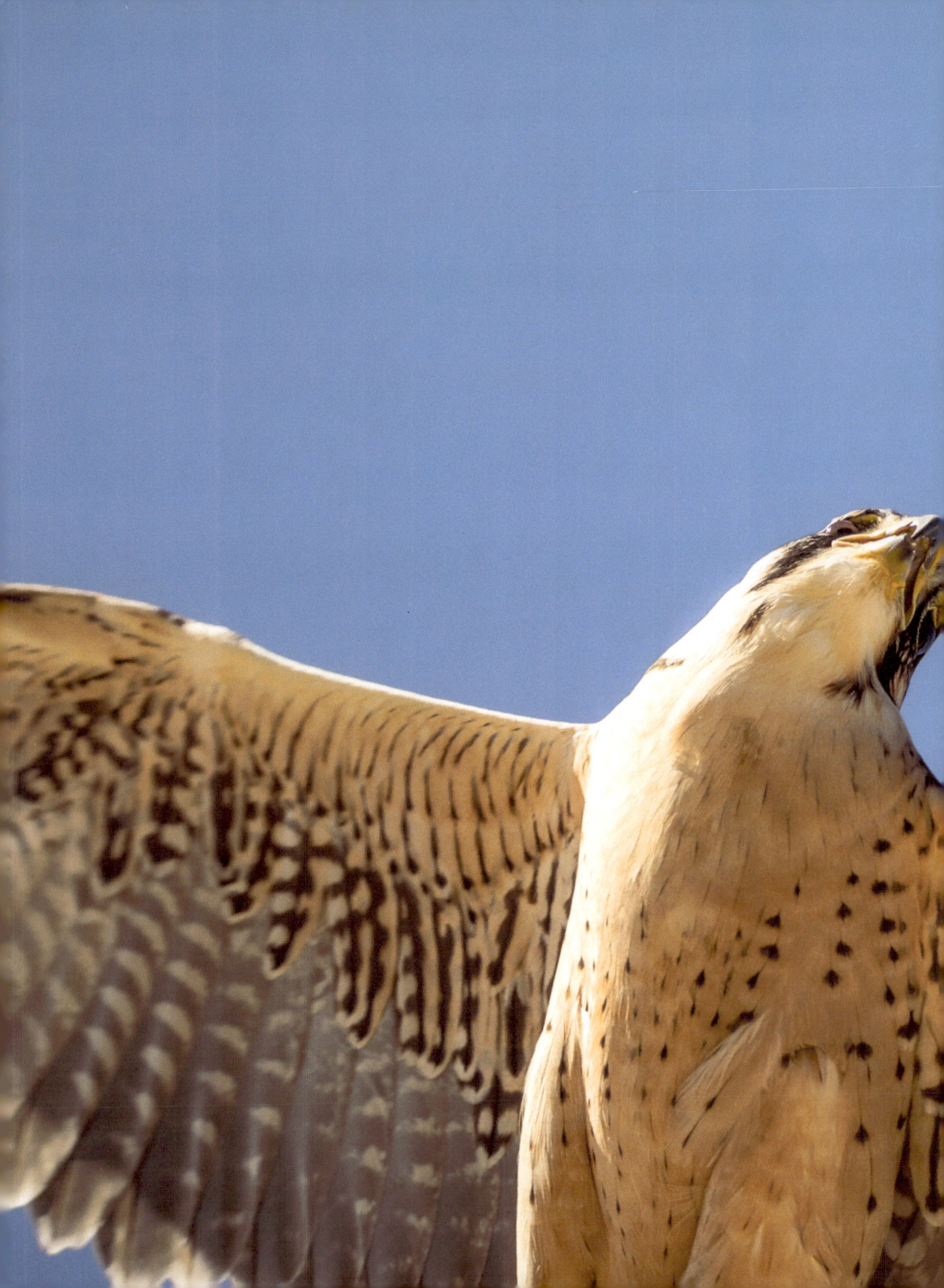

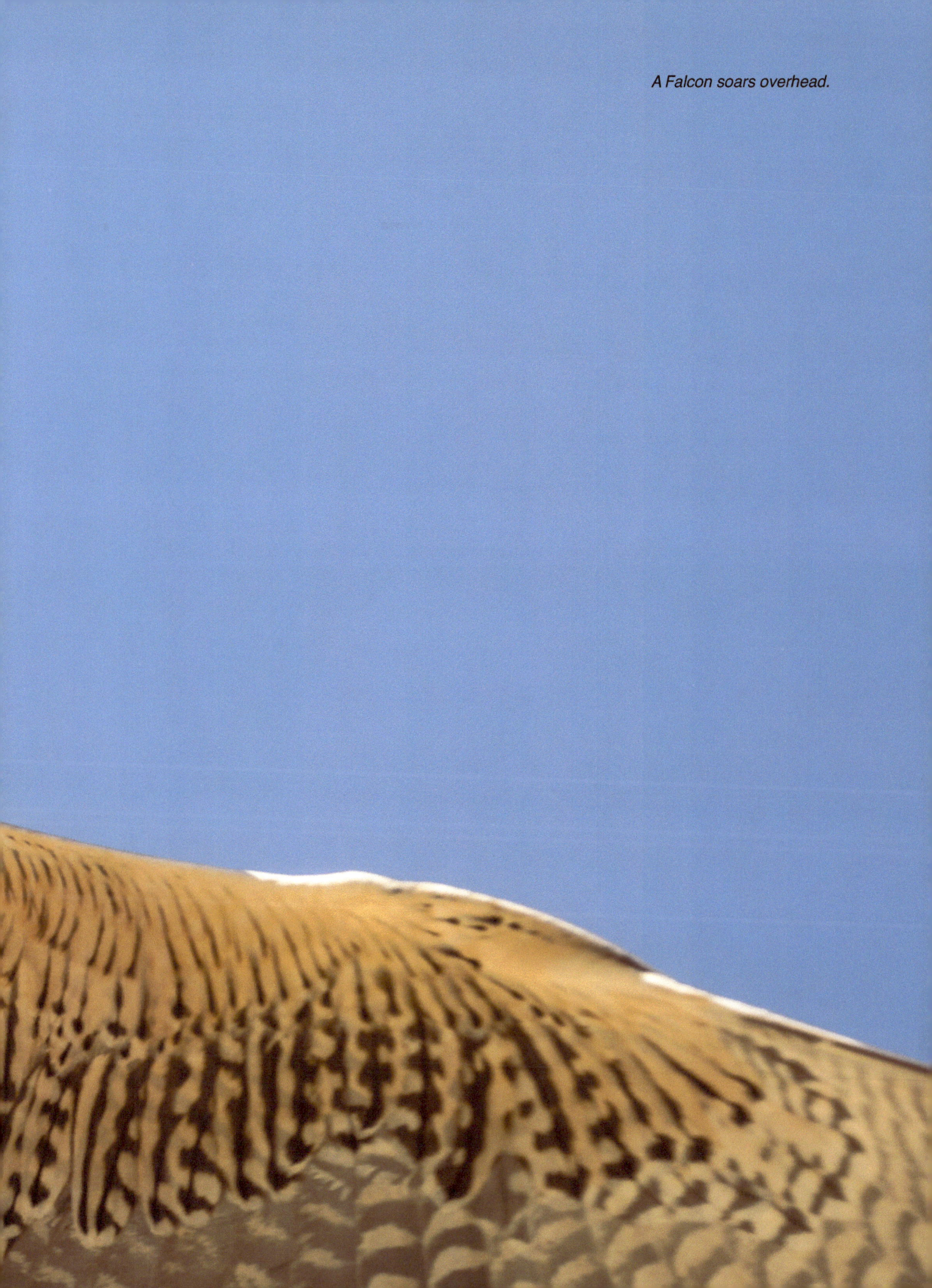

A Falcon soars overhead.

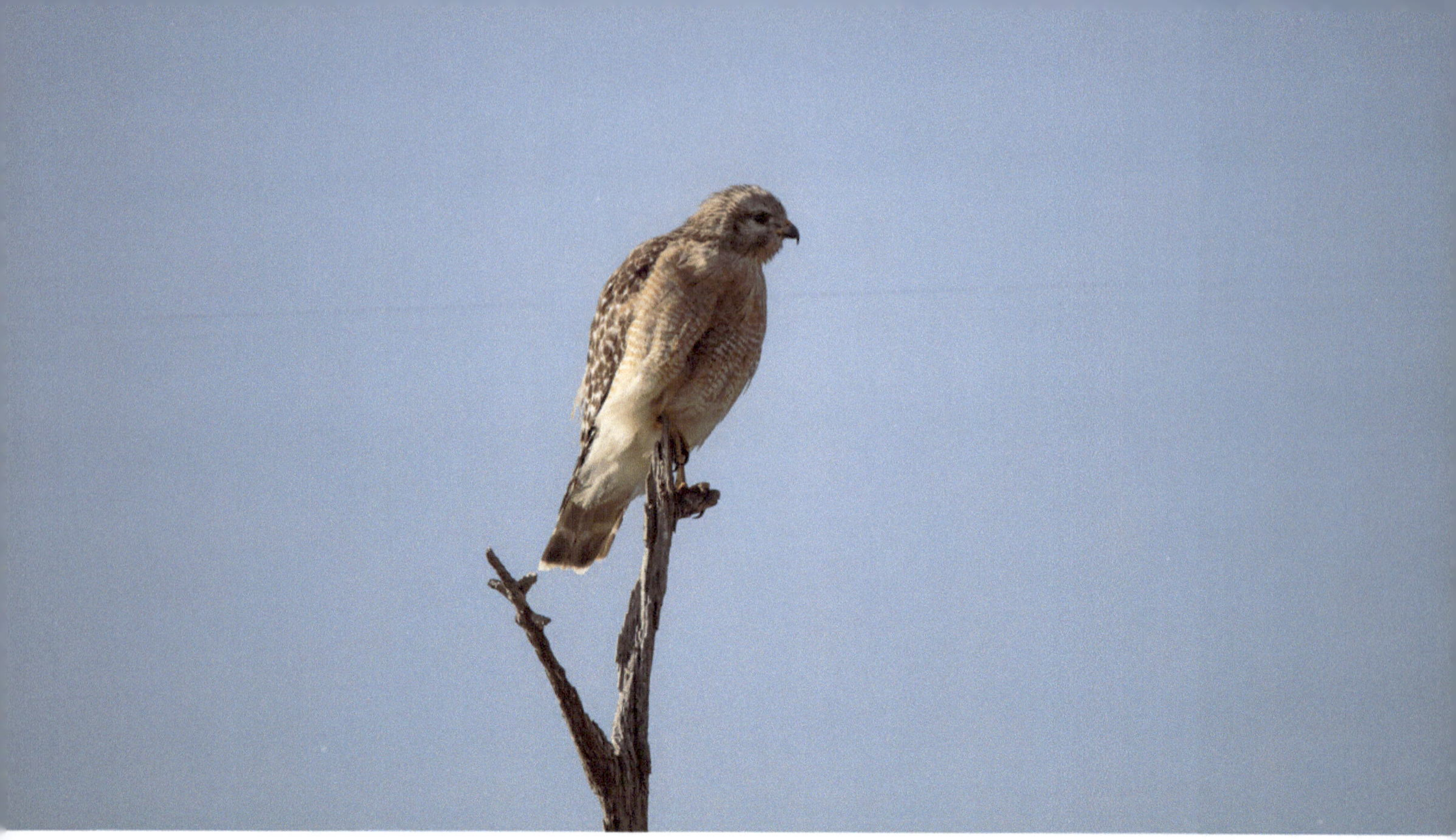

Above: This adult hawk has a sharp beak to show you.   Below: Male bald eagle is watching you.

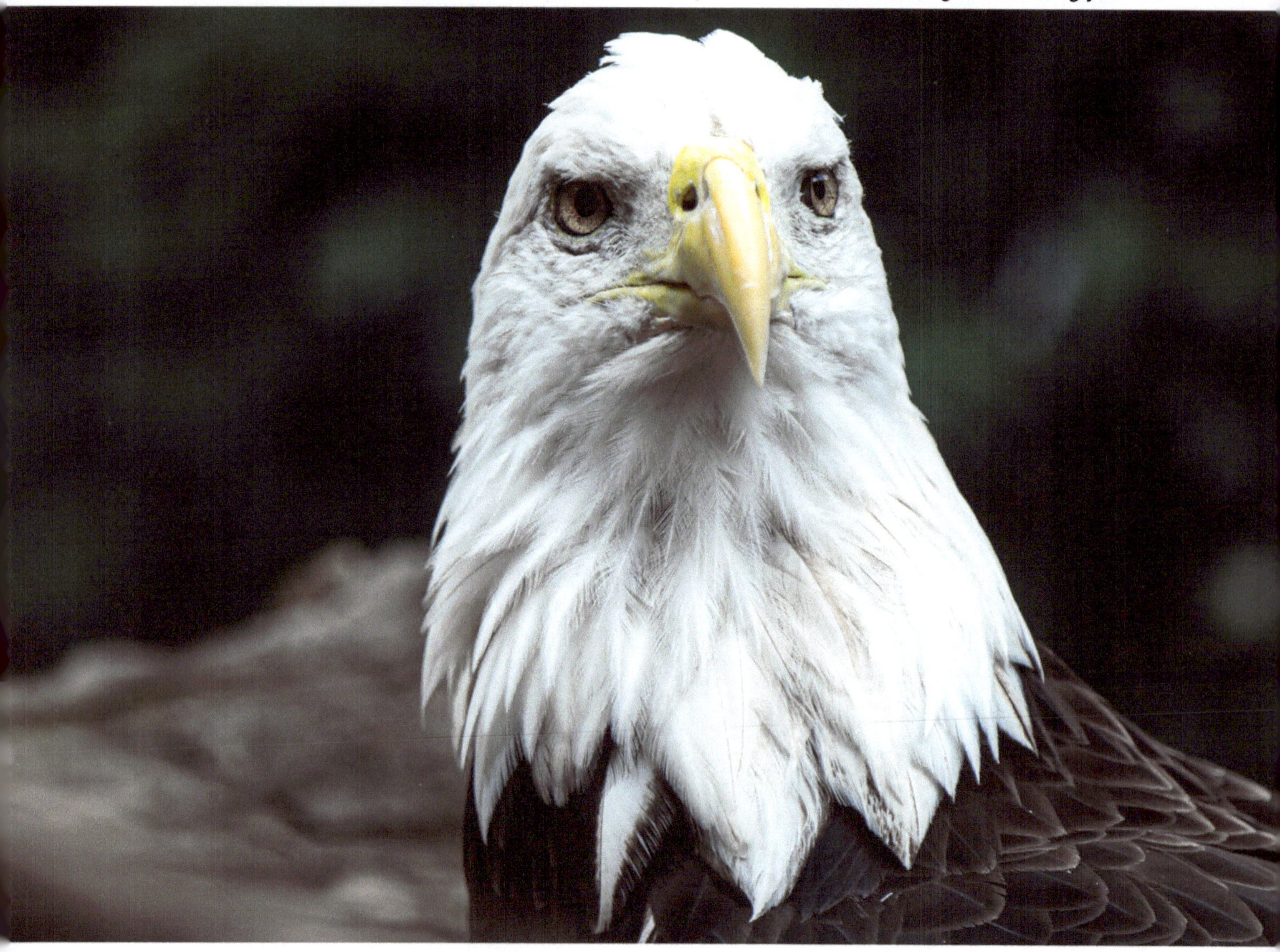

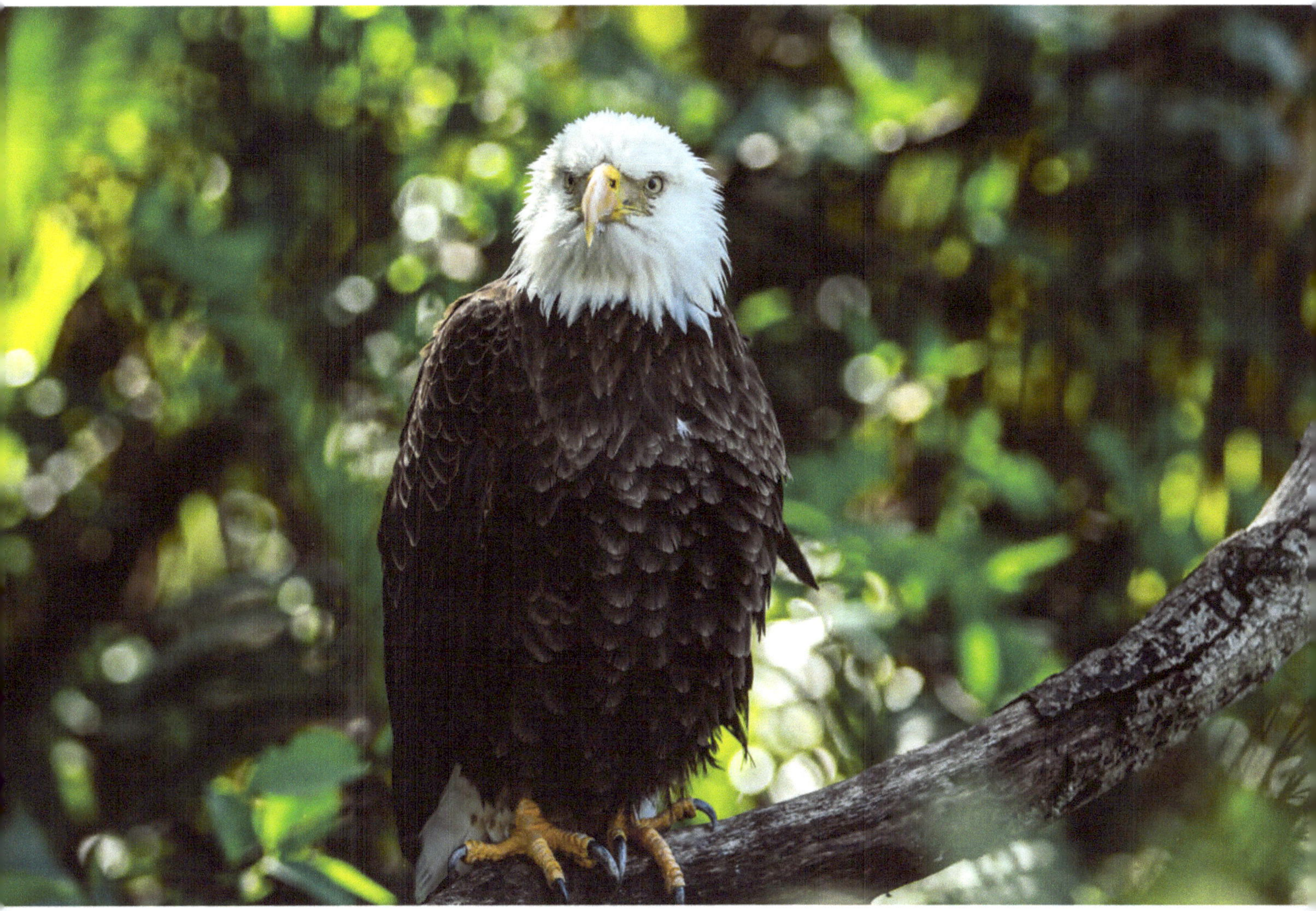

Eagle starts to puff feathers.

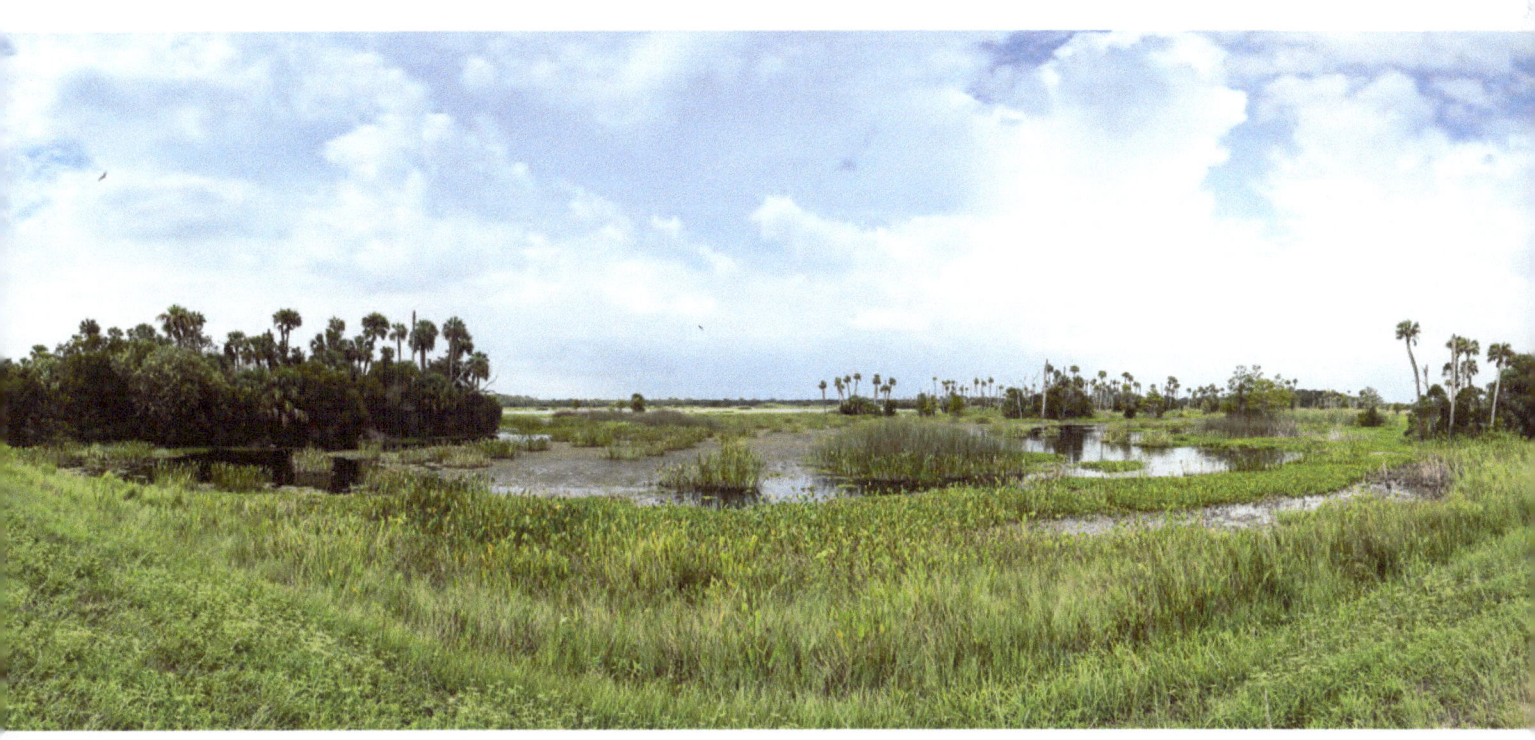

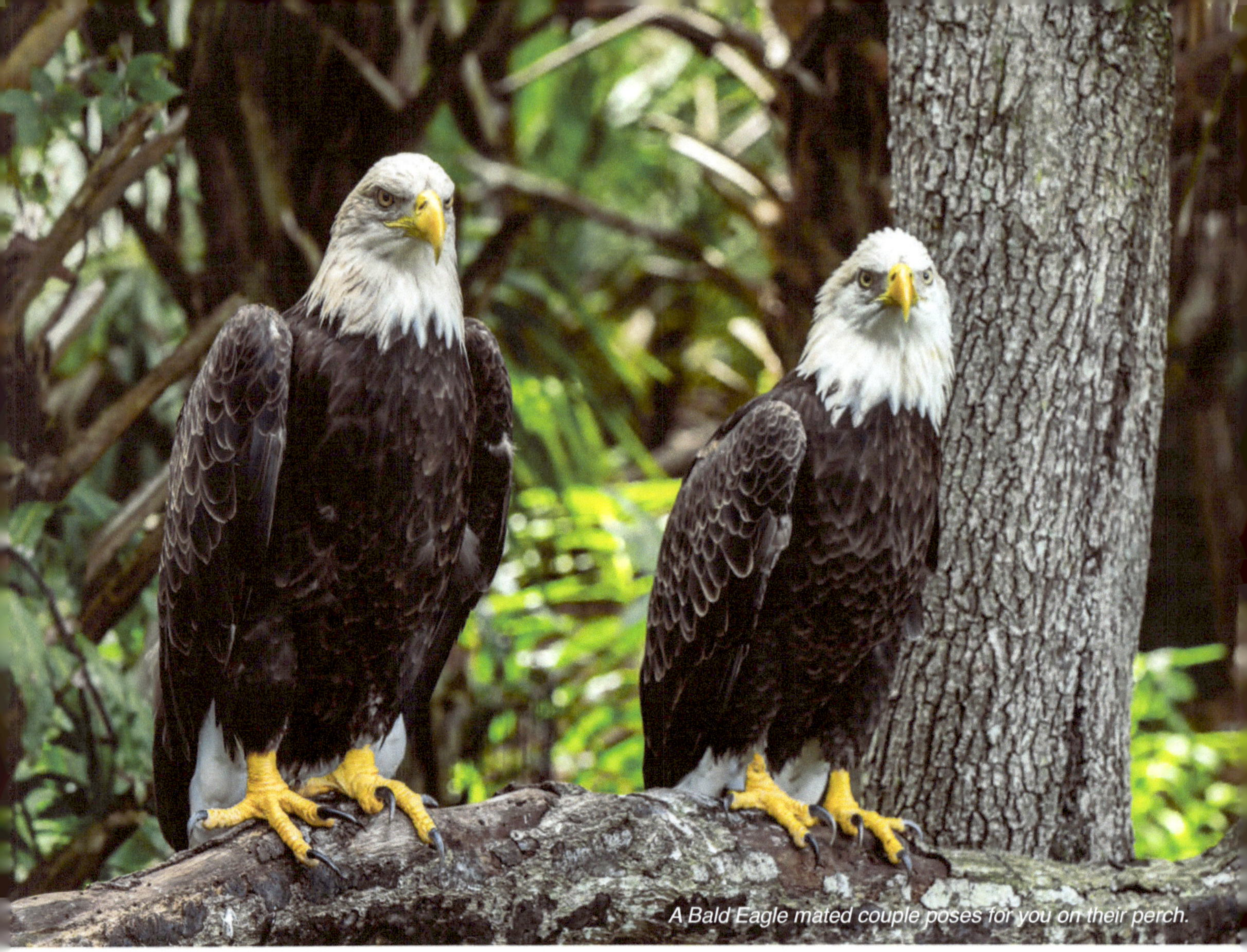

A Bald Eagle mated couple poses for you on their perch.

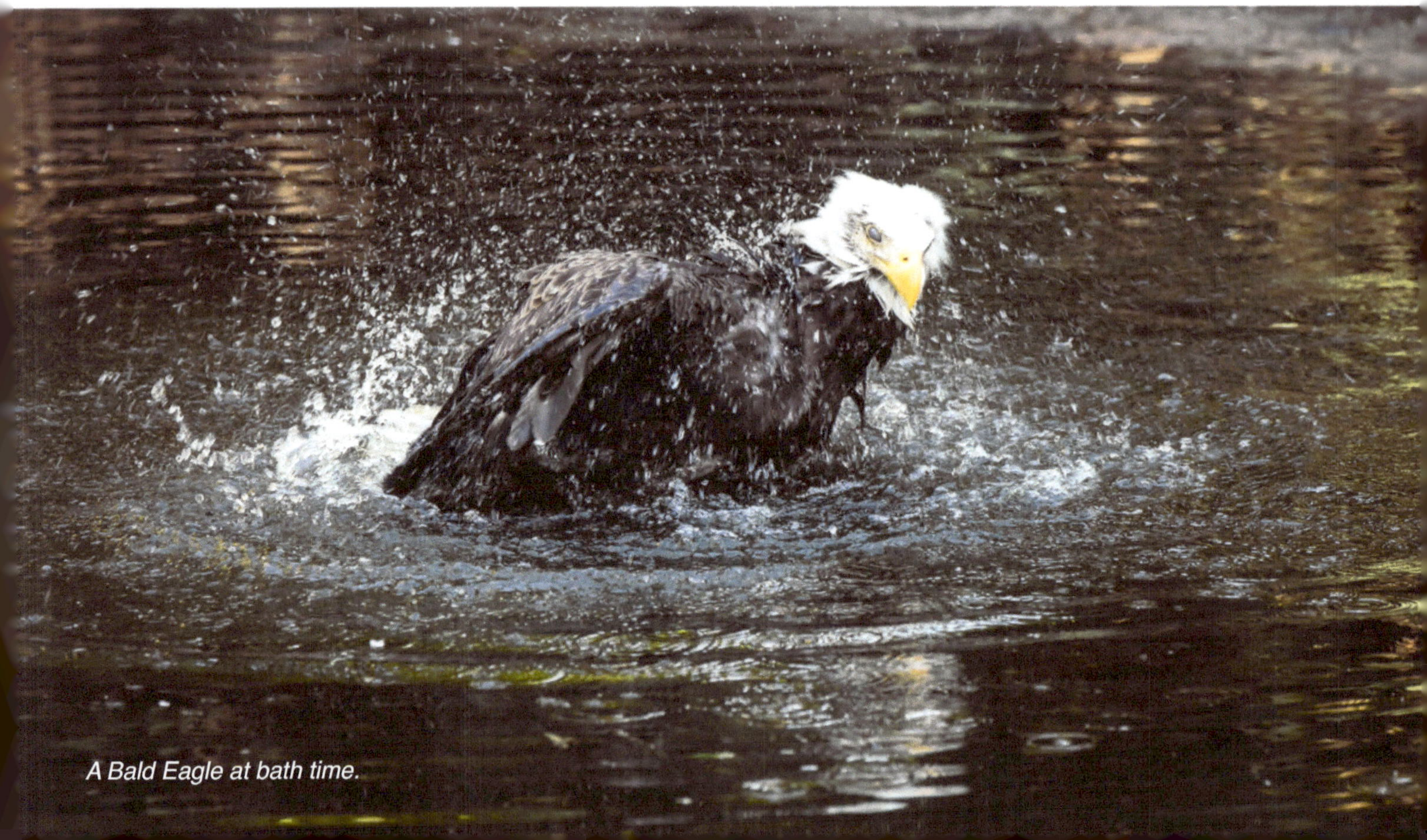

A Bald Eagle at bath time.

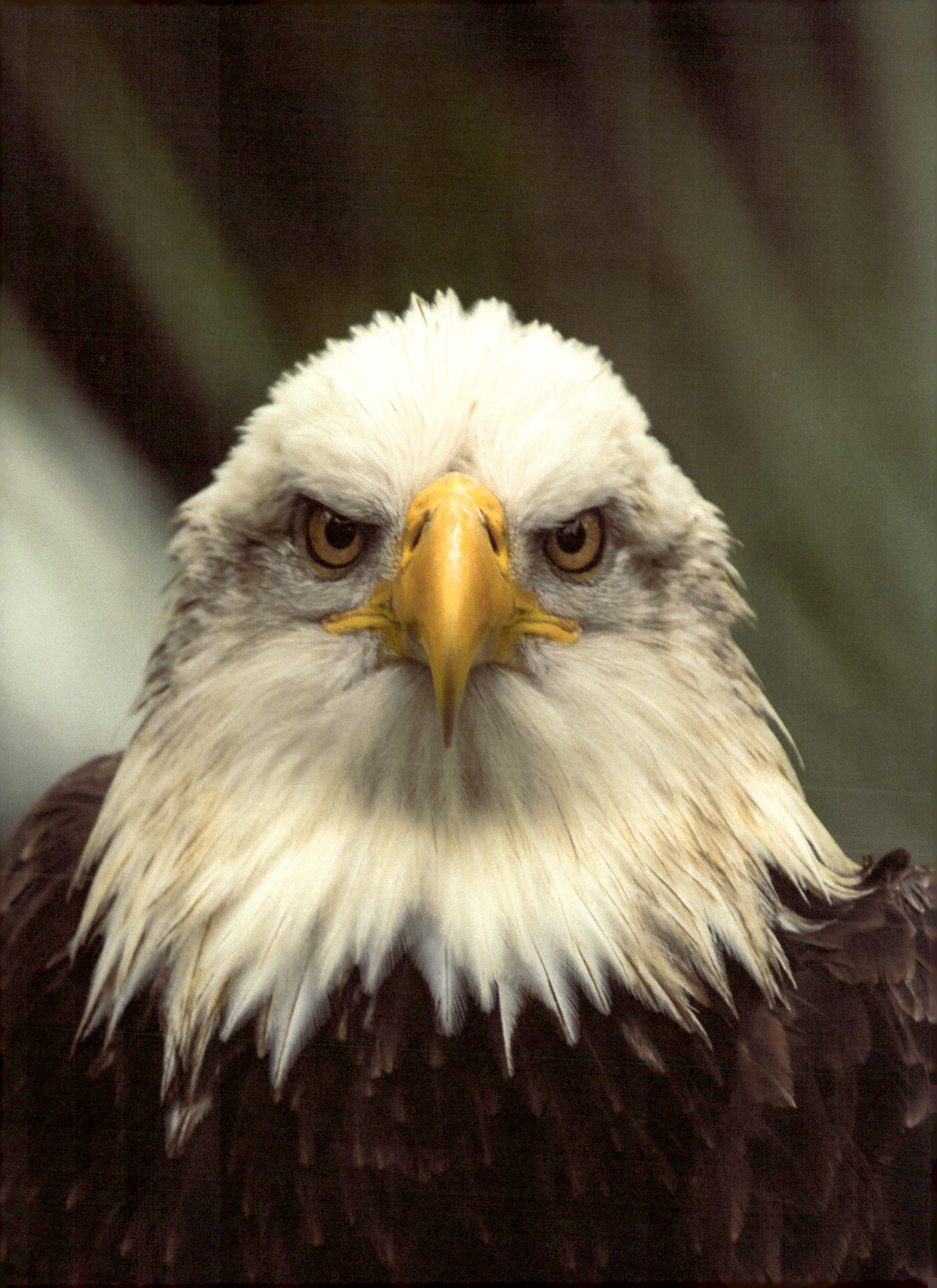

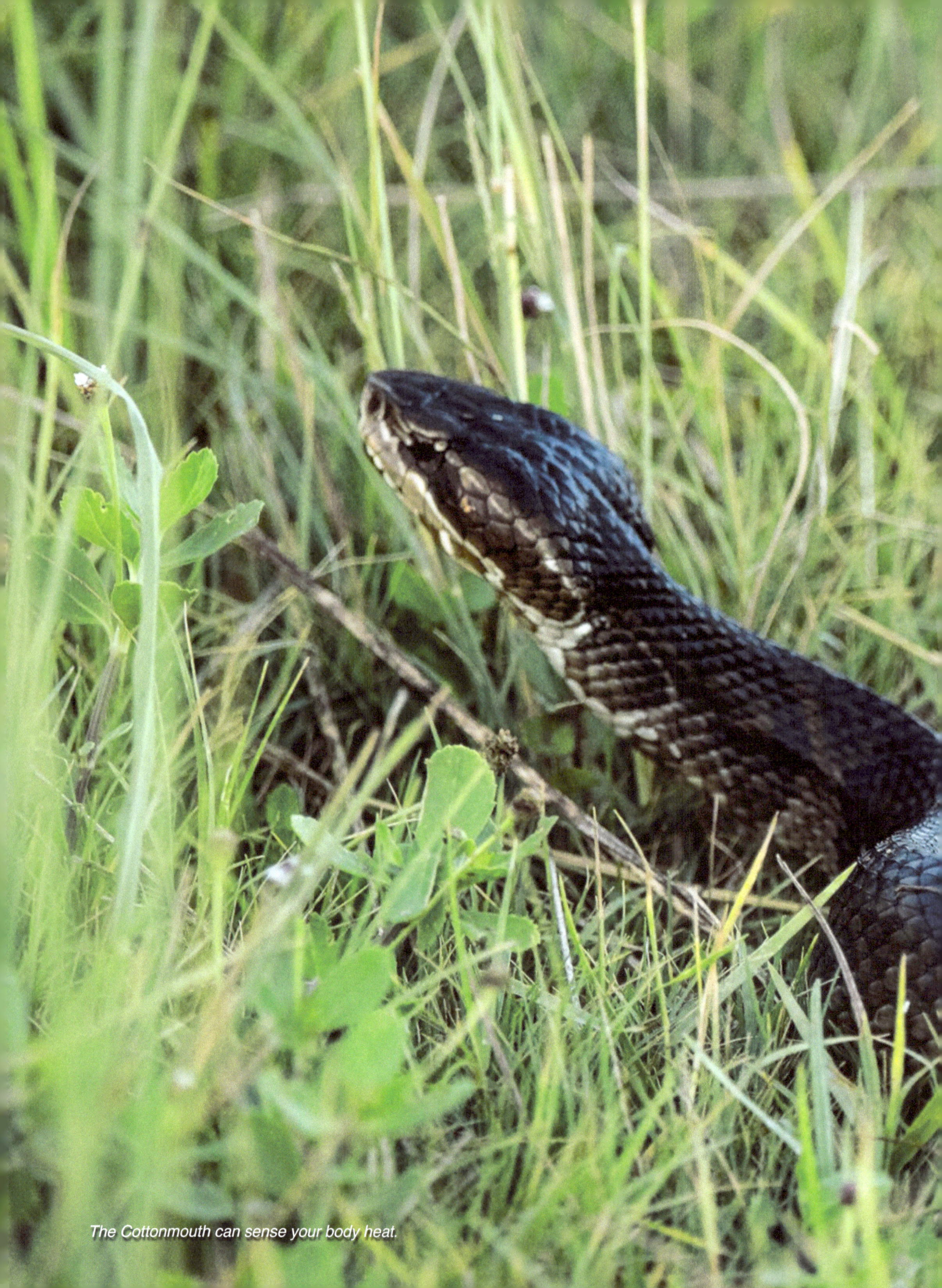
The Cottonmouth can sense your body heat.

ABOUT THE SNAKES

Snakes, ohhh, they're out there and ironically were the last members of the cast to show themselves during my expeditions. I'm sure there were several other species and flavors out there, but I frequently encountered the ribbon snakes, black snakes, garter snakes, the copperhead and cottonmouth. I had been putting efforts into one location for a few weeks and had caught a shot of a large, dark colored water snake. I would say 5 foot or larger based on the size of the scales on its back. I snagged a shot of it from a distance of one hundred yards(ish) with my 70 to 200-millimeter lens. Approximately two weeks later, I was rounding a bend on a hiking trail that had been near the siting. Low and behold a 6-foot cottonmouth slithered out of the bushes and onto my trail immediately in front of me. I froze… he or she froze… and the stand-off began. Took a minute or two to realize that it was not hunting me, and this was pure accidental coincidence. I took a couple of small stones and tossed them in the direction of the snake. Curiously enough they would drop near the head and the snake would not move at all. Come to find out there's no heat in a rock (IKR… smart one!) About three minutes into our little standoff, he or she decides to turn around and head back to the water. At that point I was pretty sure that was the same snake that I had photographed two weeks earlier. I would have a snake encounter once every two weeks and it was mostly non-poisonous small snakes on the trail.

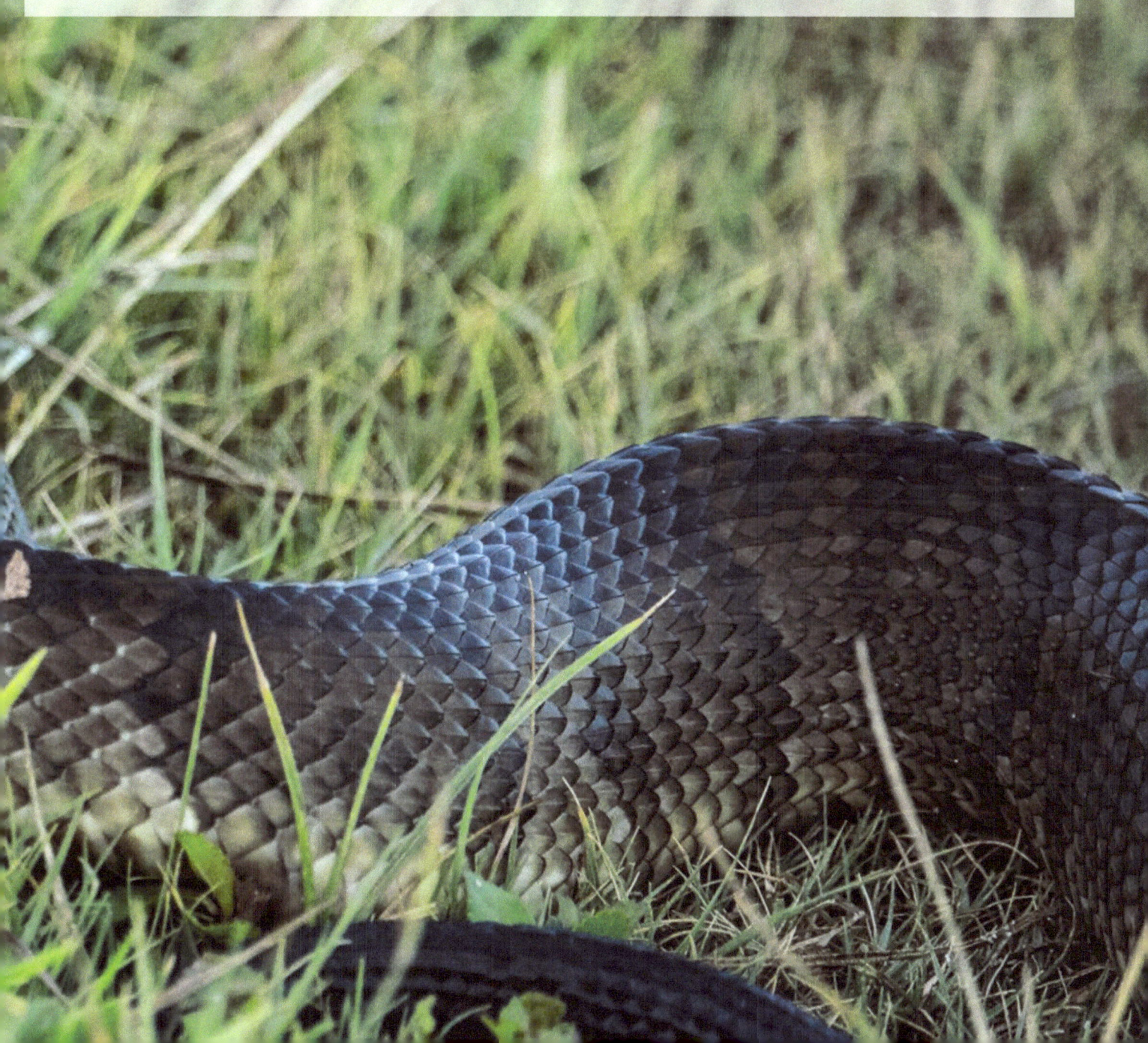

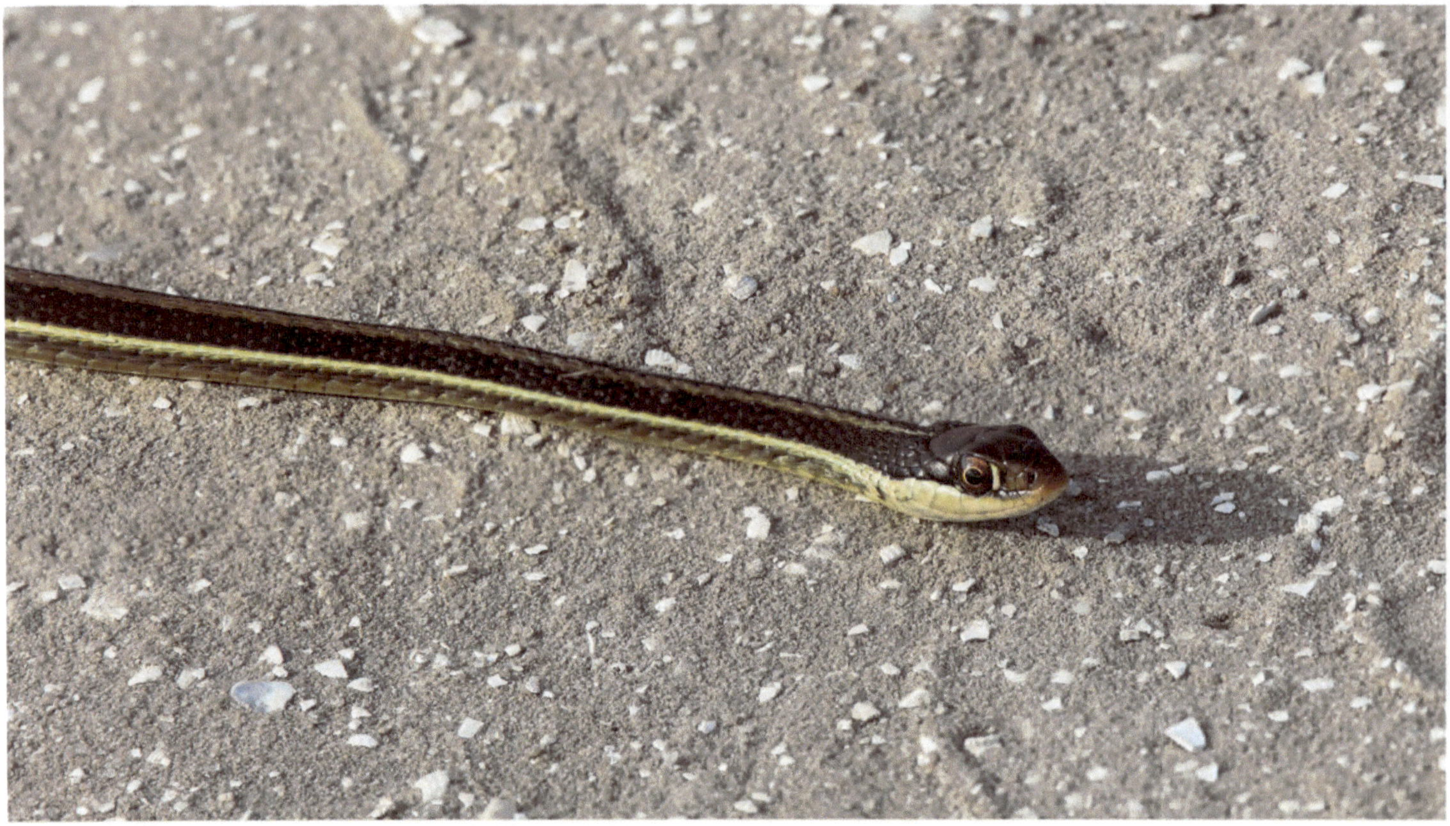

A non-venomous Ribbon Snake slithers across your path.

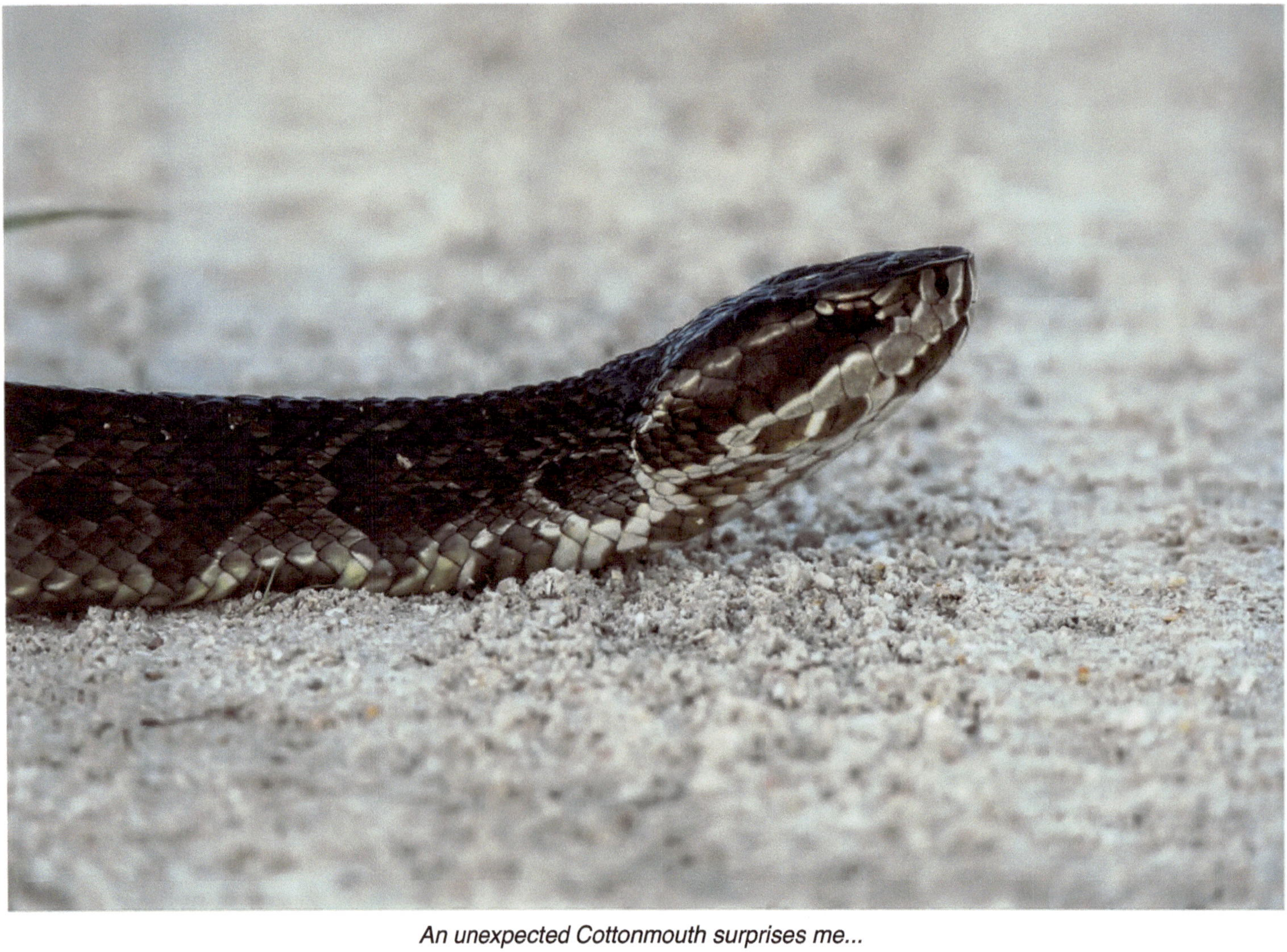

An unexpected Cottonmouth surprises me...

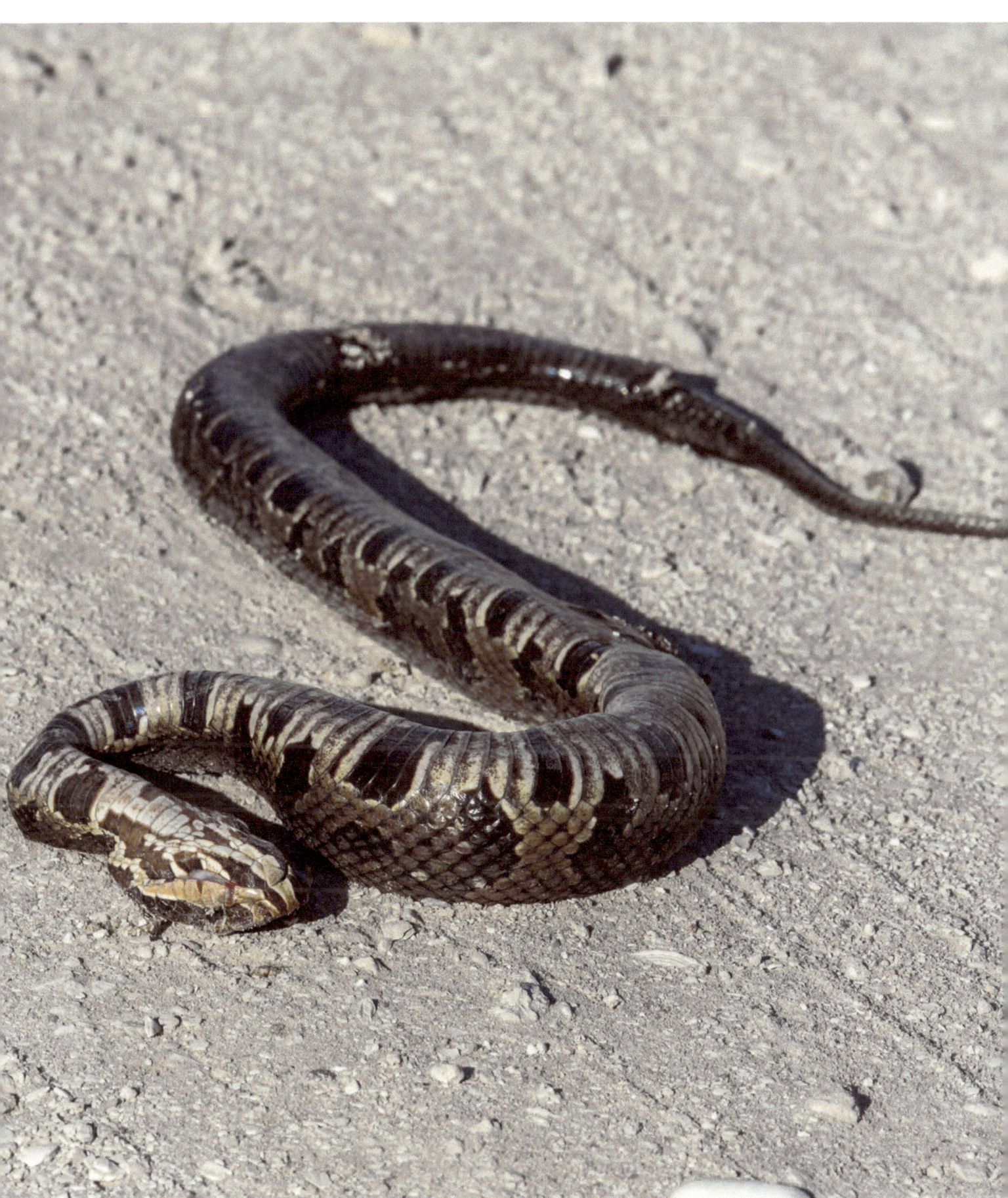

A Cottonmouth dropped from an Osprey at dinner time.

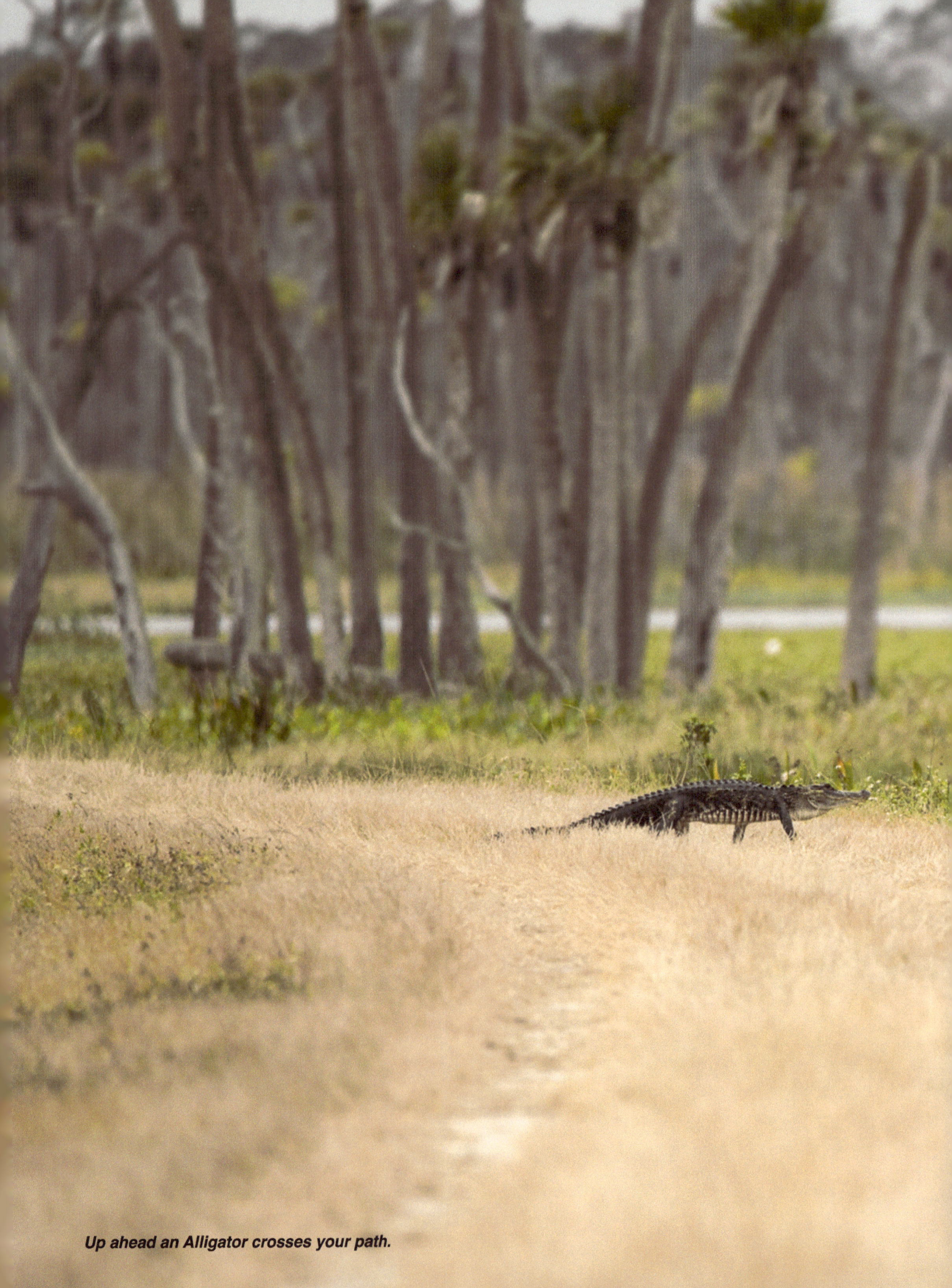

Up ahead an Alligator crosses your path.

ABOUT THE GATORS

When I was younger, I owned a baby alligator. In the mid-nineties they were taken off the endangered species list and you could actually purchase one at a pet store in Detroit. He was named Gus gator and we had a relationship that lasted approximately 9 months. I lived in a small one-bedroom apartment, and I created a habitat for him in my laundry room. It consisted of a small Kitty pool, some beach sand, a sunlamp, hot rock and a small filter. In the beginning everything was well and good, and it was quite a novelty that brought a lot of people by to gawk at him. But Gus grew, and so did my distrust for him. He was now getting out of his habitat and walking around the apartment. I would frequently find him underneath the refrigerator, as he liked to lay next to the motor to keep warm. He went from eating goldfish, to baby mice, to rats. Reptiles like this need a lot of time to interact with a human, and the more you leave them locked away in a dark room, the more of a wild animal you have. So, at an early age Gus was given a new home for 150 bucks (and I kept all my fingers.)

When I first started my wetlands project, I was most excited to see and interact with the alligators. During my first 6-mile hike, at the beginning of the alligator mating season, I saw upwards of 75 alligators in one expedition. The first three, I was pretty smitten with the "up close and personal effect" and seeing them in their natural environment. I recall walking down one particular trail that parted two small lakes, I can't put a number on how many were on the left and how many were on the right but at this point I was completely out-numbered, and as I looked over the lakes dozens and dozens of heads could be seen watching me walk by. As I would interact more with them in the months ahead, I began to realize as I would approach that their attention would turn toward me. Many cases I would witness them begin to move in my direction (only in the water…) Now this was contingent on temperatures, in anything under 75 degrees this particular behavior wasn't witnessed, in the hot months of June, July, August, *yes,* alligators in water would definitely respond to my approach. I believe this is a result of idiots hiking in the wetlands, and feeding them. In the 18 months that I spent on their turf, none of them left the water to come onto land to confront me. In all cases, the two responses were either stand their ground, or to retreat back into water. As the winter months would approach, there would be an increase in sedentary activity, with the alligators laying in close proximity to trails, with no movement at all. Just after the mating season and into the hatchling phase (the first part of September,) a mother alligator had about eight hatchlings with her, in the shallows. I spotted the hatchlings before the mother, in fact she was about 200+ yards away from me. She could clearly see me and was on a path coming directly toward me. I politely snapped a few pics of her young and got on my way before her arrival. We would meet again…. several weeks later, I came through the same area, and caught two of the small ones napping on her back. I was able to locate two more in the reeds nearby. I believe by this point the local predators, osprey, eagle and other alligators had thinned her herd.

The typical length that you would encounter here would range between 4 to 7 feet. The large, old alligators are frequently sought after during the Florida Alligator nuisance hunts. So when you see a large alligator 9 to 11 feet in length, not only are they old but they have outfoxed the hunter at some point. That leads me to my next encounter, with Mr. Godzilla. I would estimate him easy 10 and a half (if not more) feet in length. As an alligator crosses the seven to eight foot mark their girth begins to expand massively. This old fella took a whole bank to himself. Over the next five weeks, I had the opportunity to photograph him 12 times. The encounters were in close proximity, with what common sense would allow with a 70 to 200mm lens. However, my last encounter was memory: I was standing near Mr. G (within 25 feet) and it decided it would retreat into the water. You hear stories about how fast an alligator can move, and they climb fences, and they climb trees, and they will outrun you on land, but during 18 months this was the only time I'd ever seen something close to that. Mr. Godzilla, evacuated the area in less than a second., to my recollection the majority of the movement came from his tail and it was kind of like a launch into the water... this had an "oh shit" factor of + 2, much respect Mr. Godzilla. And for me, well…lesson learned and from that day forward I doubled my reactionary distance. 2018 was not a good year for the state of Florida from a critter standpoint. They had the most alligator attacks, as well as the most shark attack bites on the record books. Press reports had indicated water temperatures had increased, causing aggression in both alligator and the shark. During my travels, I would frequently see a newscast about an elderly woman walking a dog who'd been attacked, or a hiker who had been attacked or a golf boy shagger. But the common denominator was: t*hey got into the water.* Come on now, this is *their* hood, not ours. I have never experienced one advance on land to come after me, they always return to the water… that's their home. But if you want to go in there and you know they're there, don't complain if you come back missing a toe, your dog, or simply ***don't*** come back.

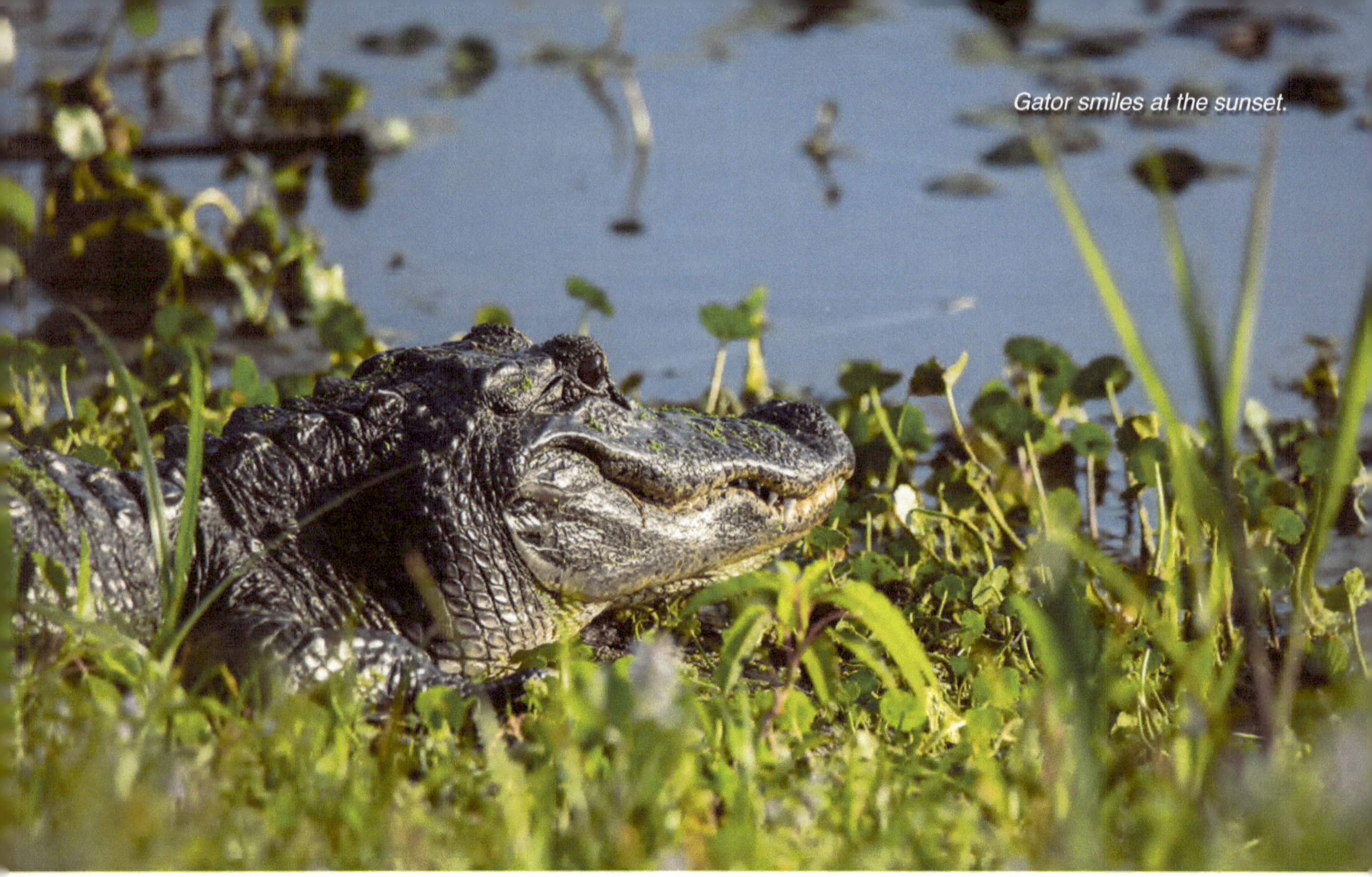

Gator smiles at the sunset.

Below: This alligator is camouflaged and closer than you think...

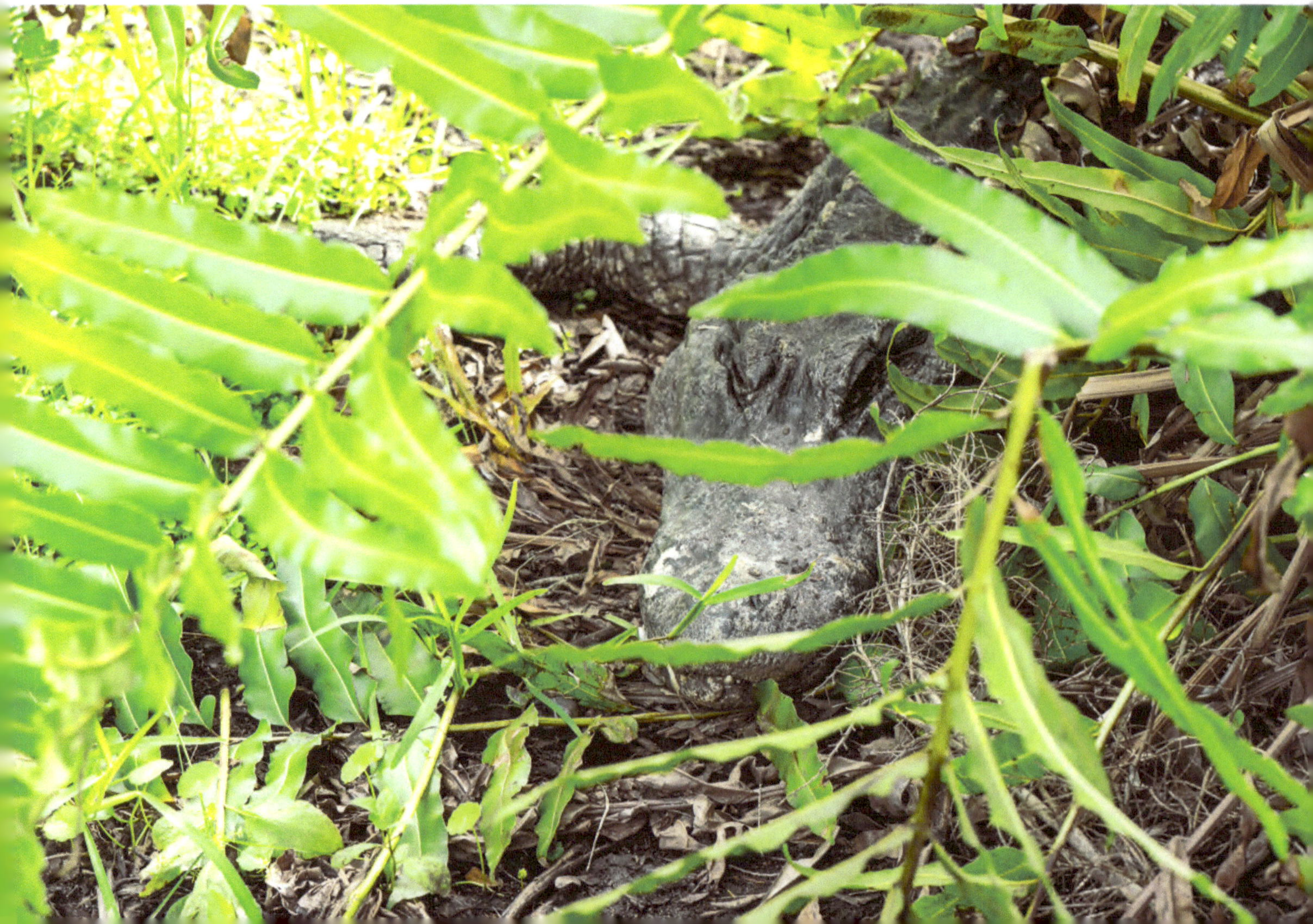

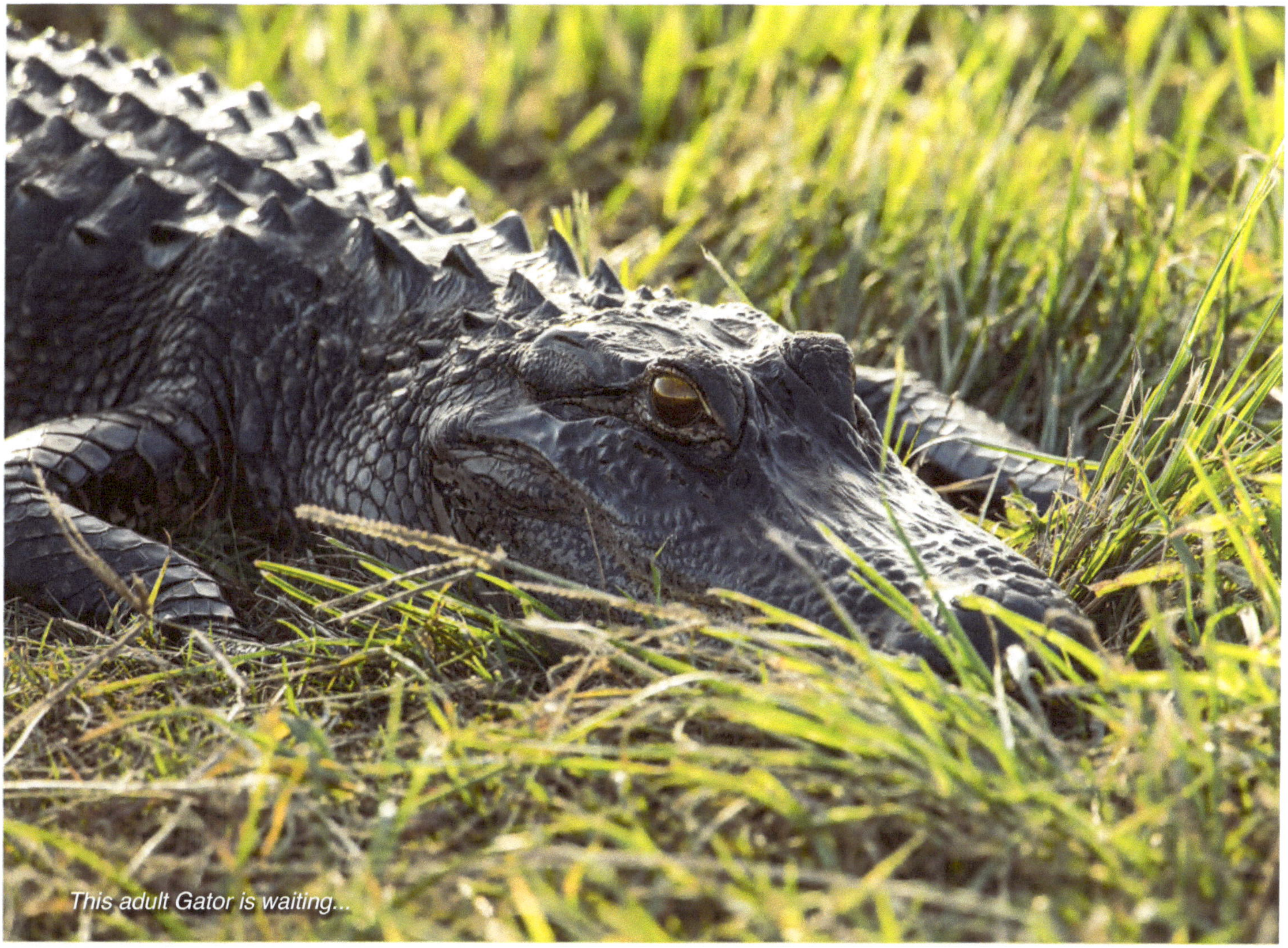

This adult Gator is waiting...

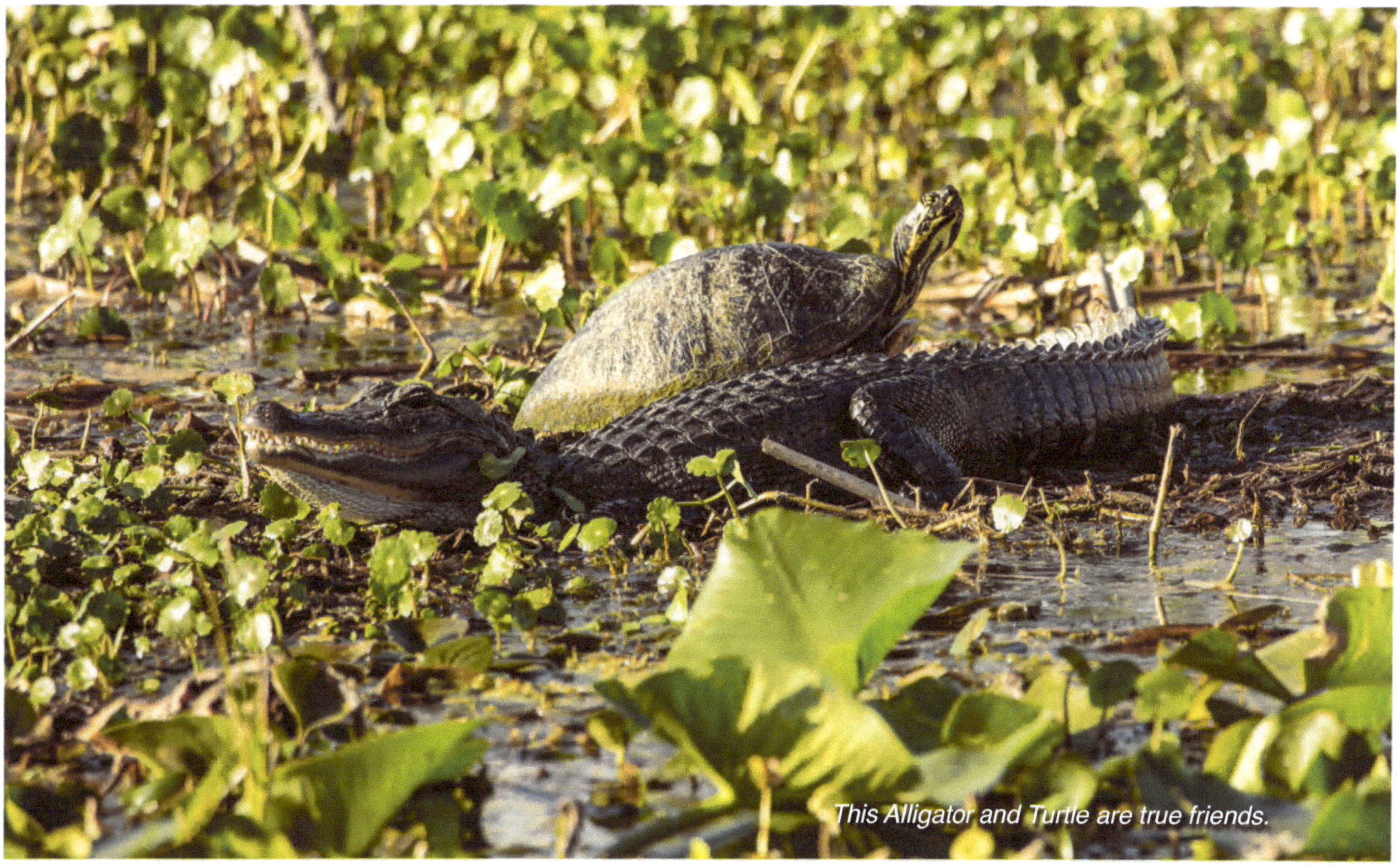

This Alligator and Turtle are true friends.

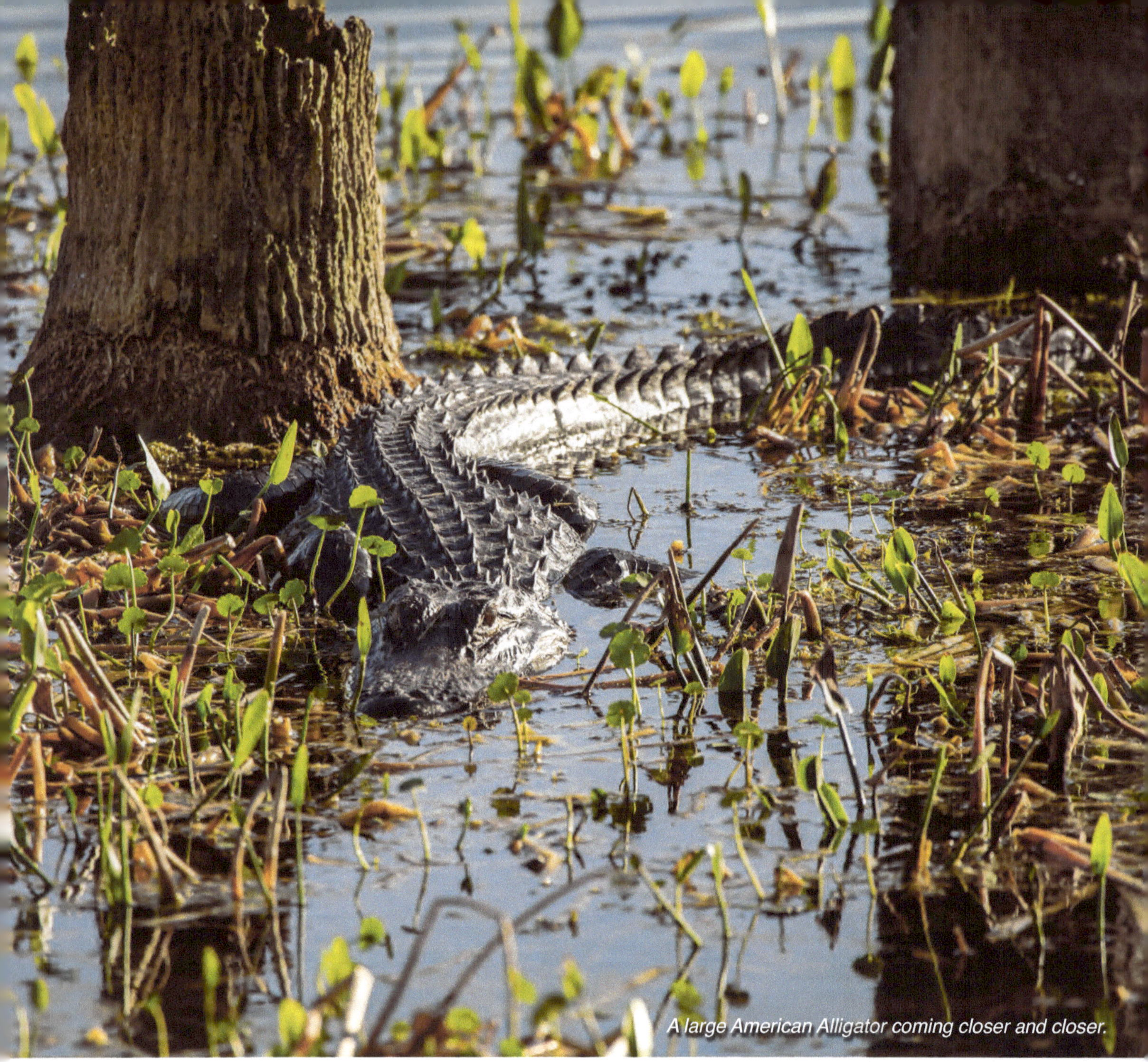

A large American Alligator coming closer and closer.

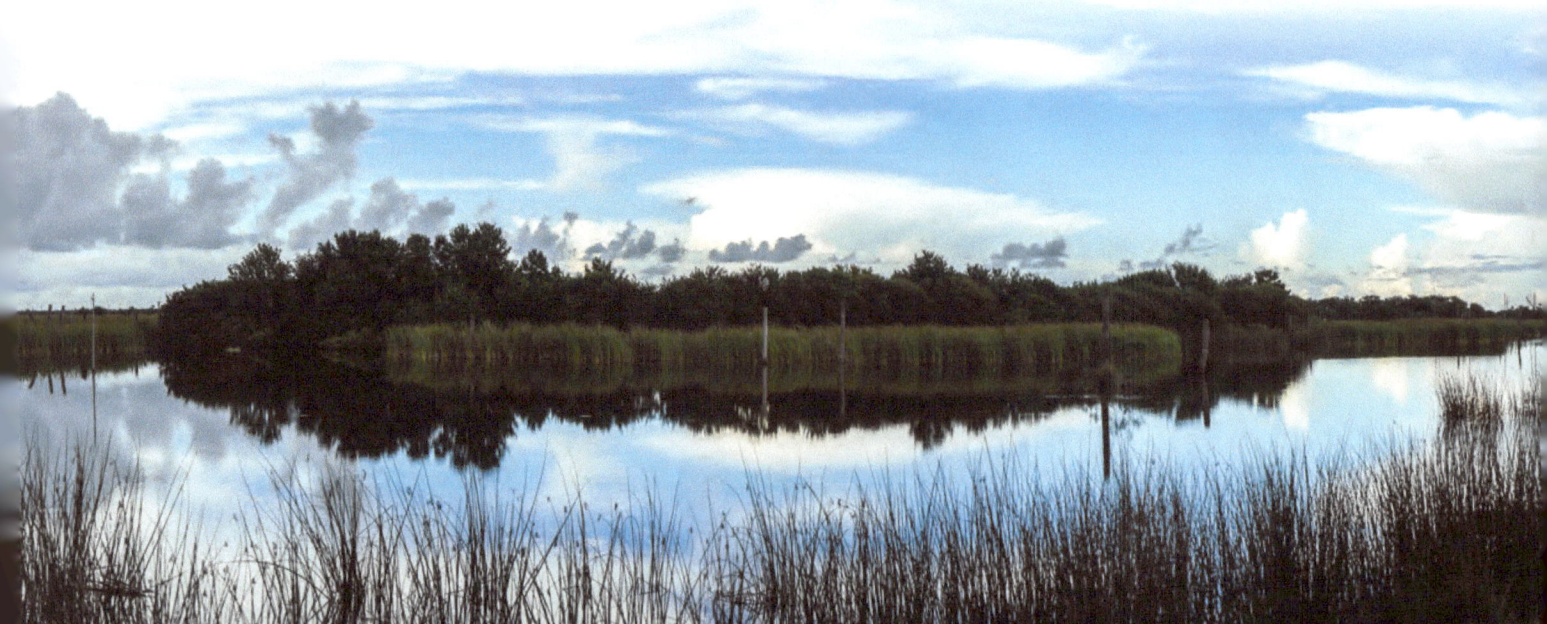

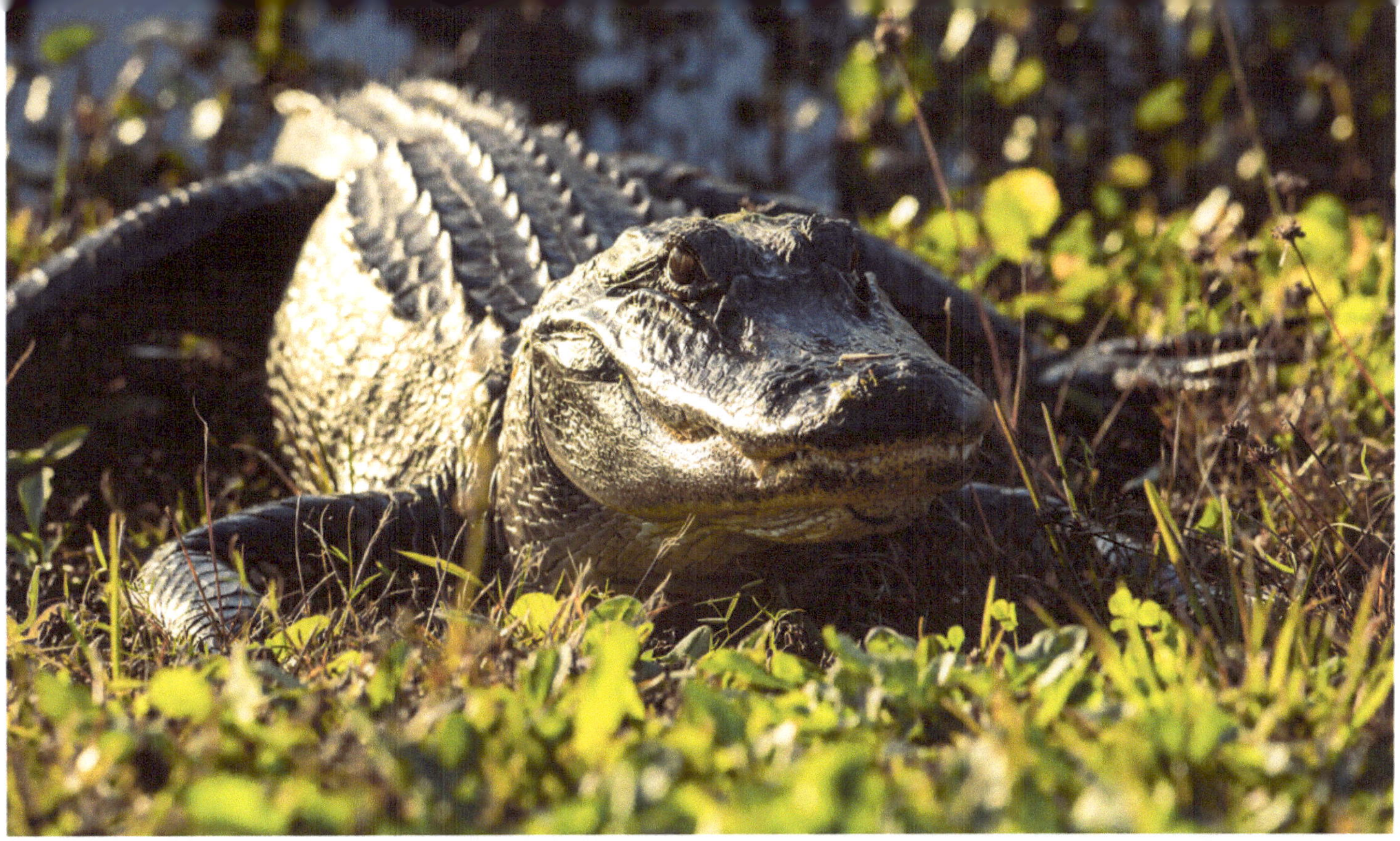

Above: A golden Gator suns nearby you.

Right: A mud Gator slips back into the muck.

Below: A large Gator smiles big for you as it basks in the glow of the setting sun.

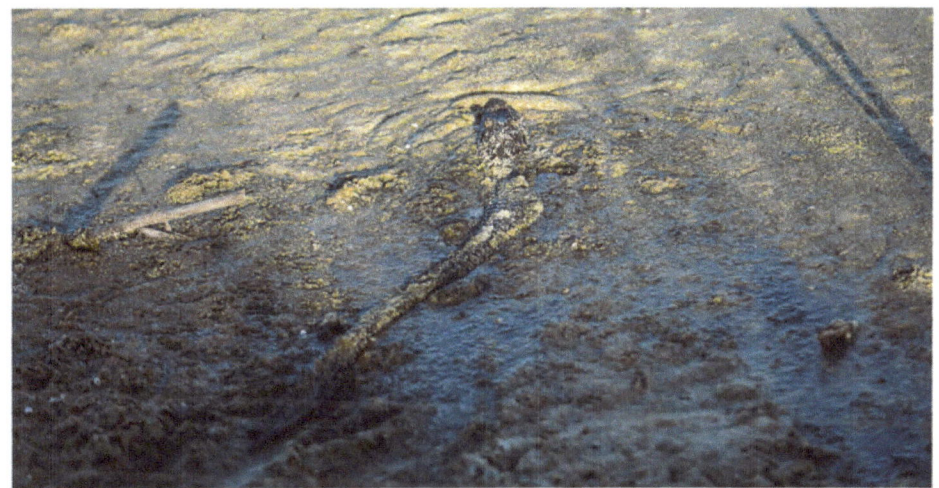

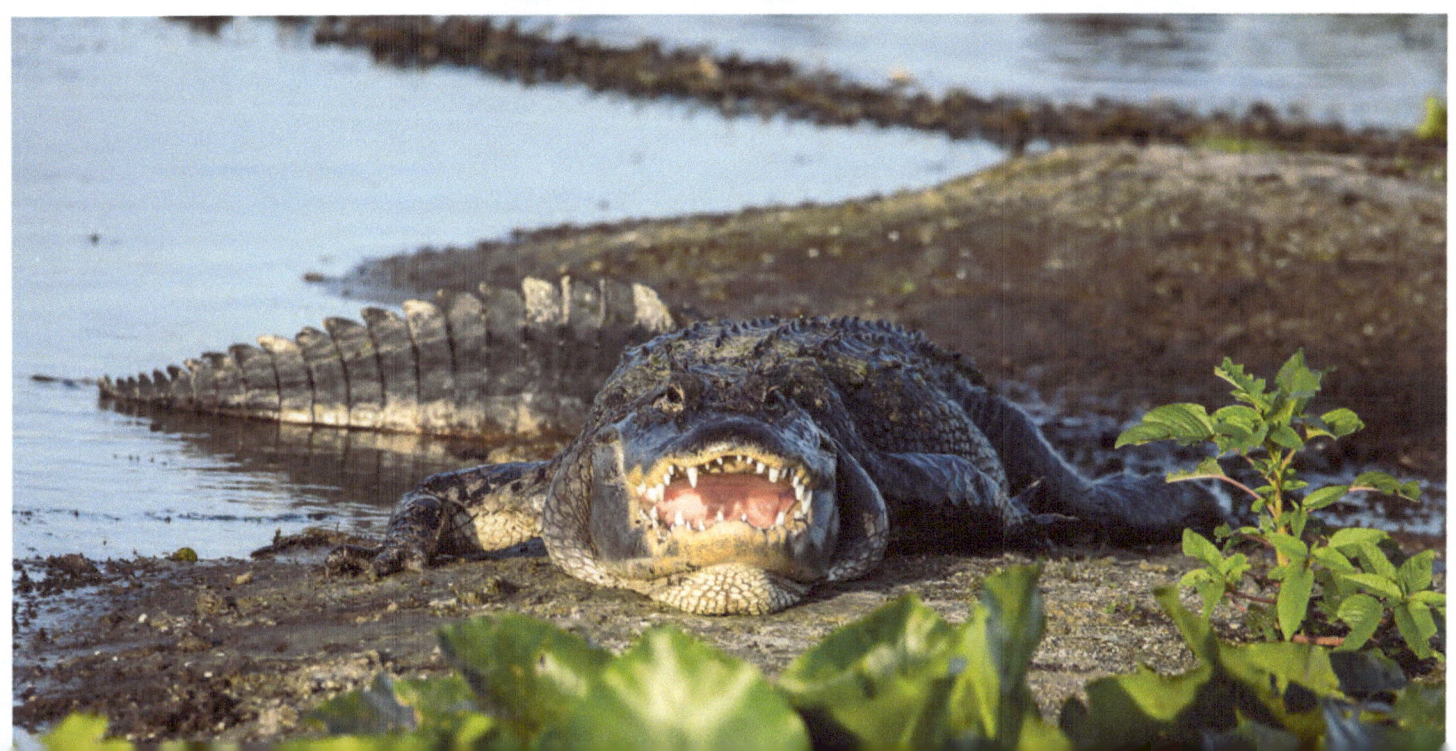

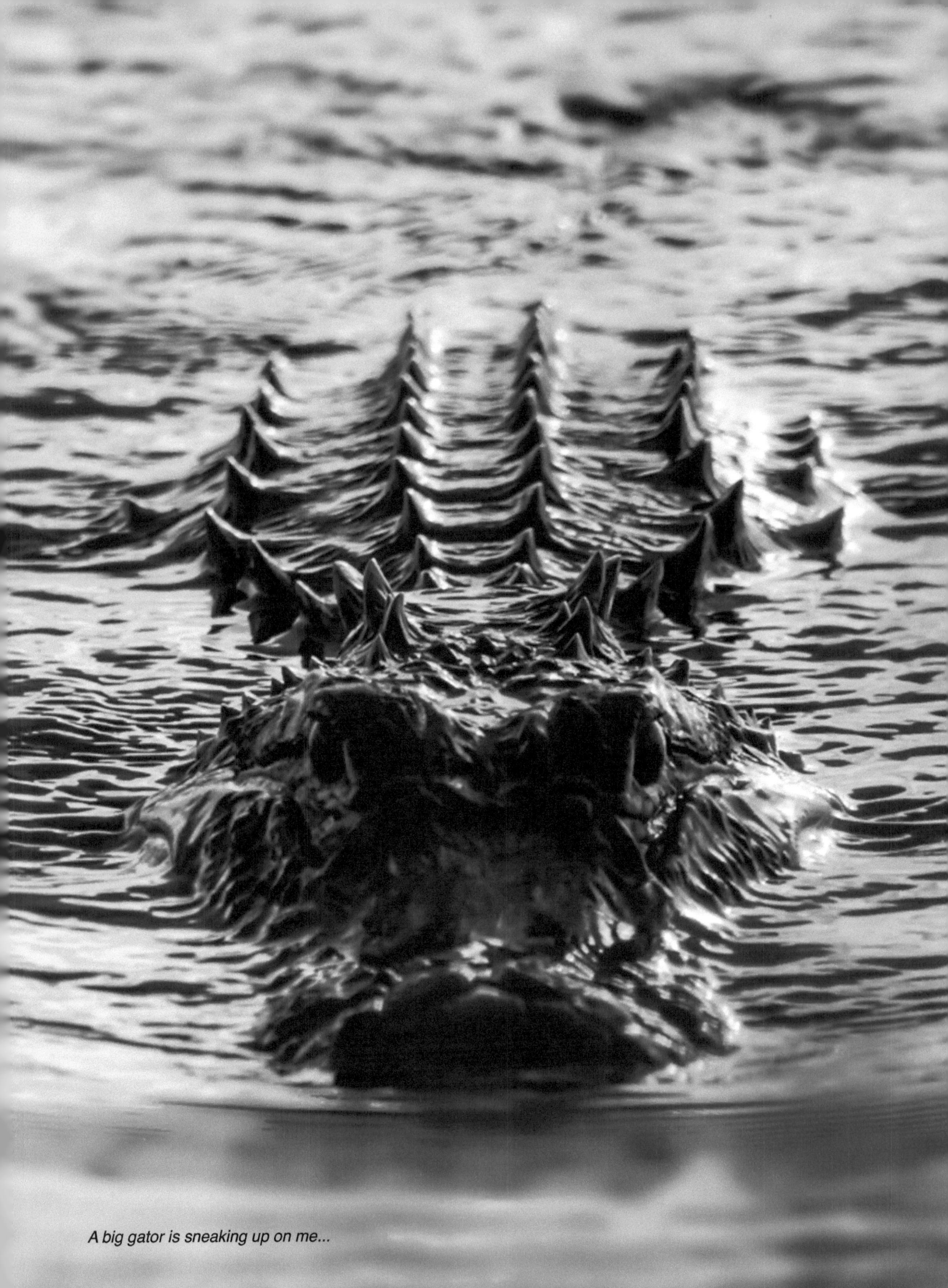

A big gator is sneaking up on me...

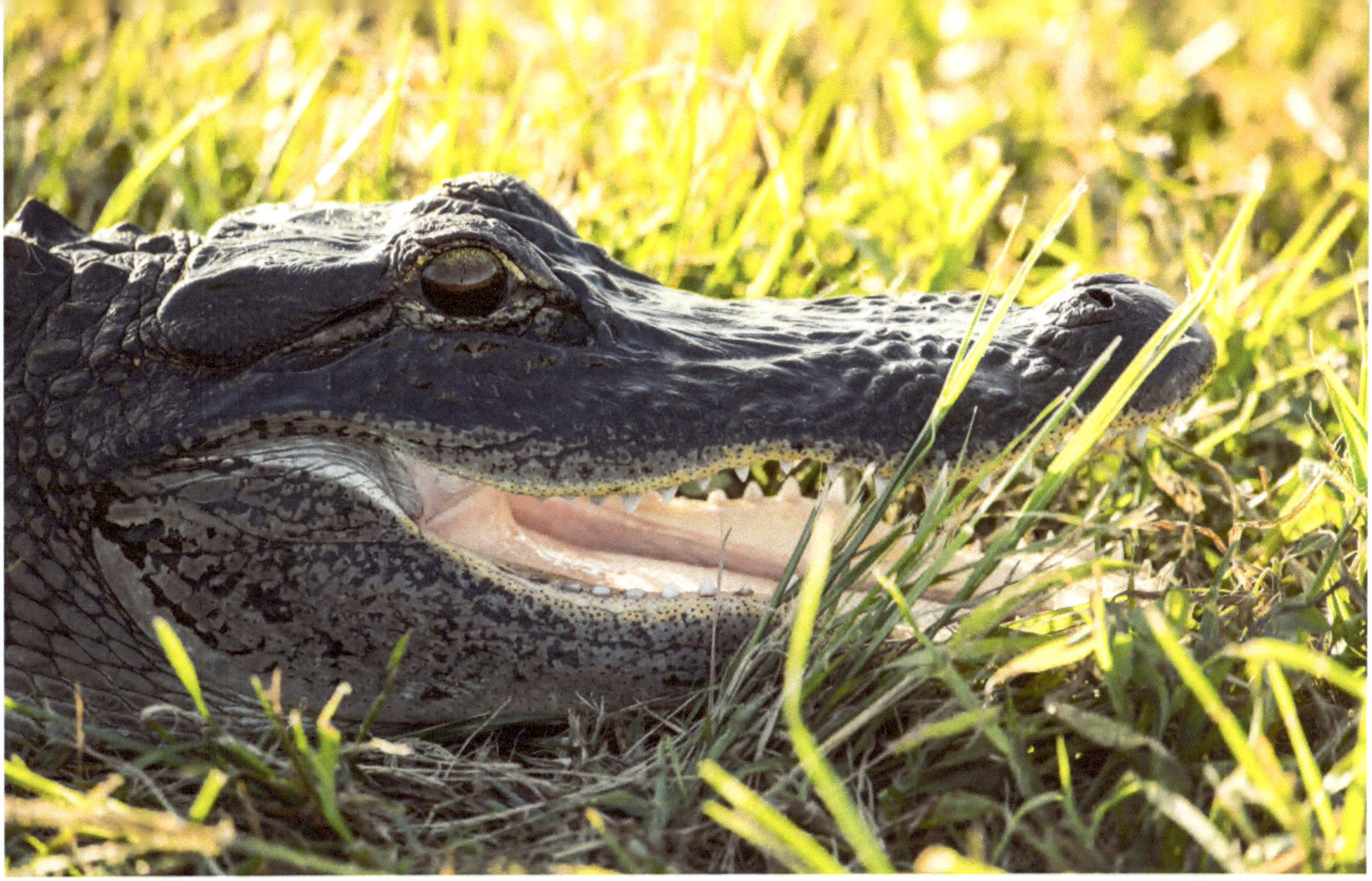

Above: An Alligator gives you a warning hiss. Below: A massive Alligator is hiding in your bushes to surprise you...

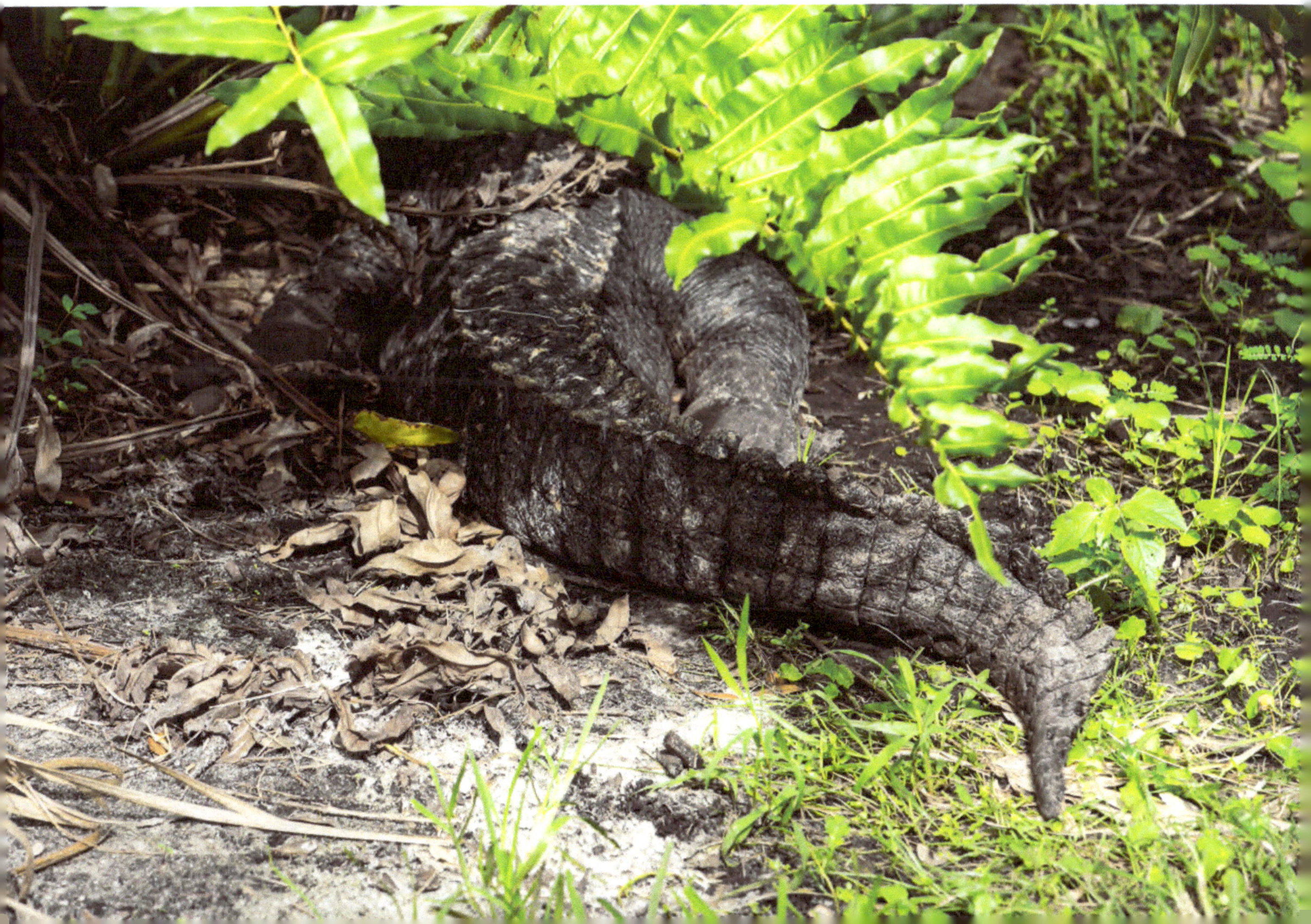

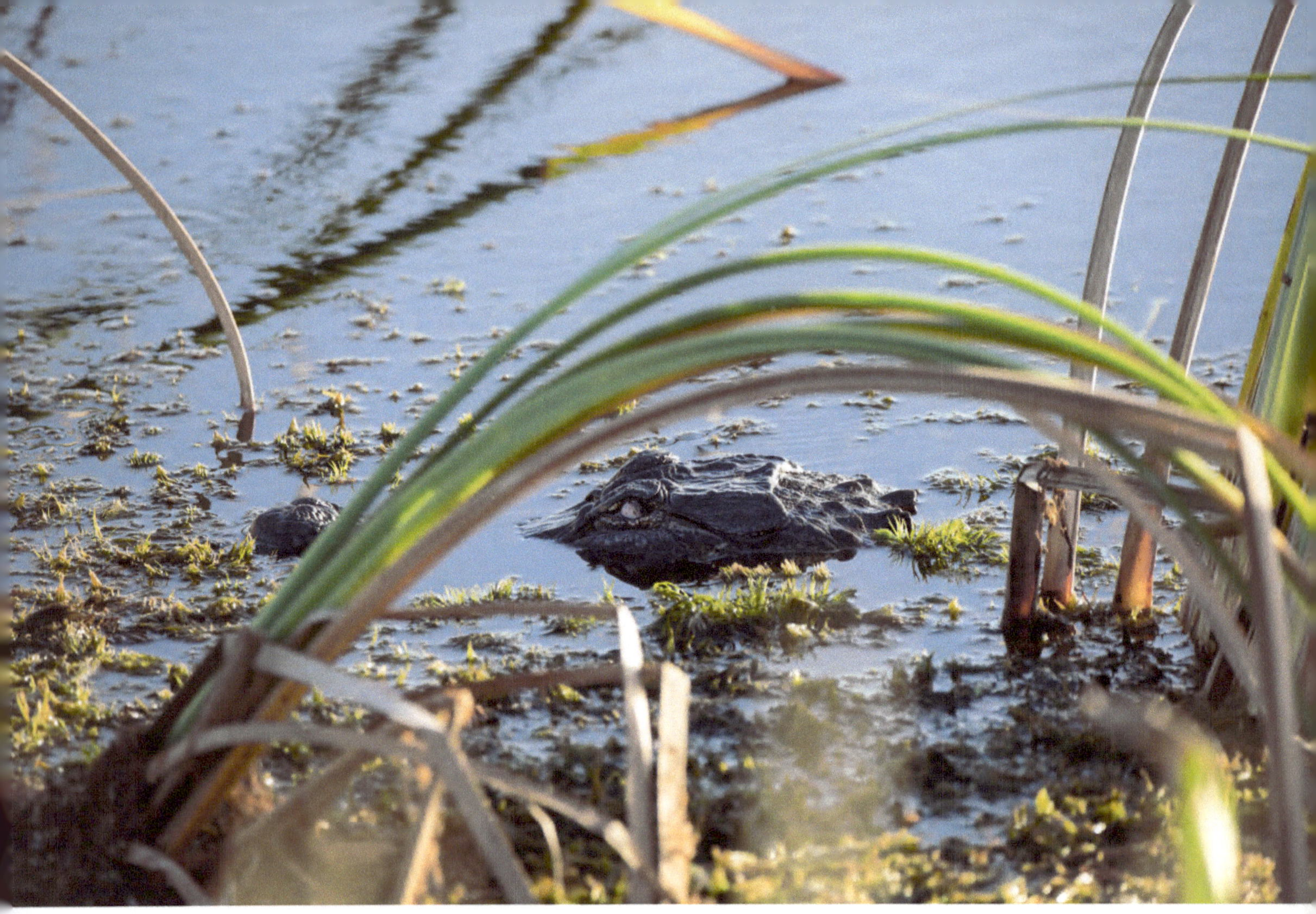

Above: This Alligator has been blinded in one eye. Below: A monster dinosaur is blocking your path.

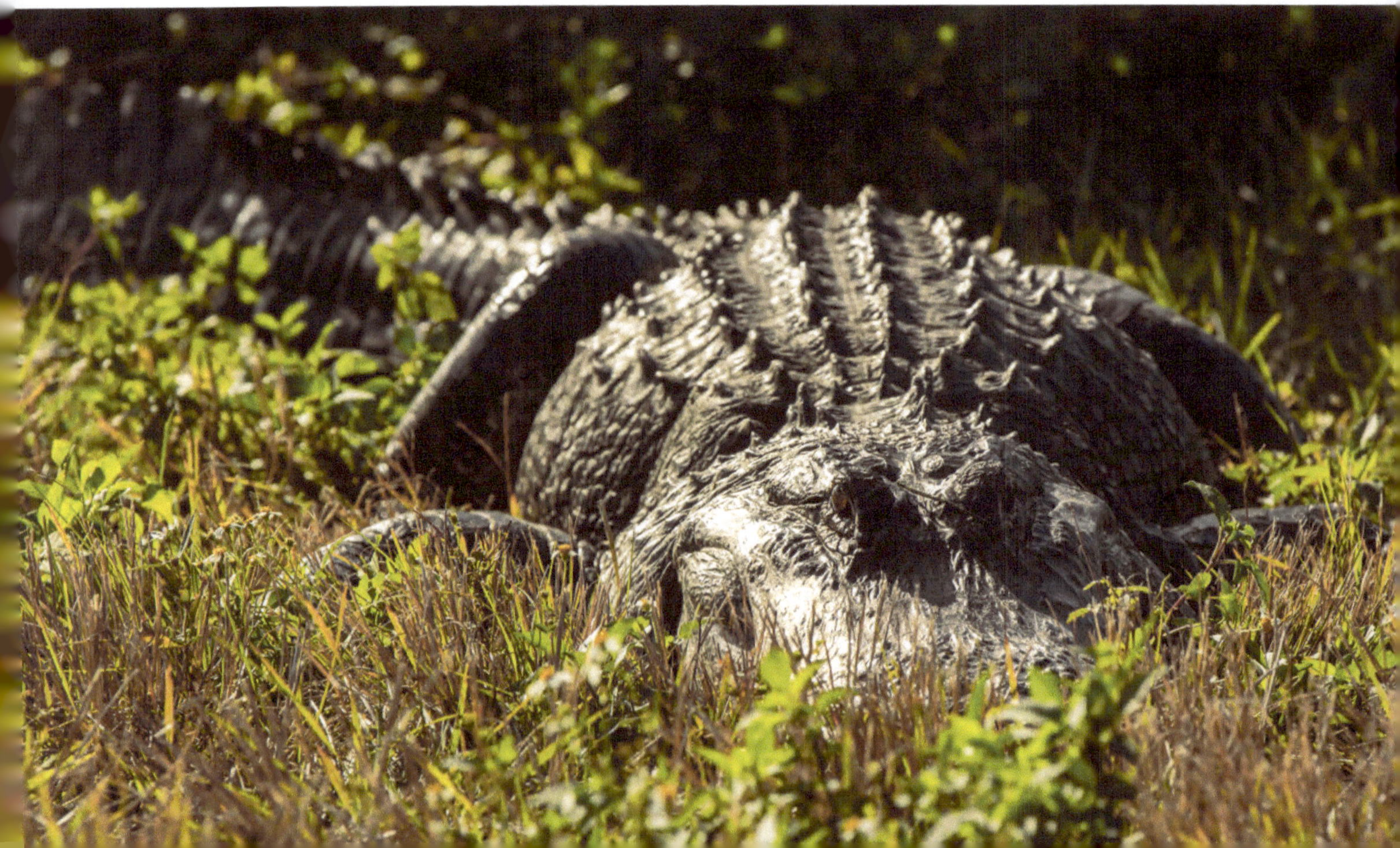

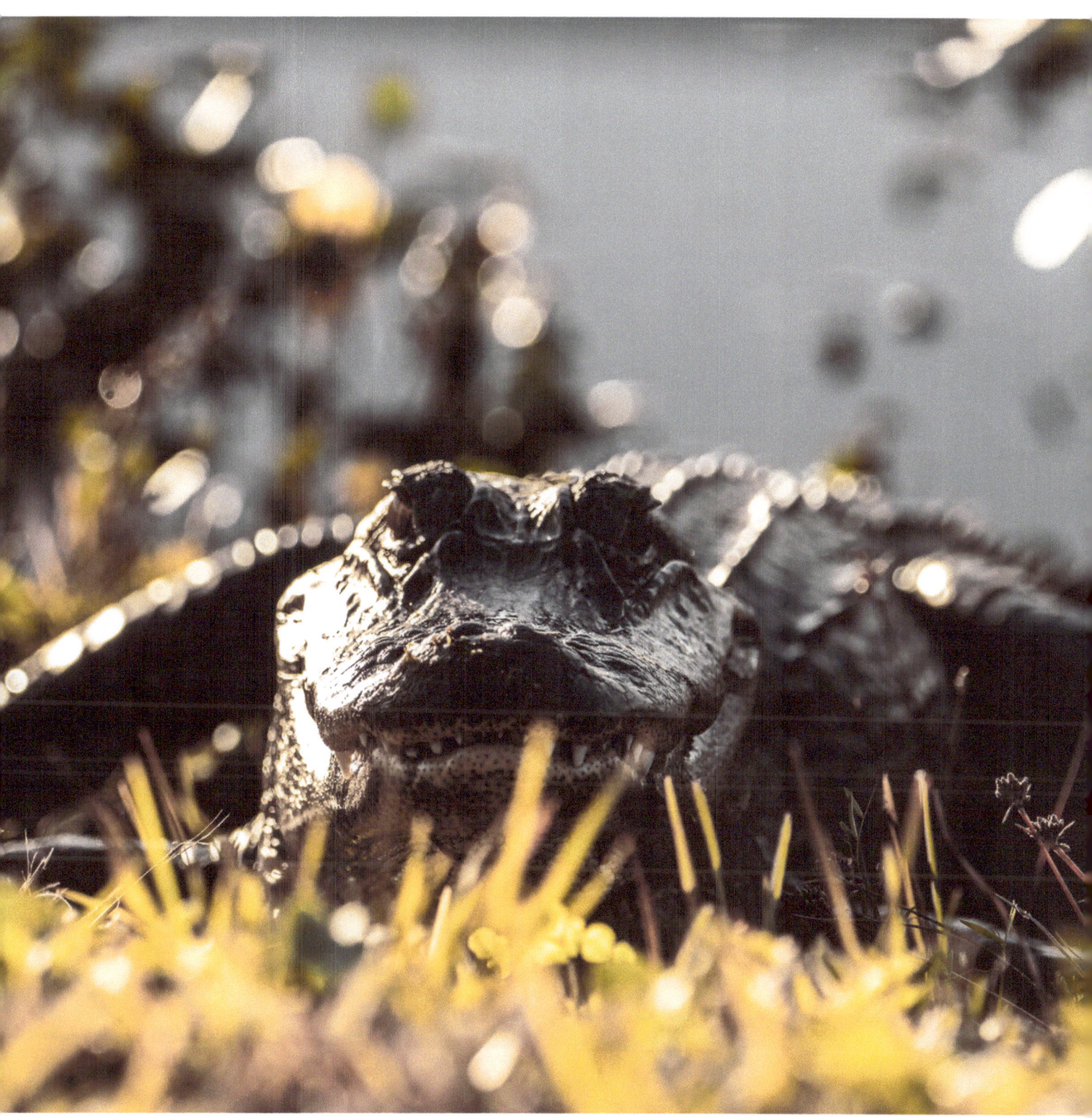

A grinning Gator is looking for you...

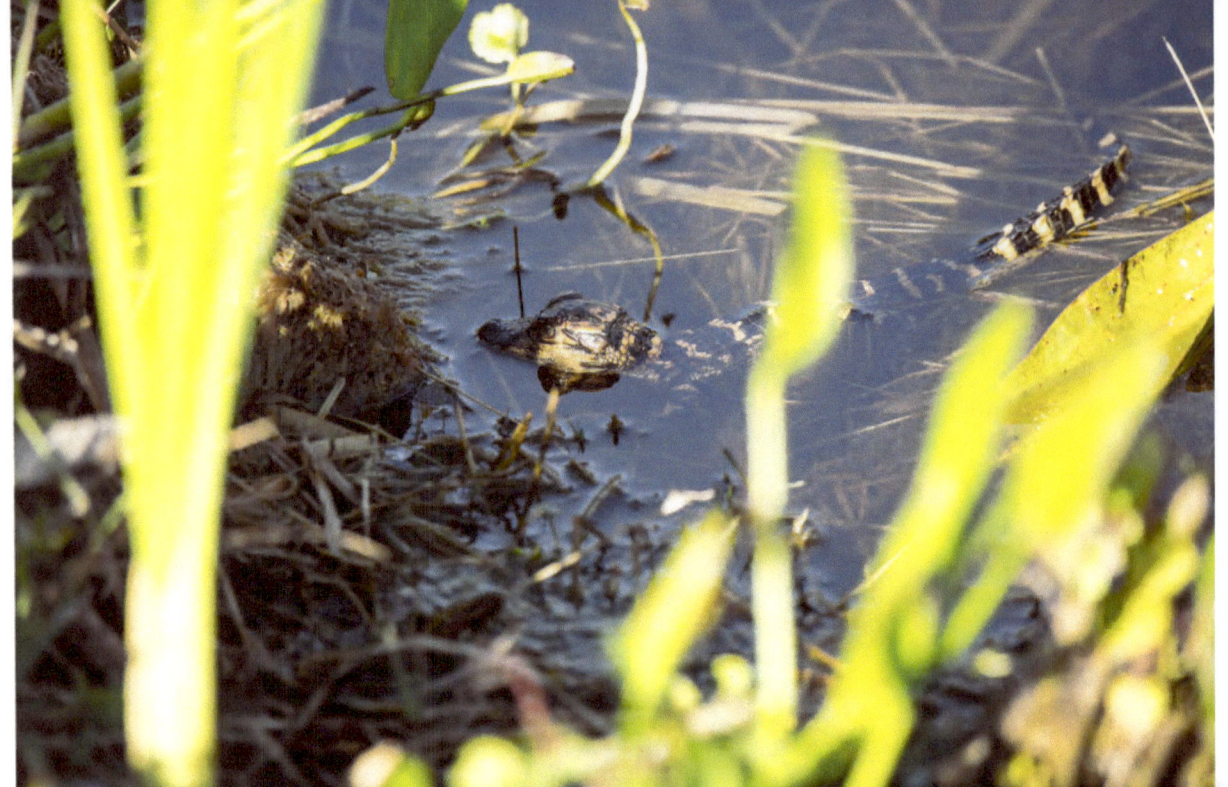

Above: Baby Gator looks for food.

Right: "Are you my mama?"

Below: Mama Gator announces herself.

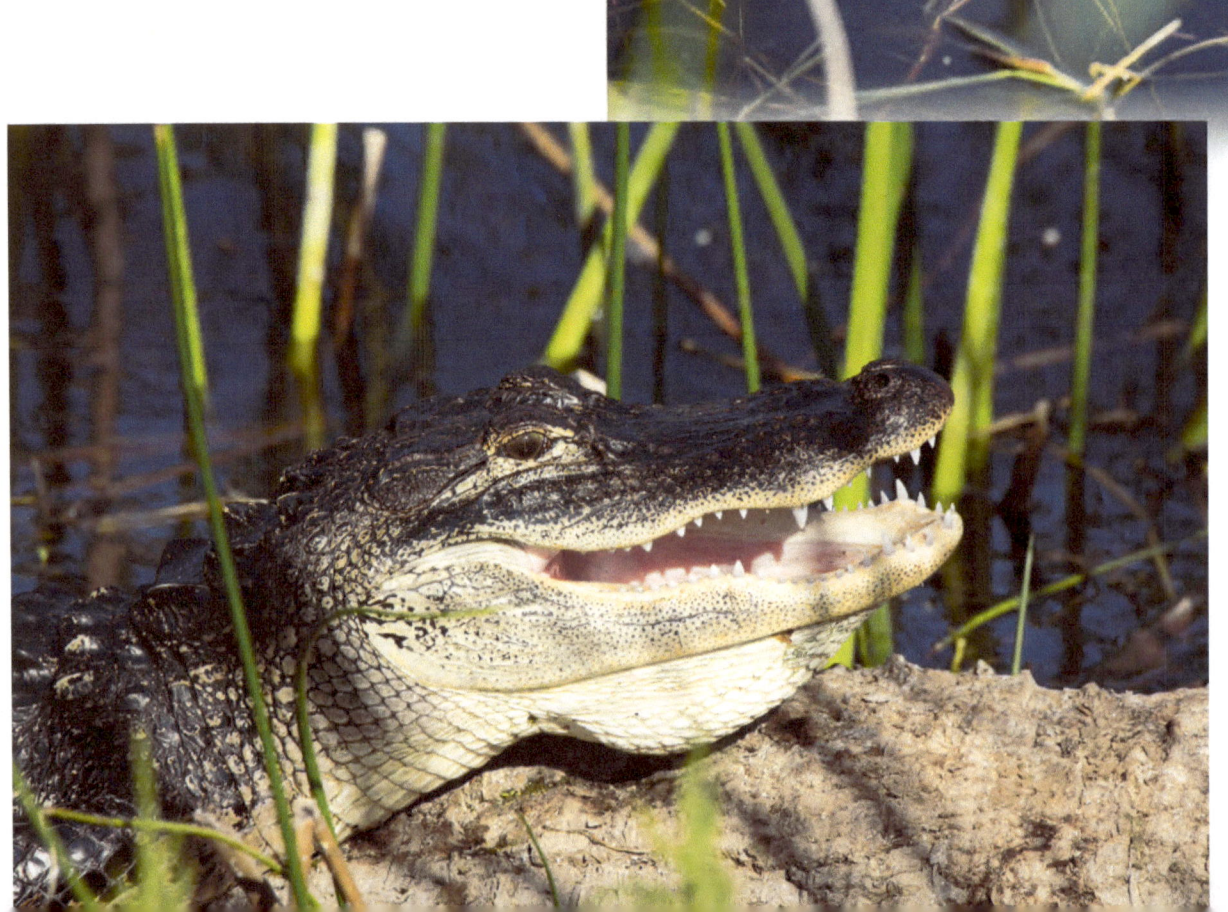

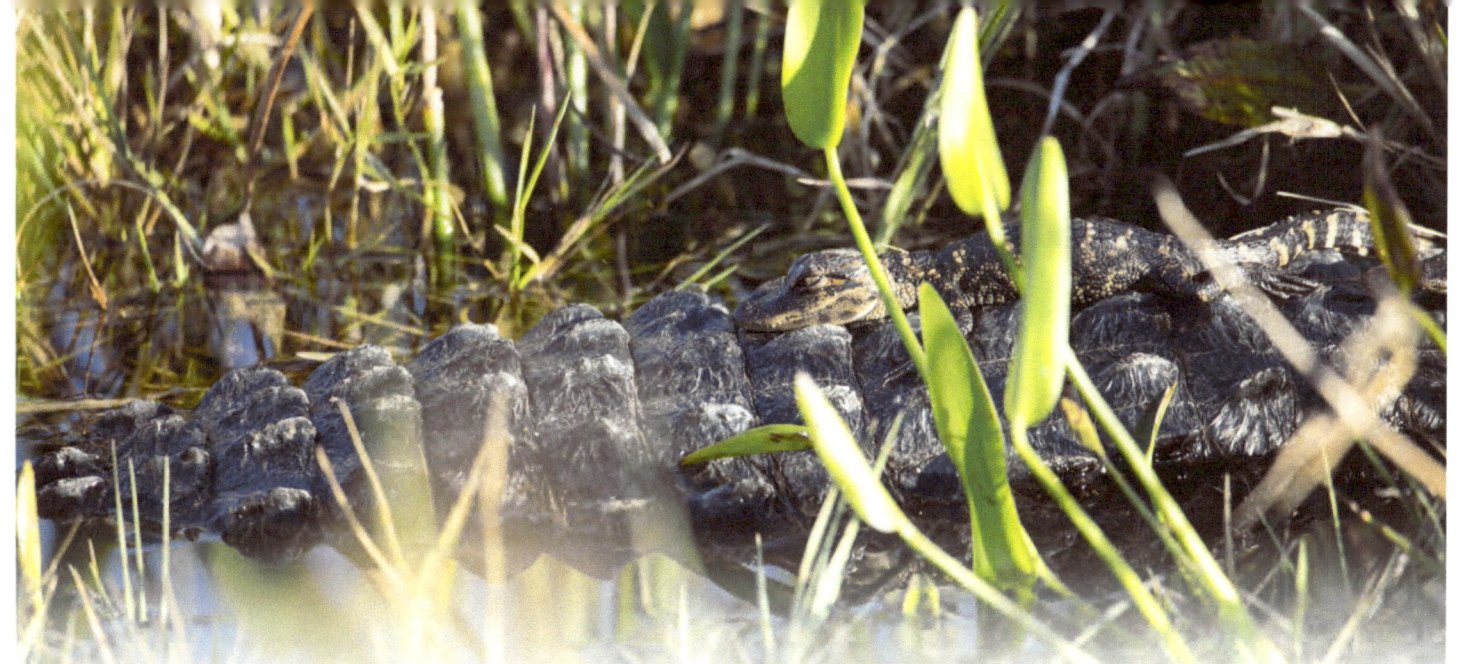

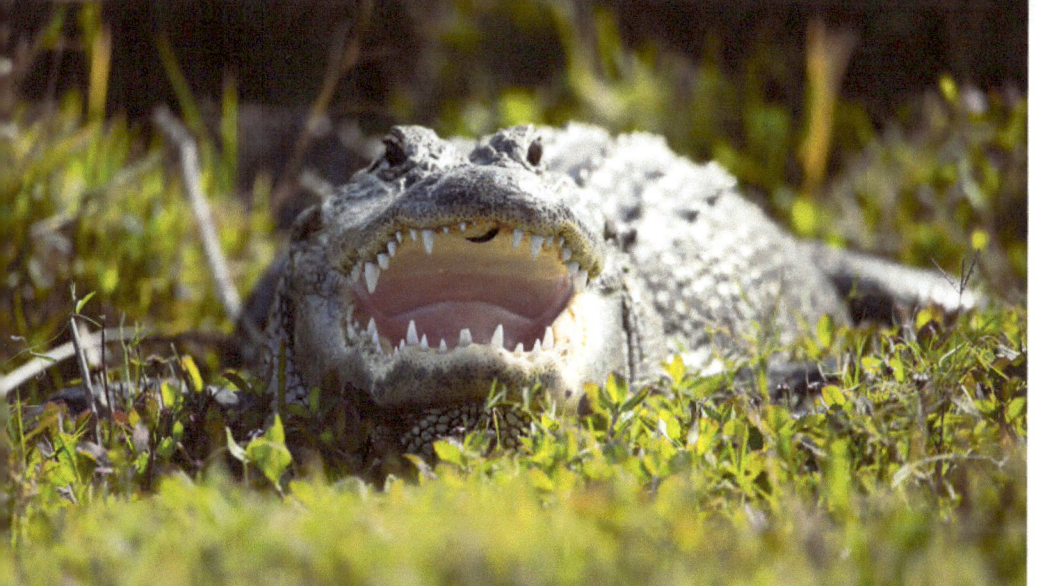

Above: Baby Gator is safe at home on Mama.

Left: Leech is happy inside this Gator's mouth.

Below: Godzilla has been spotted!

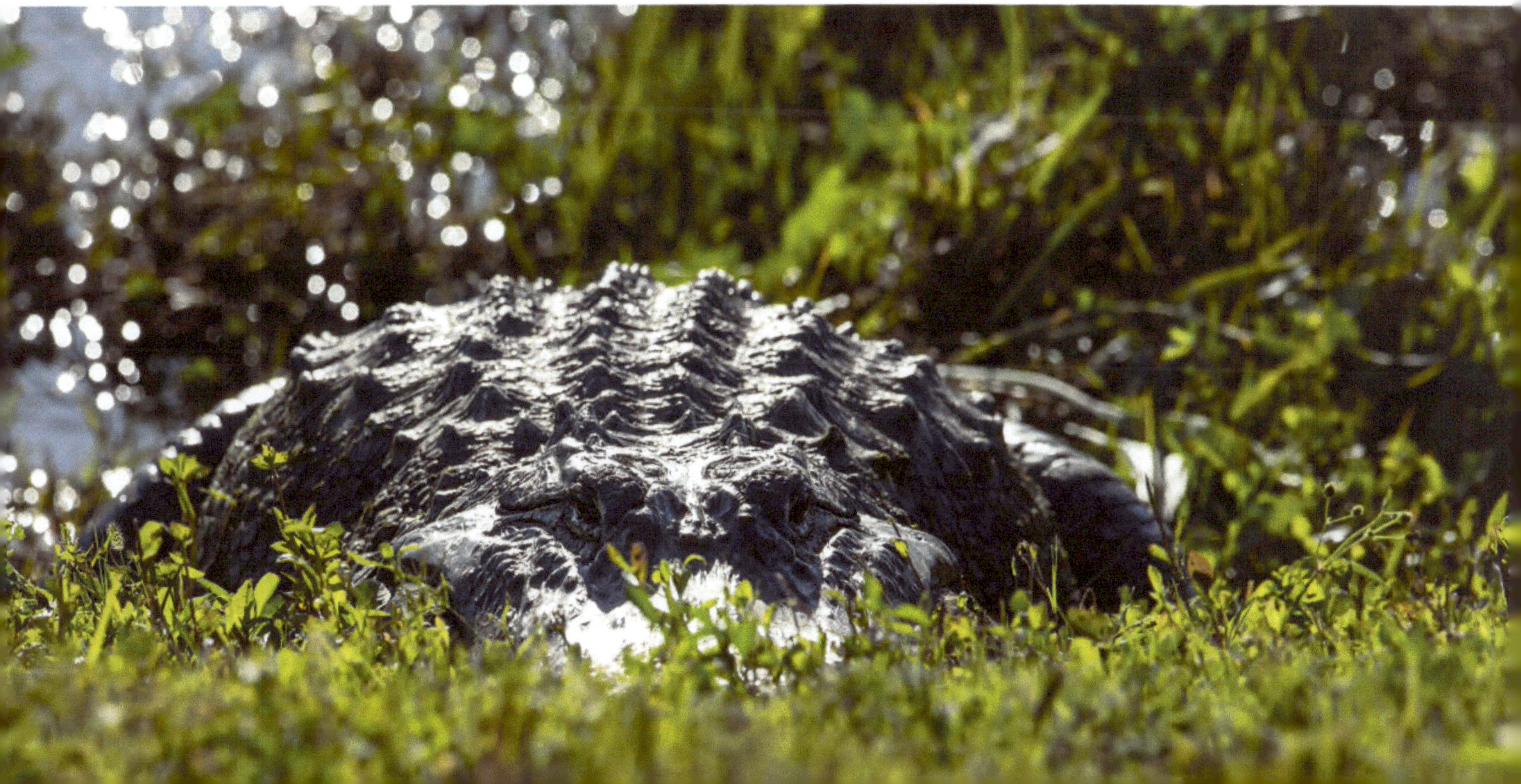

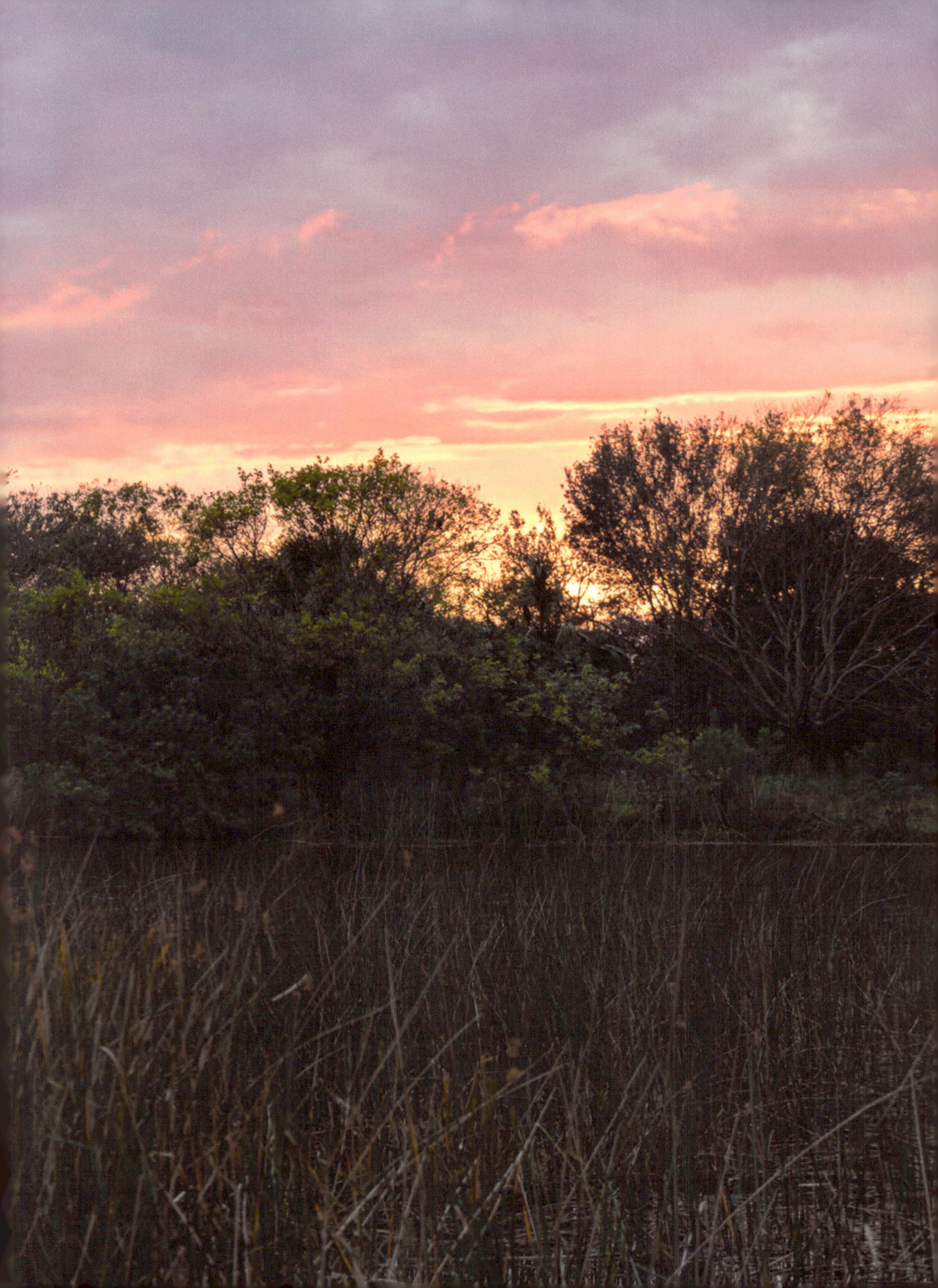

ABOUT THE OTHER CHARACTERS, CREATURES, AND OCCASIONAL ENCOUNTERS

During my 18 months I spent in this environment, I ran across a whole host of honorable mentions. The armadillo was an interesting character and would show his face for a week at a time and then disappear for months. They truly are blind. I would stand very still and they stumble all around you until they catch your scent. Keep in mind getting too close isn't recommended as they're known to carry leprosy. It would always amaze me when I would run across a lone rabbit in the wetlands. Not that they're there, but more like "you haven't been eaten yet?" In the whole scope of the apex predator ecosystems they are the walking cheeseburger out there. I had the occasion to run across several deer, wild hogs complete with long pointy tusks, raccoons, black widow spiders, various assorted turtles and reptiles, and of course the *vultures*. These guys are everywhere, every hour of every day. They do not get out of the way and are quite bold in their curiosity. Two occasions I have watched a large group of vultures work a large kill for several days. The first occasion, an adult doe had expired near a trail, and a dozen or so black vultures proceeded to buffet style this young creature over the next couple of days. The group would create a defense circle around the kill and stand watch as they would take turns getting their fill. I then ran into a large turtle that had been tipped over and could not right itself (freshly expired.) This particular crime scene drew 20 + adult vultures. My third day through and I spotted the end result… resembling that of an empty Tupperware container. Both the black vulture and the red-headed turkey vulture are present in numbers in the wetlands. The redheaded version being least common and oddly enough the two wouldn't co-mingle at the dinner table.

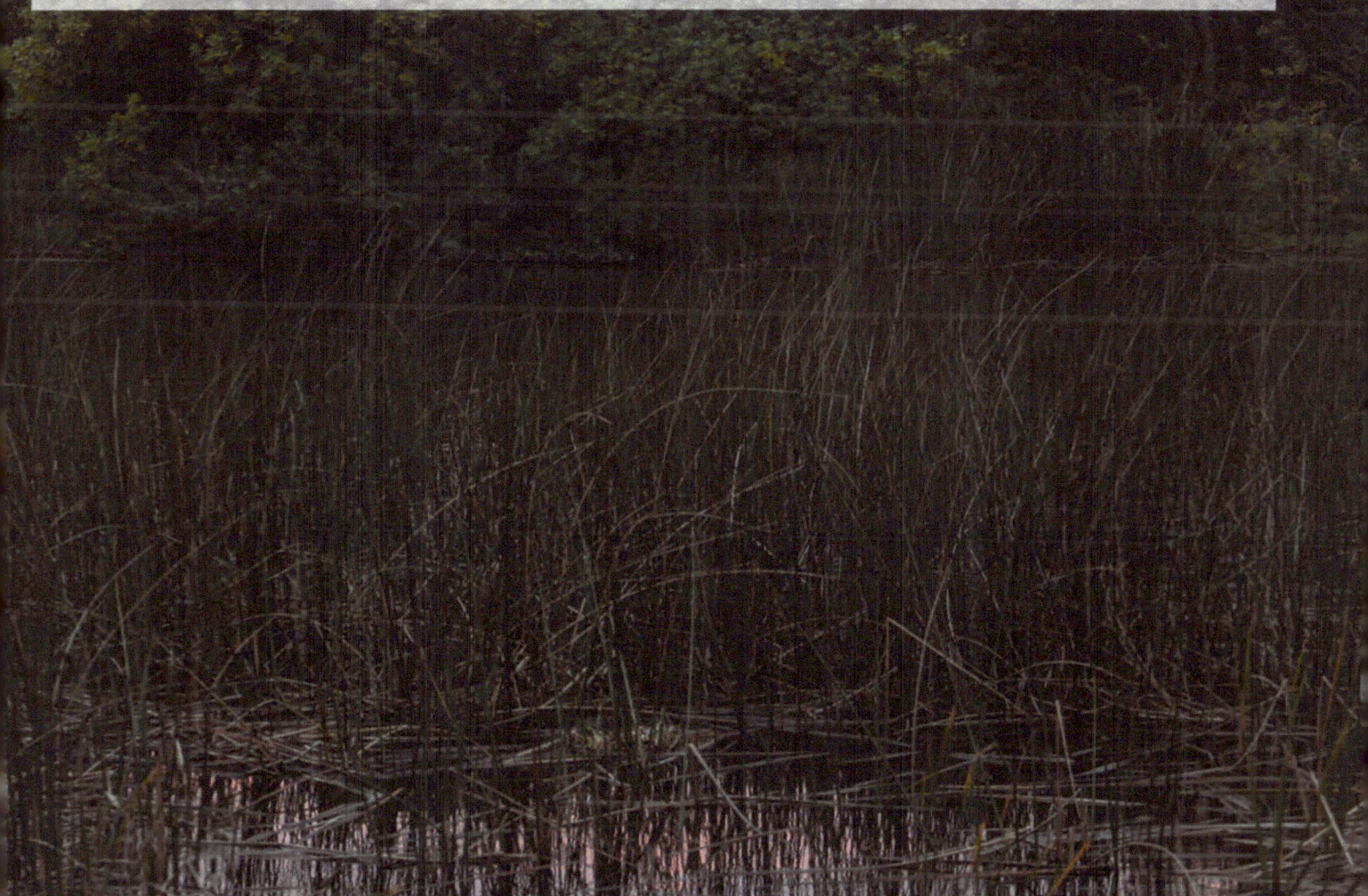

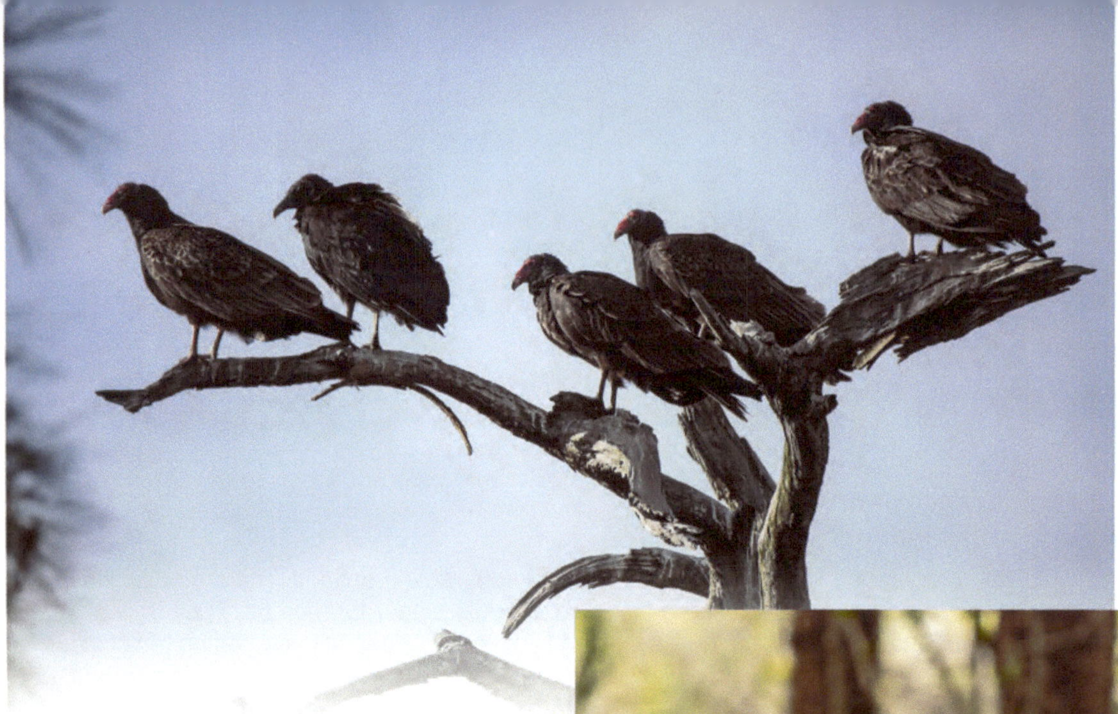

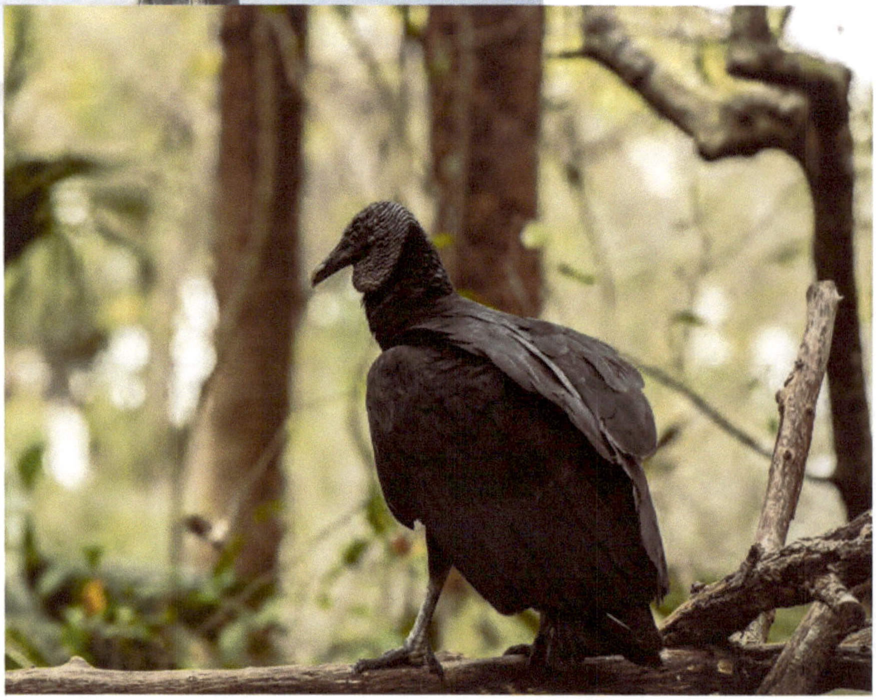

Above: A tree of buzzards waiting for death.

Right: Black Headed Turkey Vulture.

Below: A bad day to be a turtle.

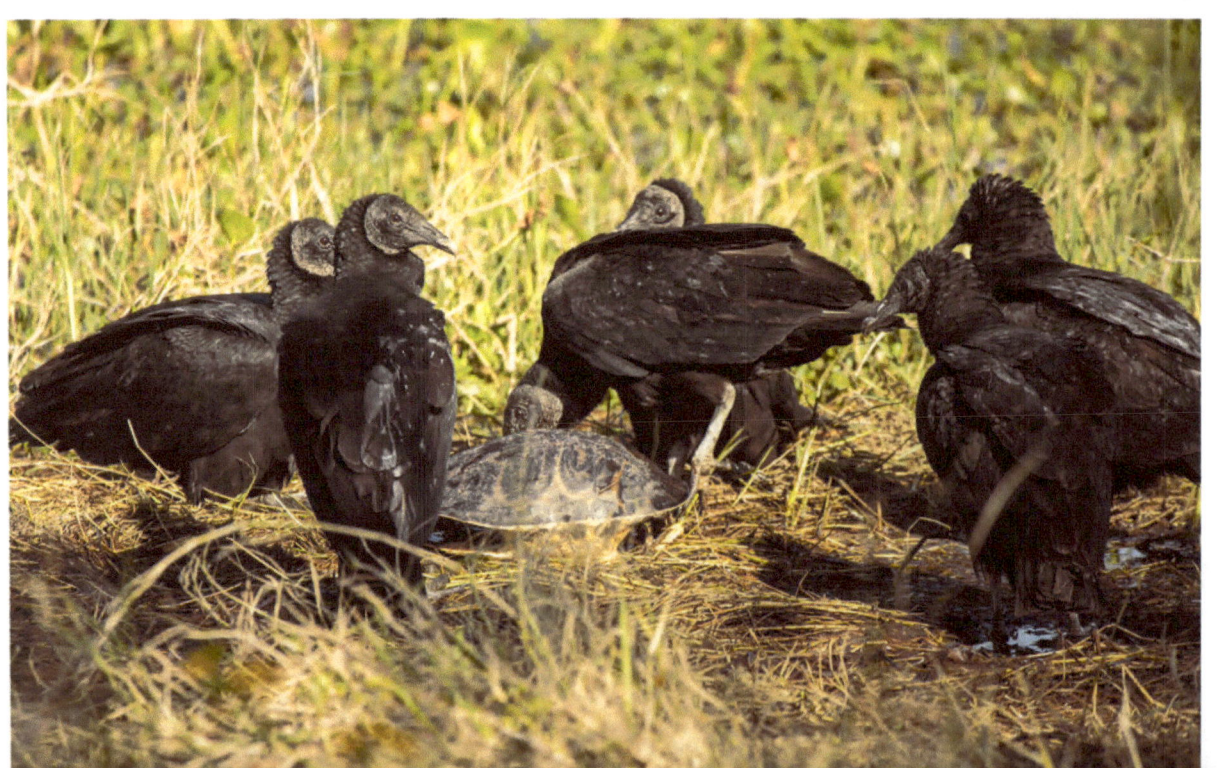

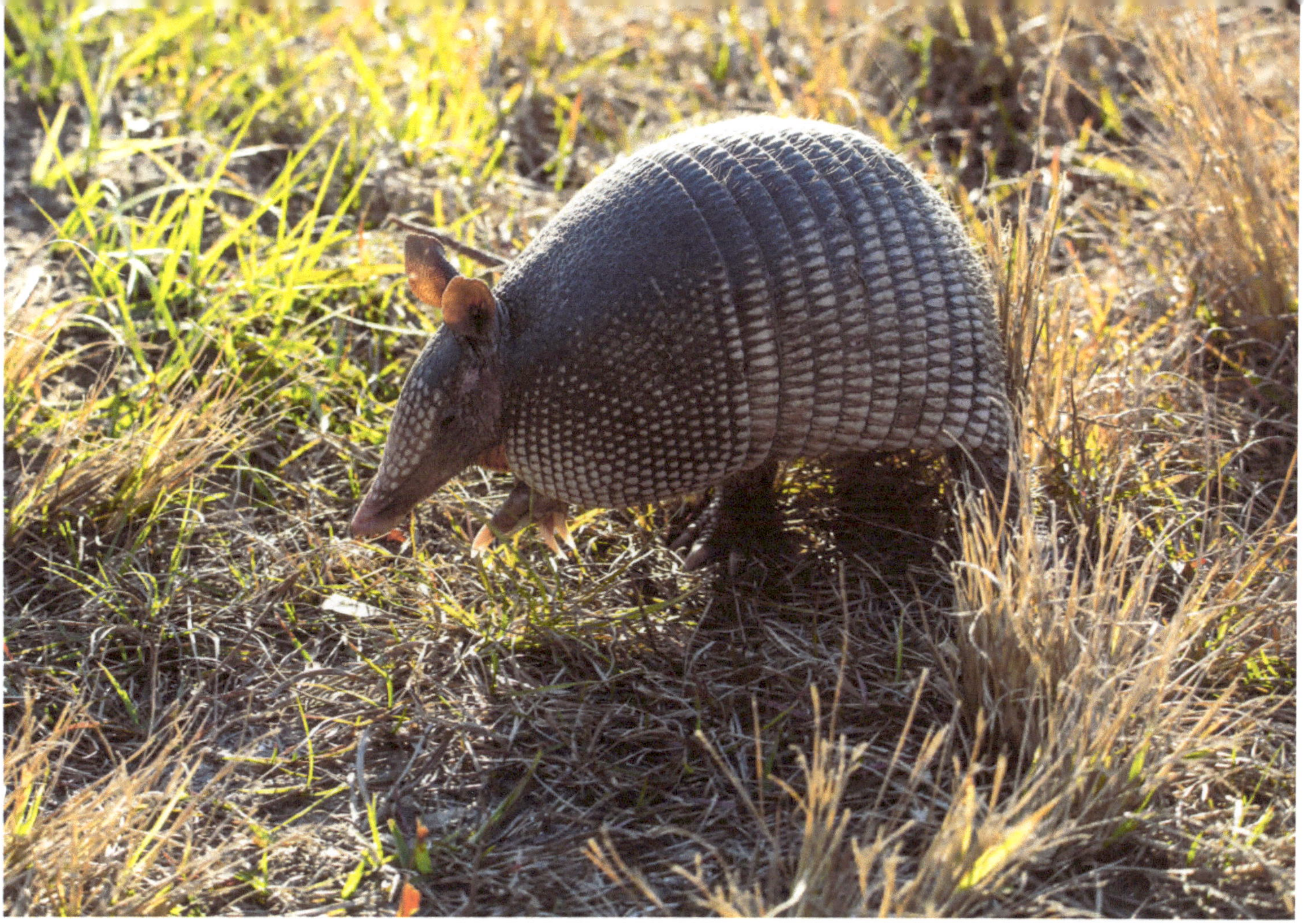

Above: An Armadillo is looking for a snack.   Below: Mr. Armadillo makes his escape.

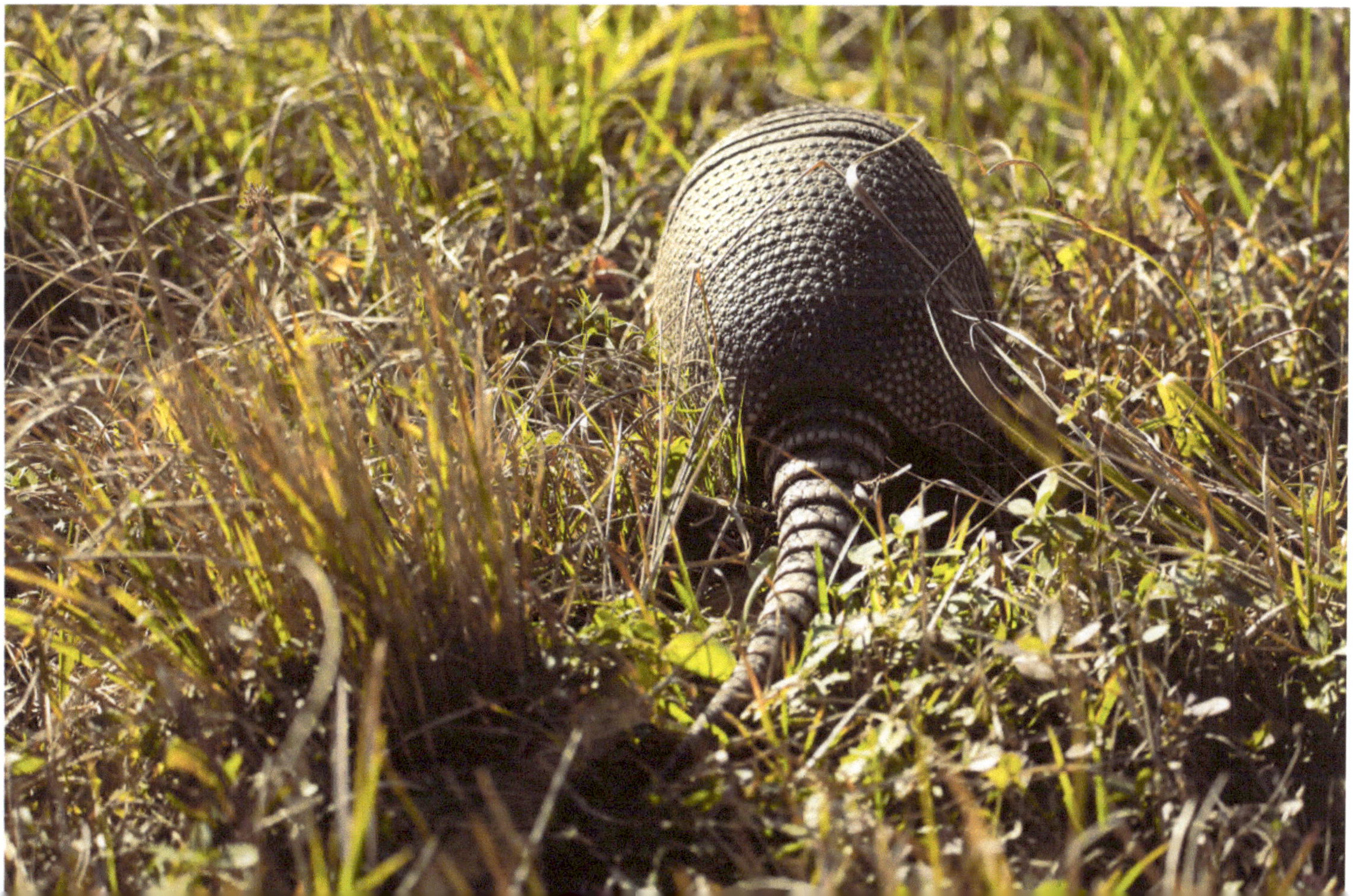

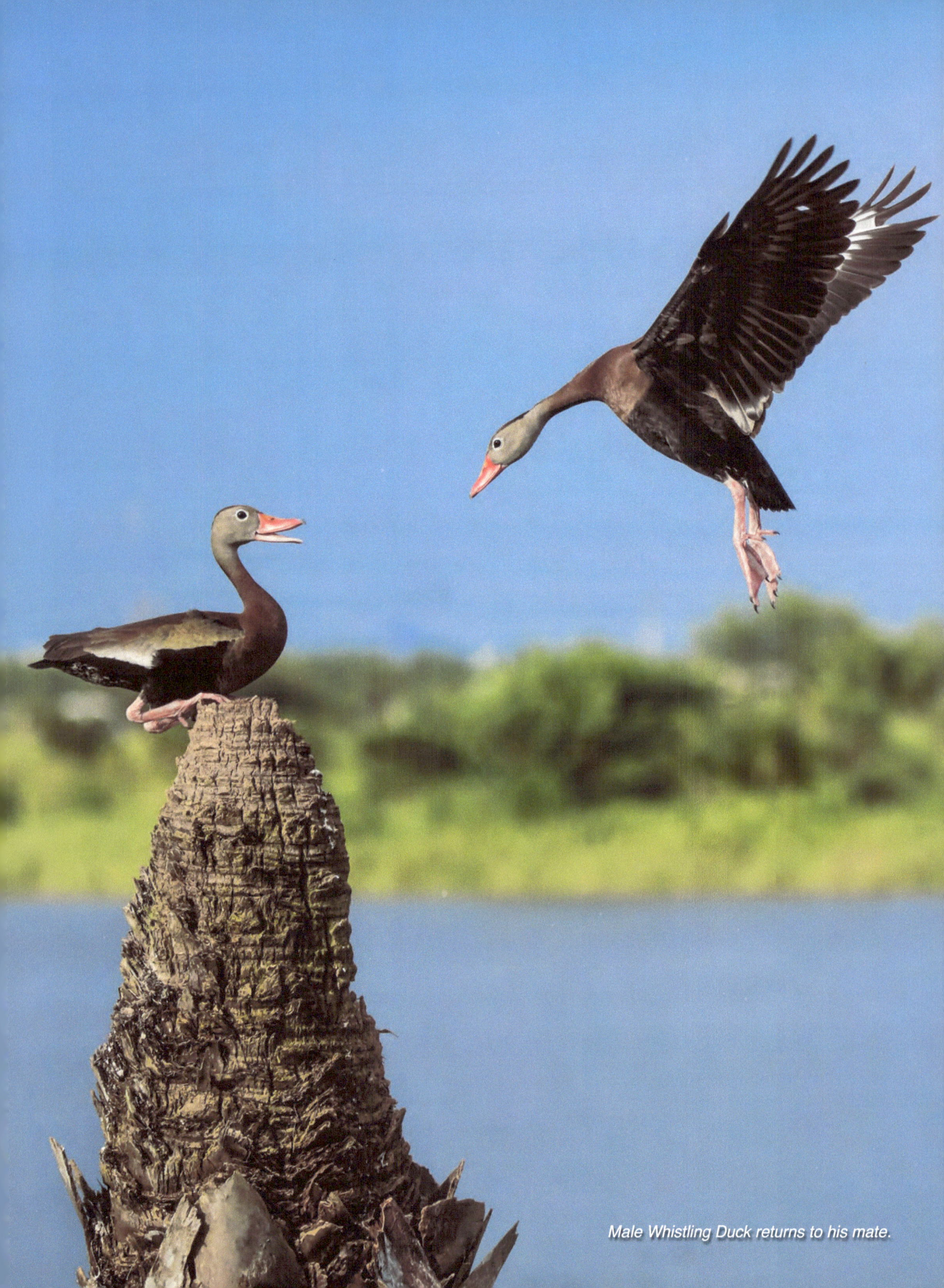

Male Whistling Duck returns to his mate.

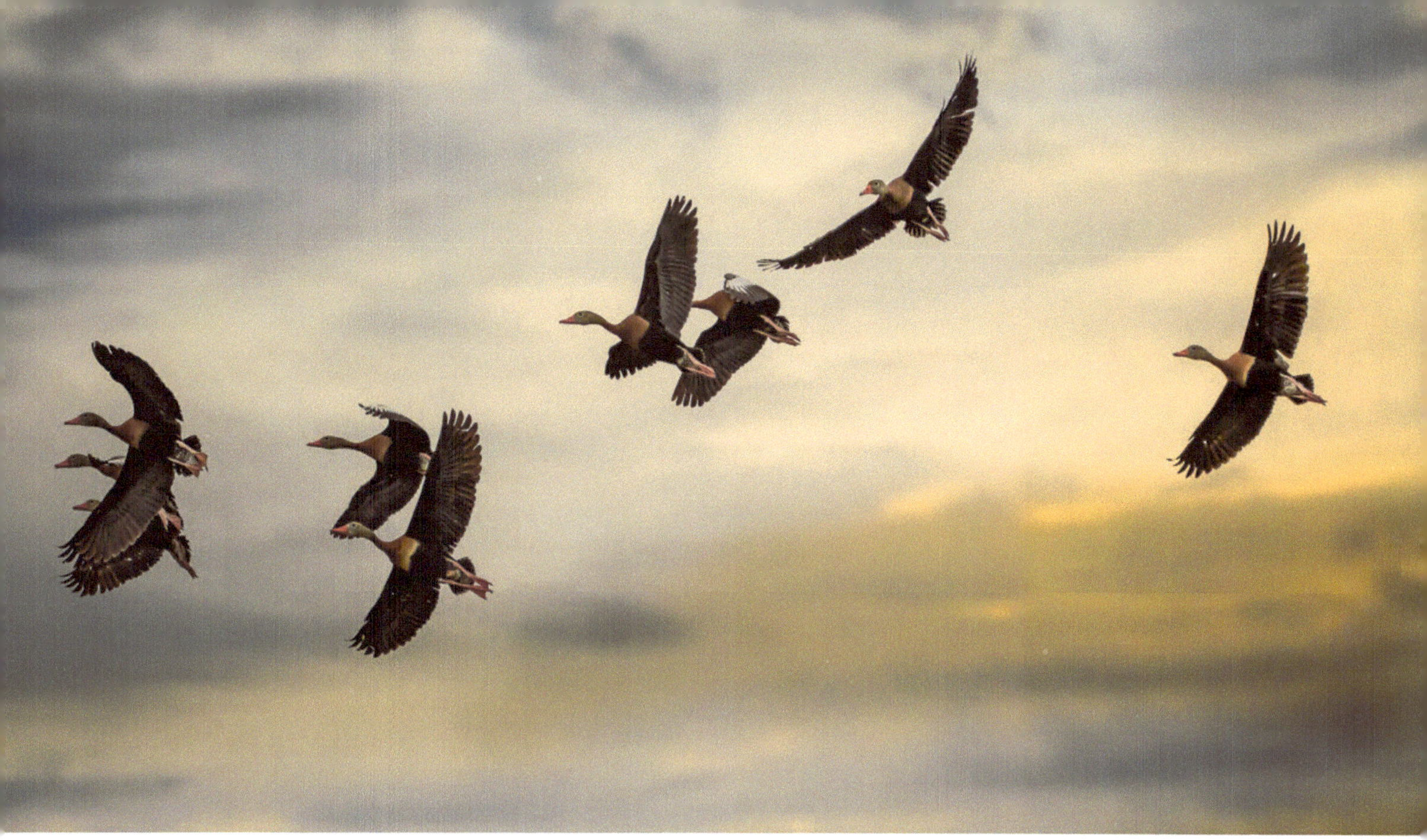

*Above: Black-bellied Whistling Ducks fly off into the sunset.
Below: A mated pair of Black-bellied Whistling Ducks.*

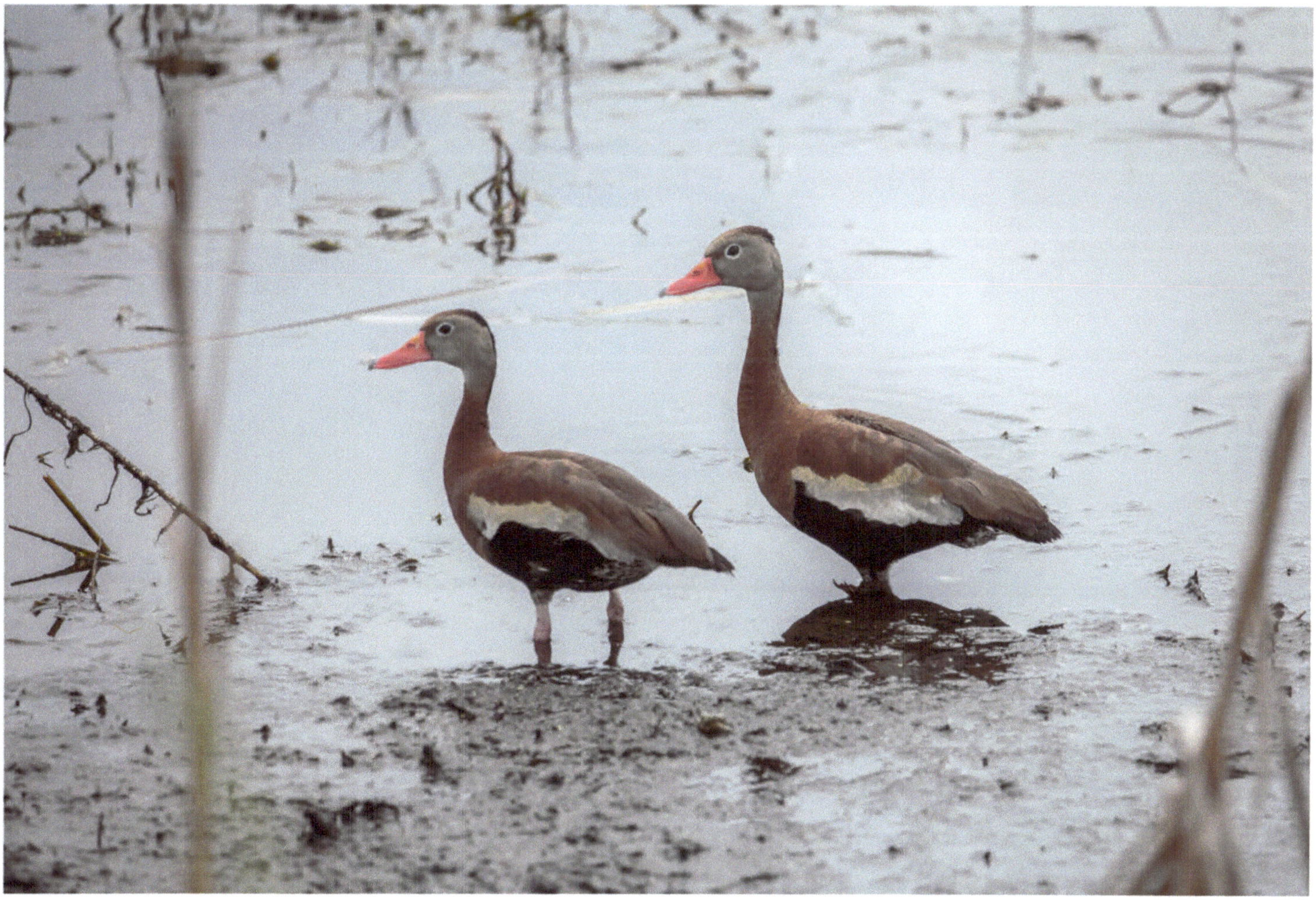

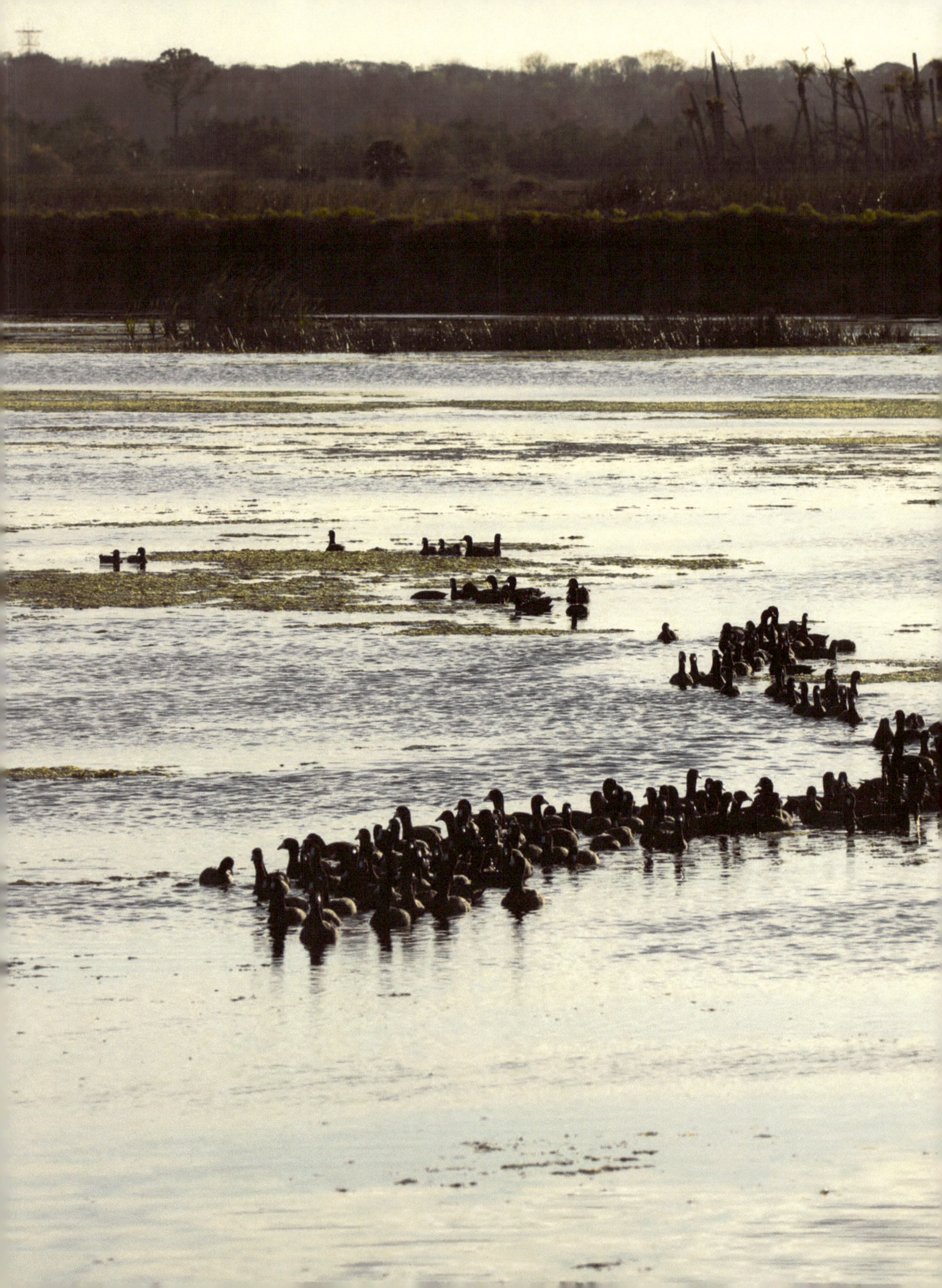

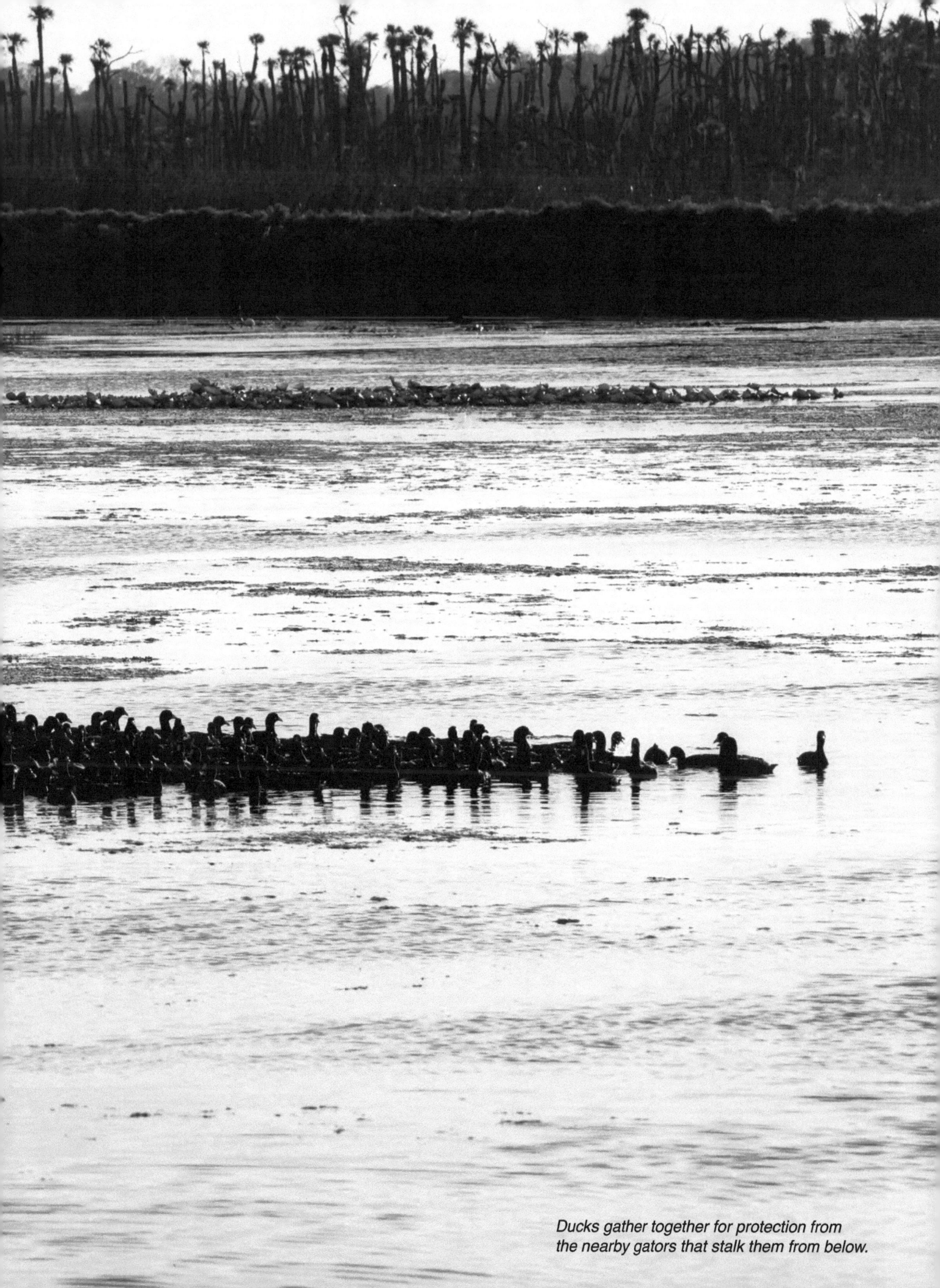

Ducks gather together for protection from the nearby gators that stalk them from below.

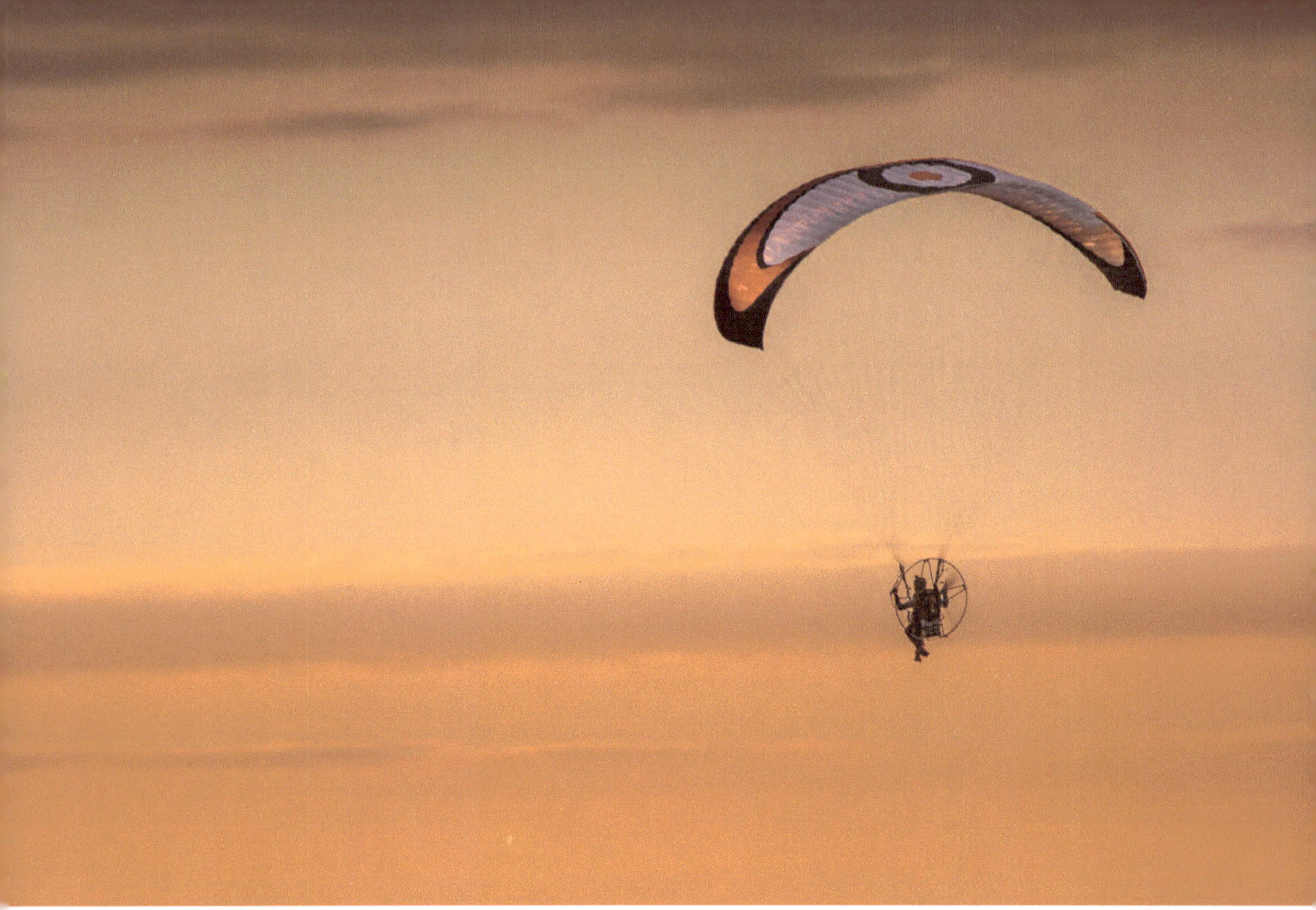

Above: A paraglider soars over Alligator infested waters at sunset.　　Below: This baby bunny has caught your scent.

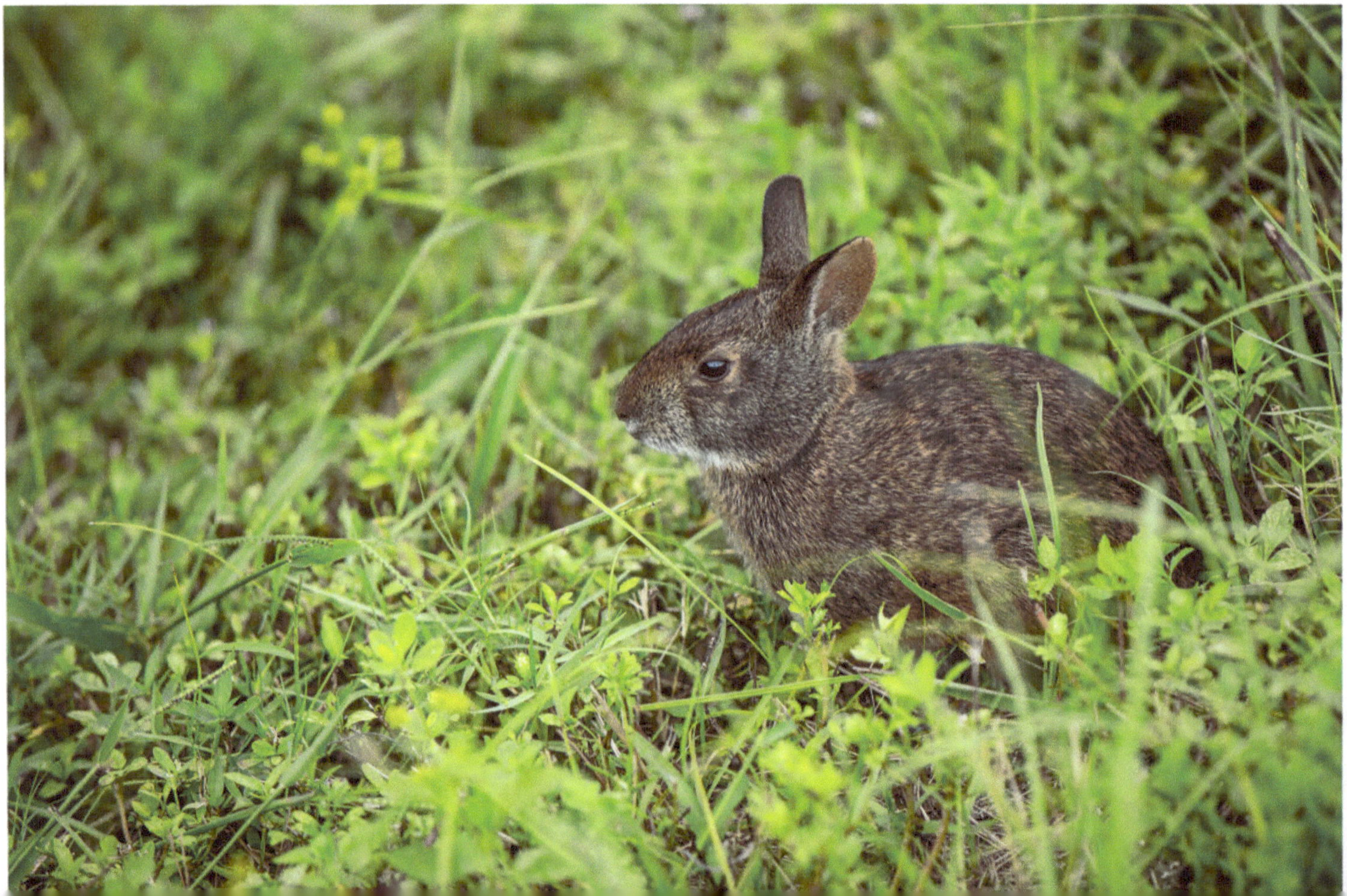

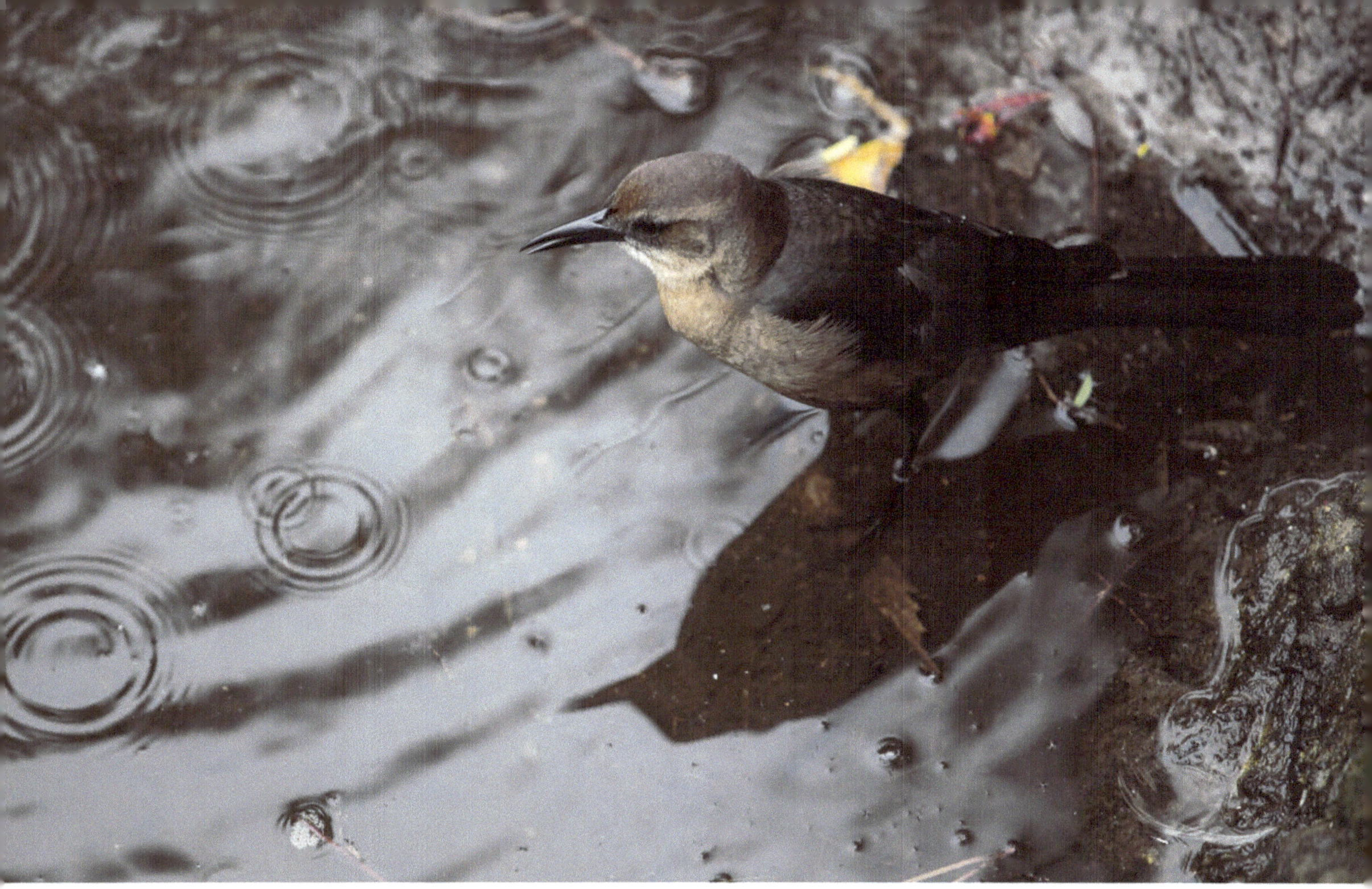

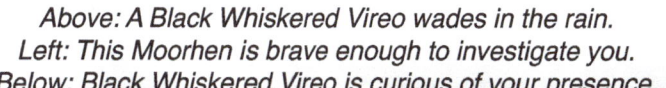

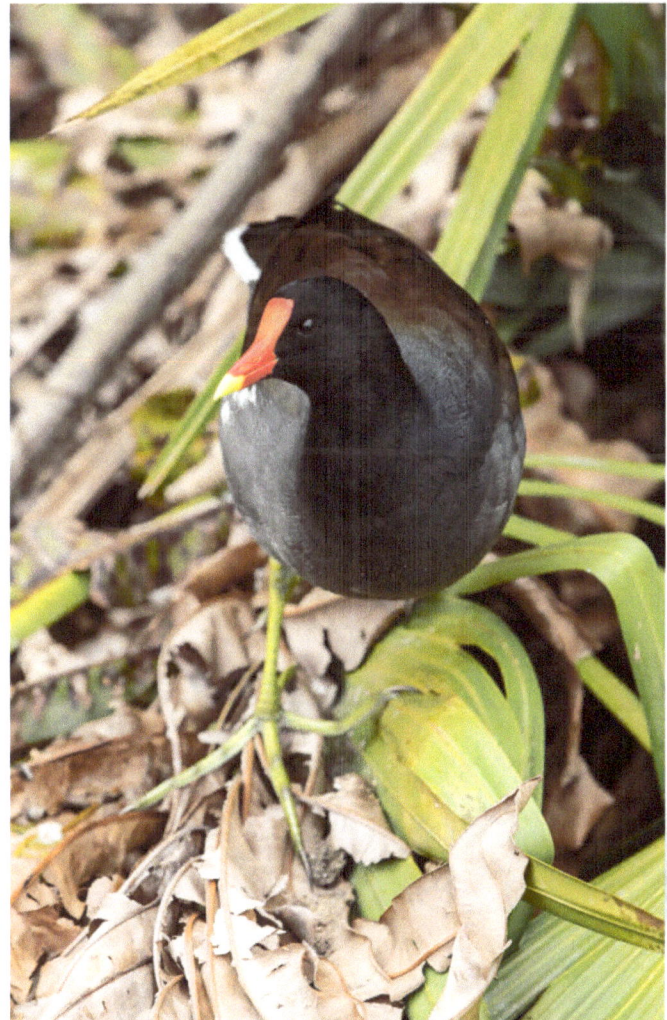

Above: A Black Whiskered Vireo wades in the rain.
Left: This Moorhen is brave enough to investigate you.
Below: Black Whiskered Vireo is curious of your presence.

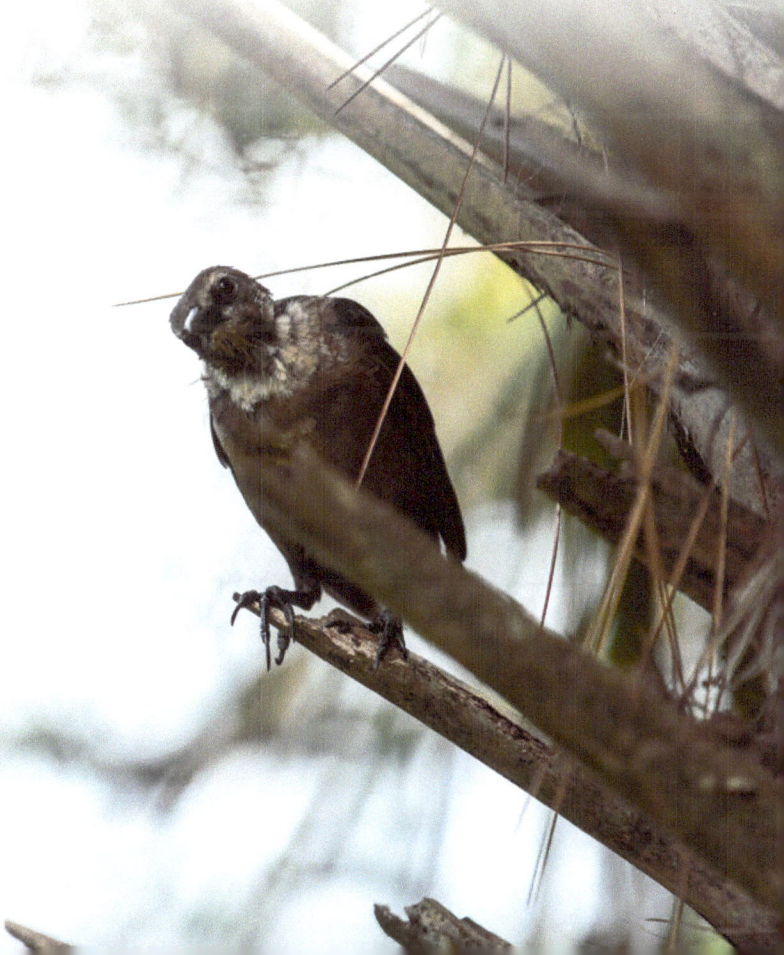

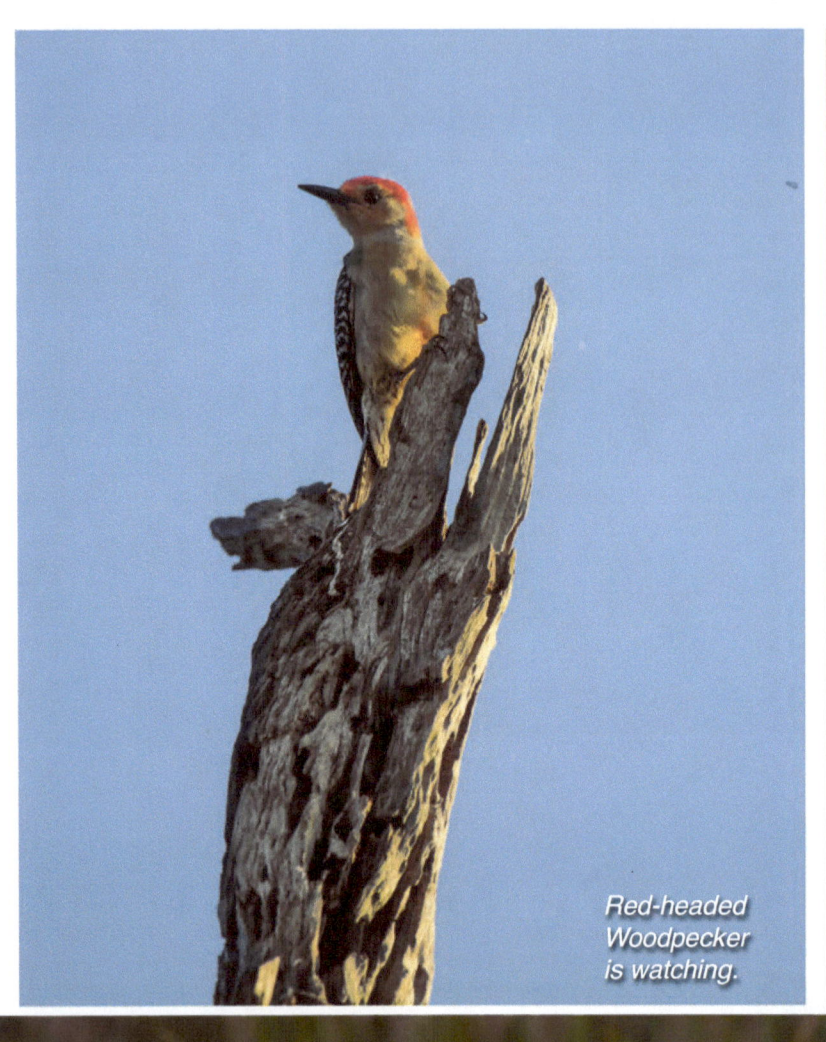

Red-headed Woodpecker is watching.

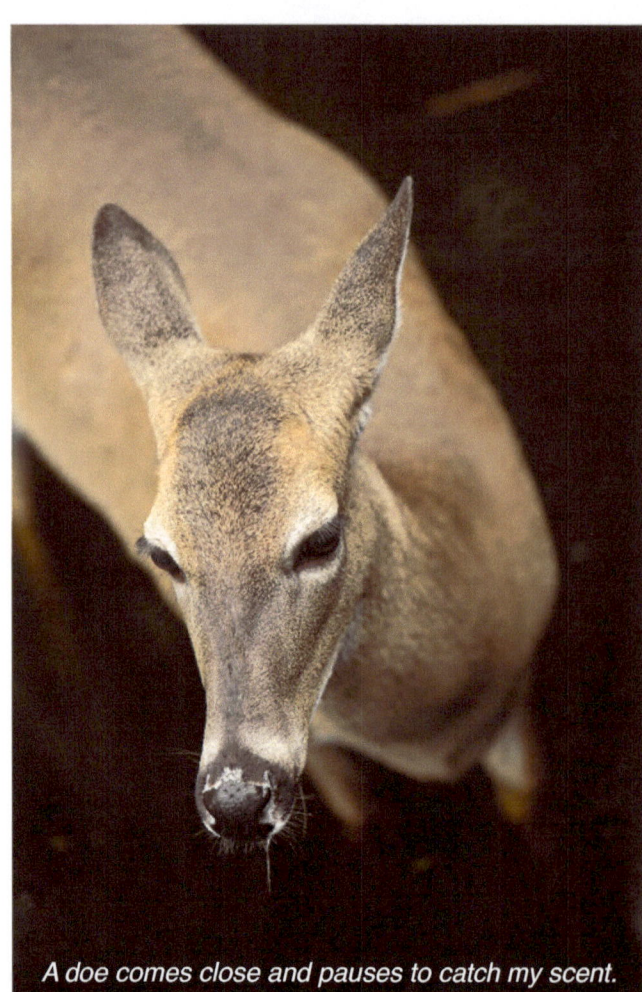

A doe comes close and pauses to catch my scent.

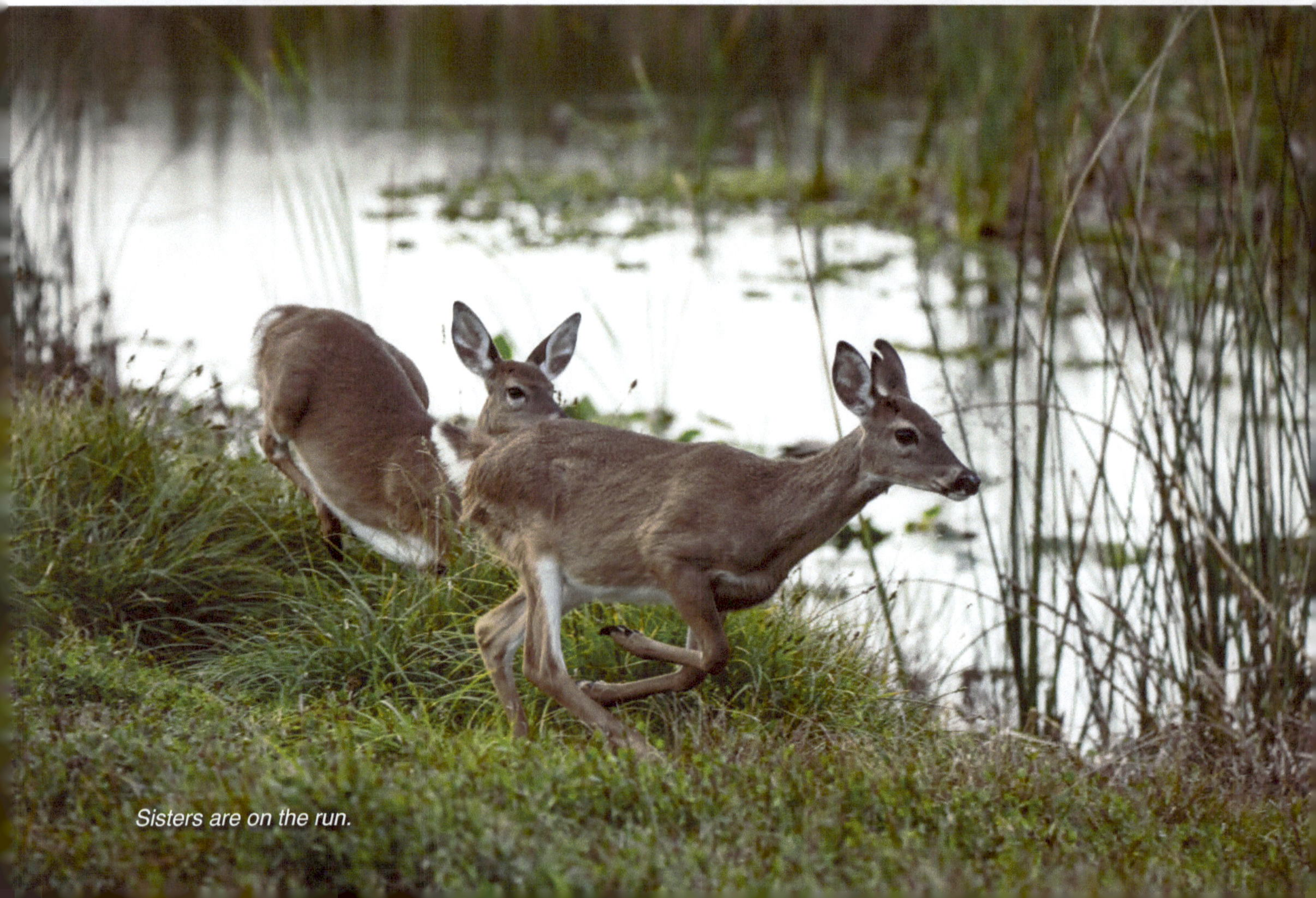

Sisters are on the run.

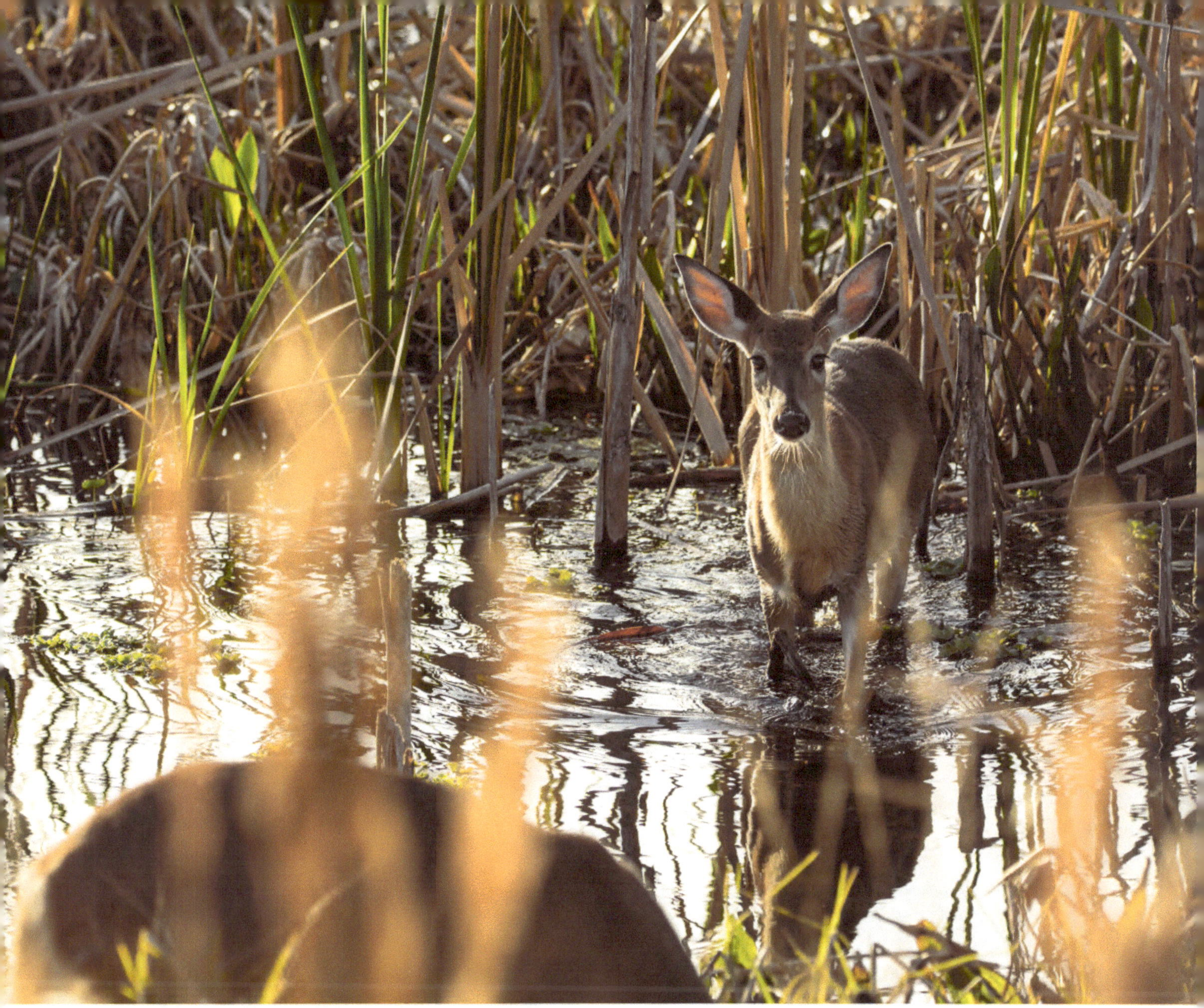

Above: After getting very close she finally caught me.

Left: The family has spotted you.

Below: A Turtle takes a break on a log.

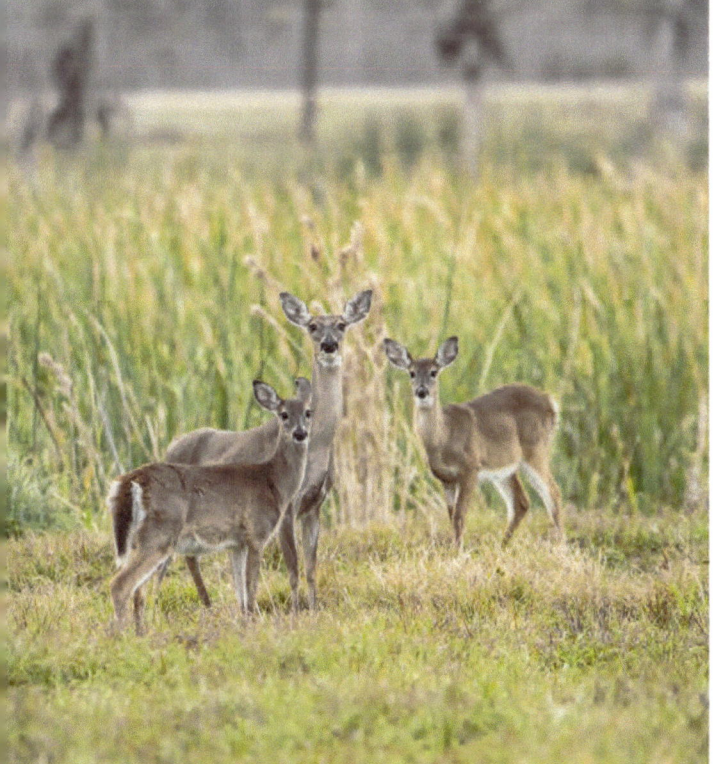

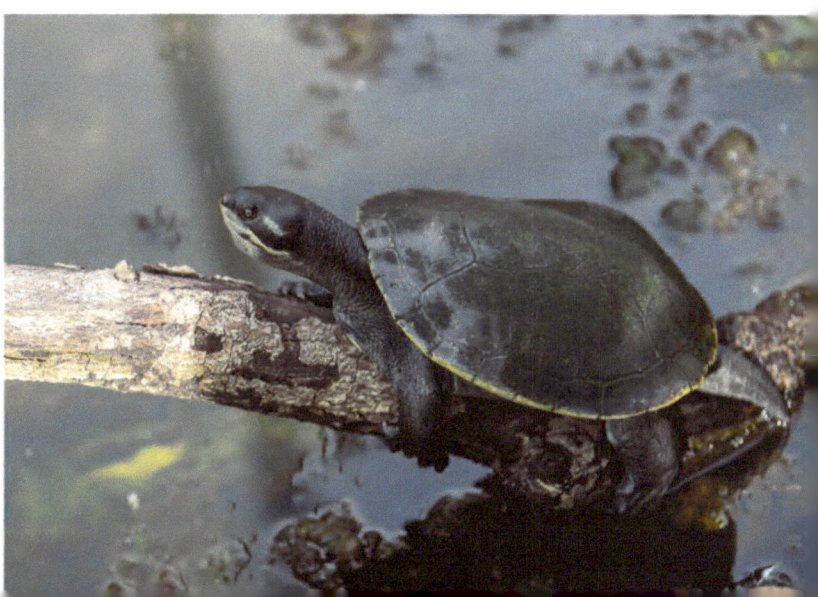

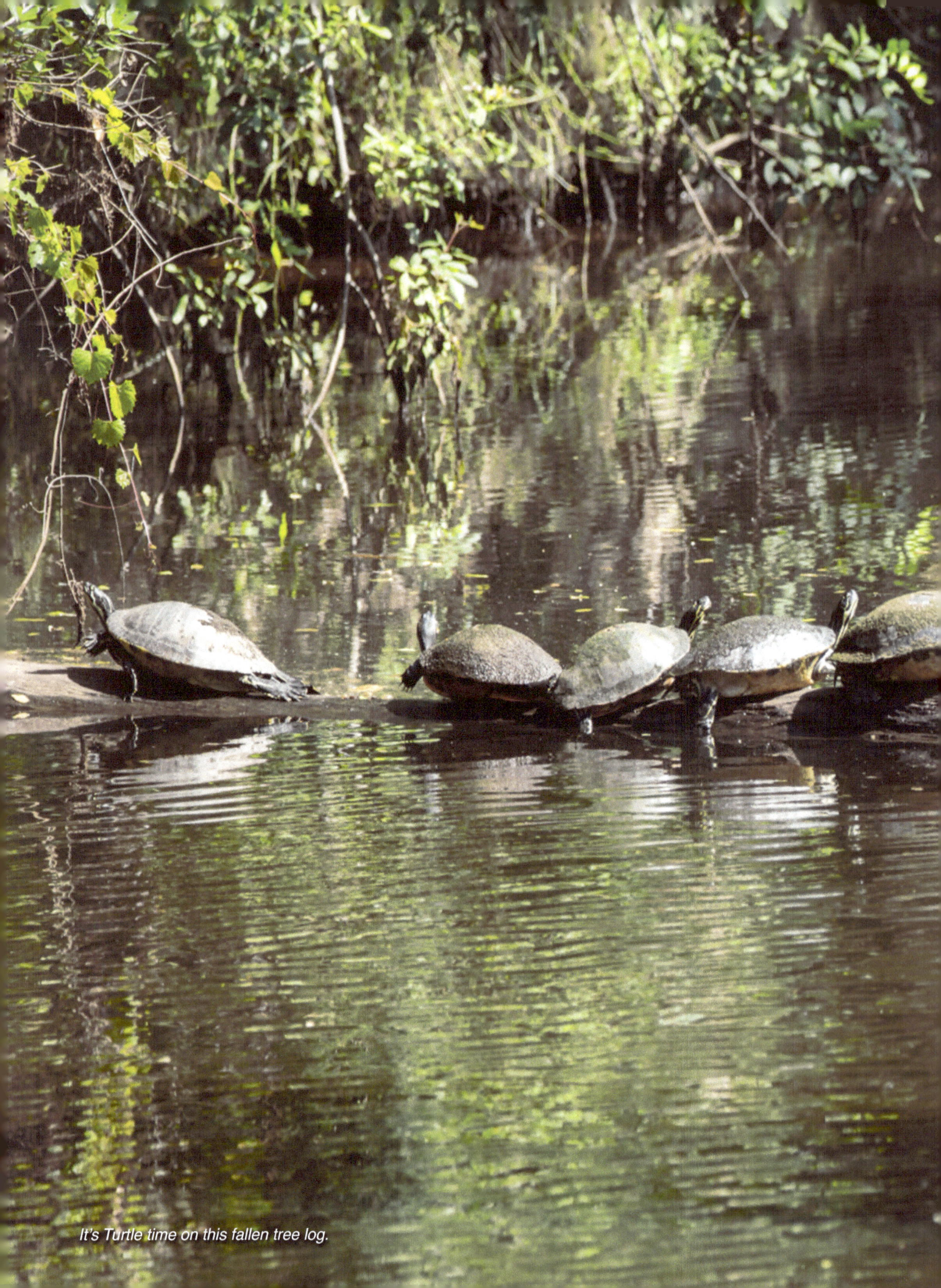
It's Turtle time on this fallen tree log.

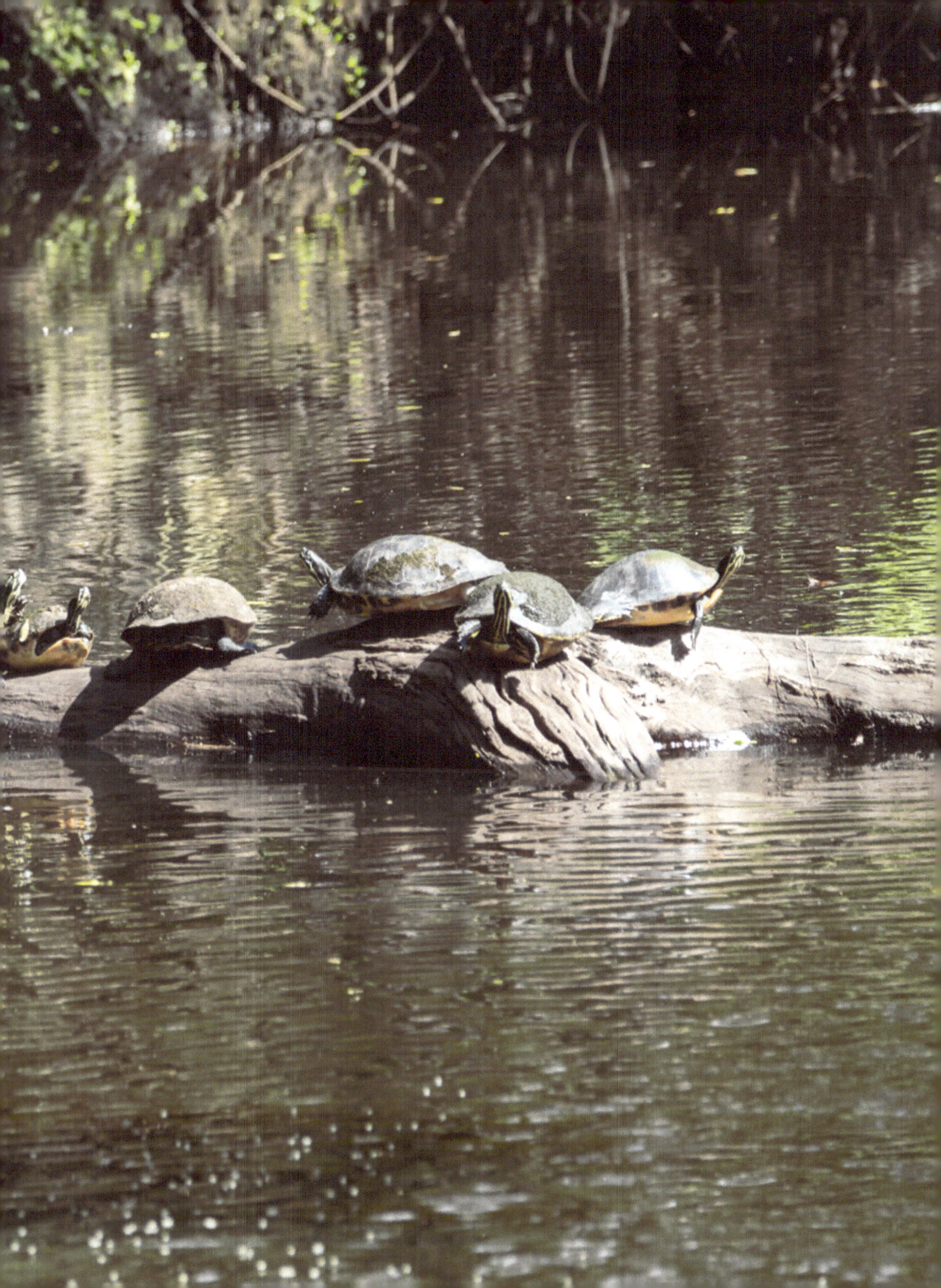

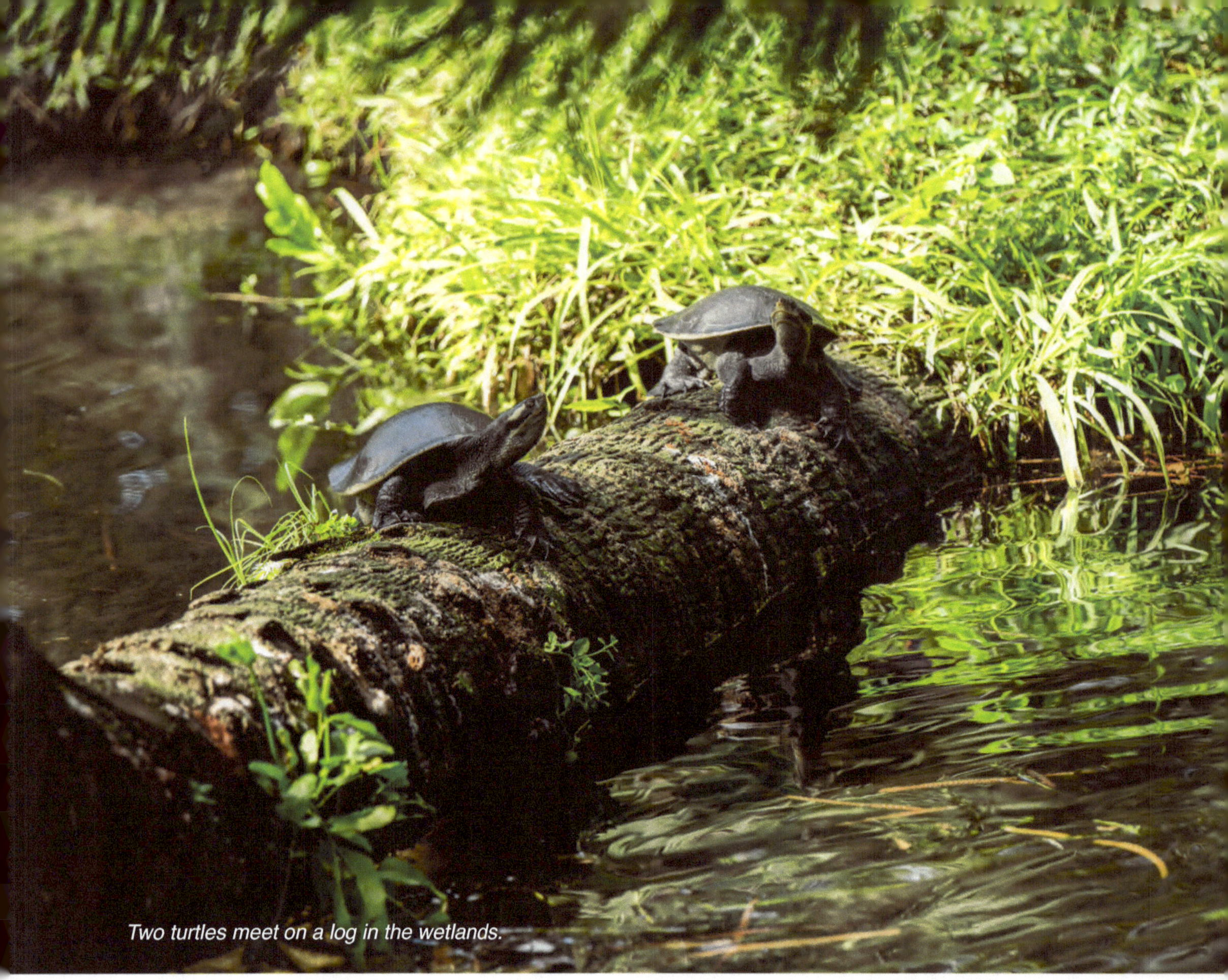

Two turtles meet on a log in the wetlands.

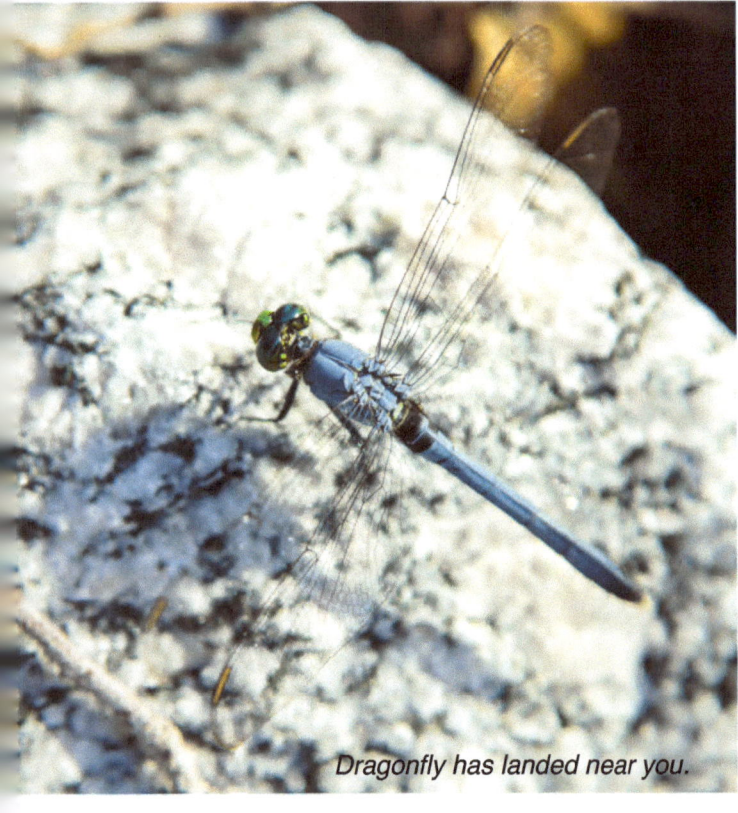

Dragonfly has landed near you.

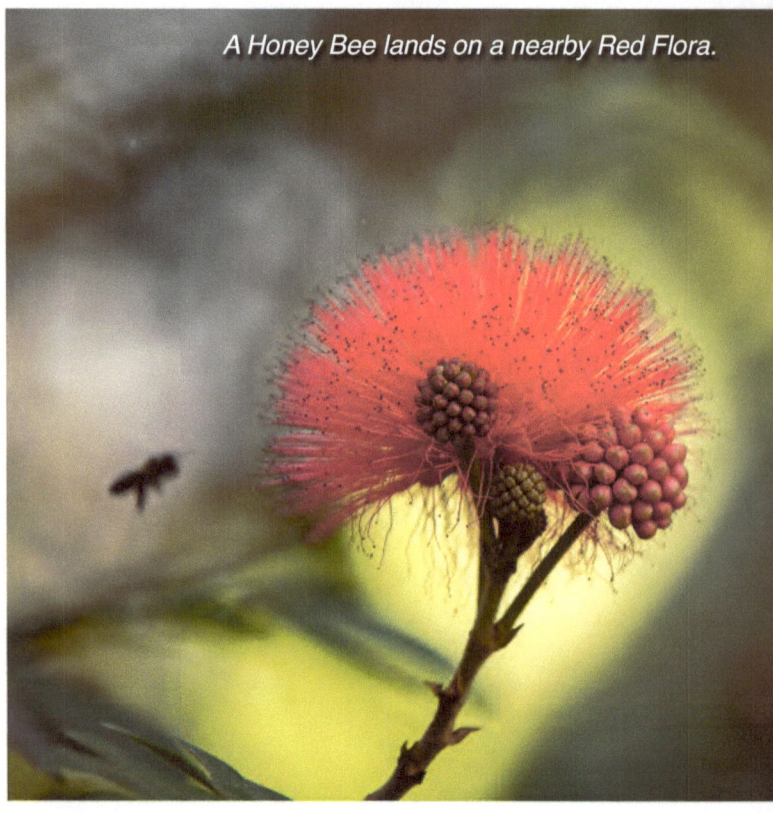

A Honey Bee lands on a nearby Red Flora.

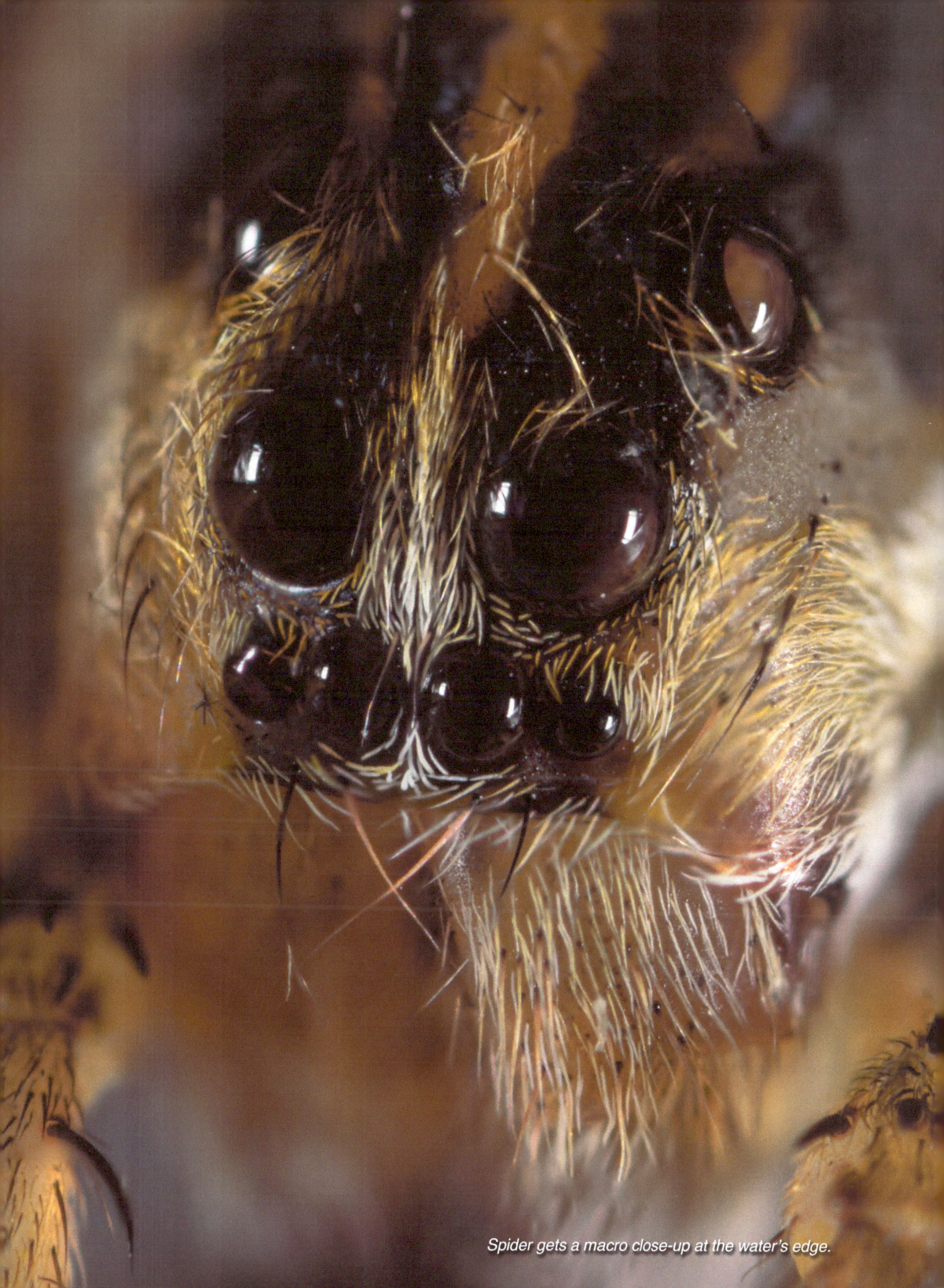
Spider gets a macro close-up at the water's edge.

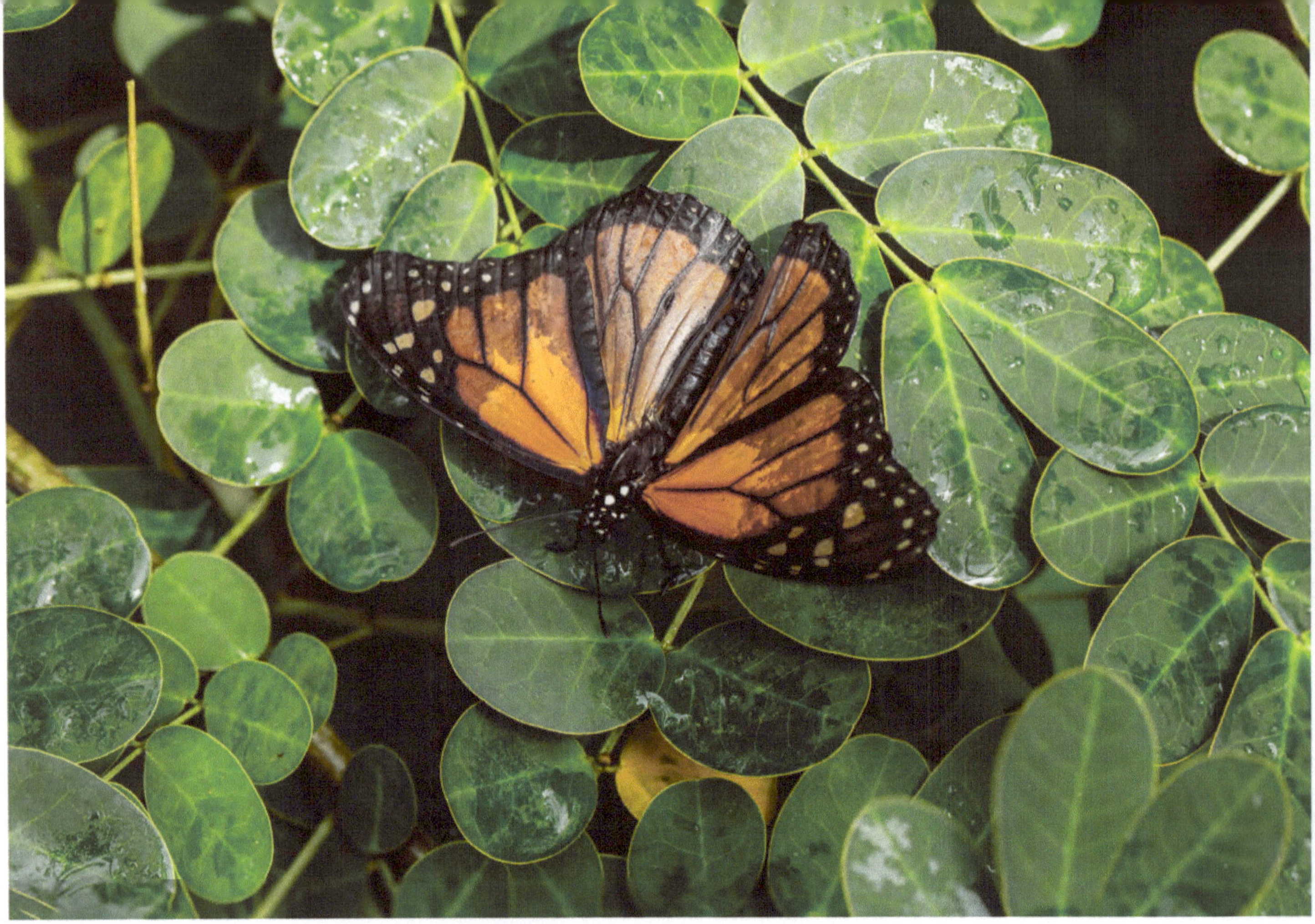

Above: Monarch Butterfly has landed after the rain.
Below: Green Caterpillar travels across a leaf.

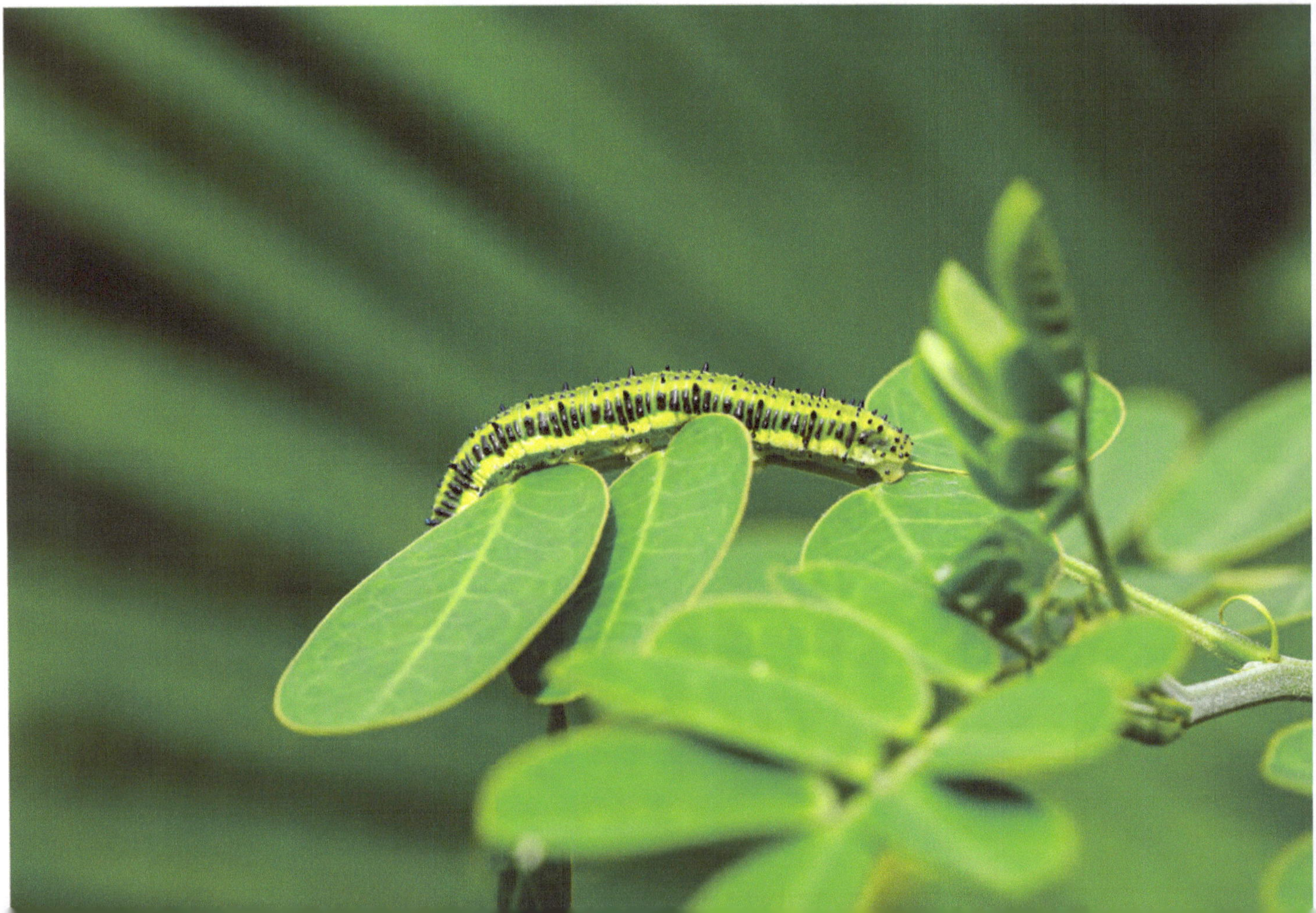

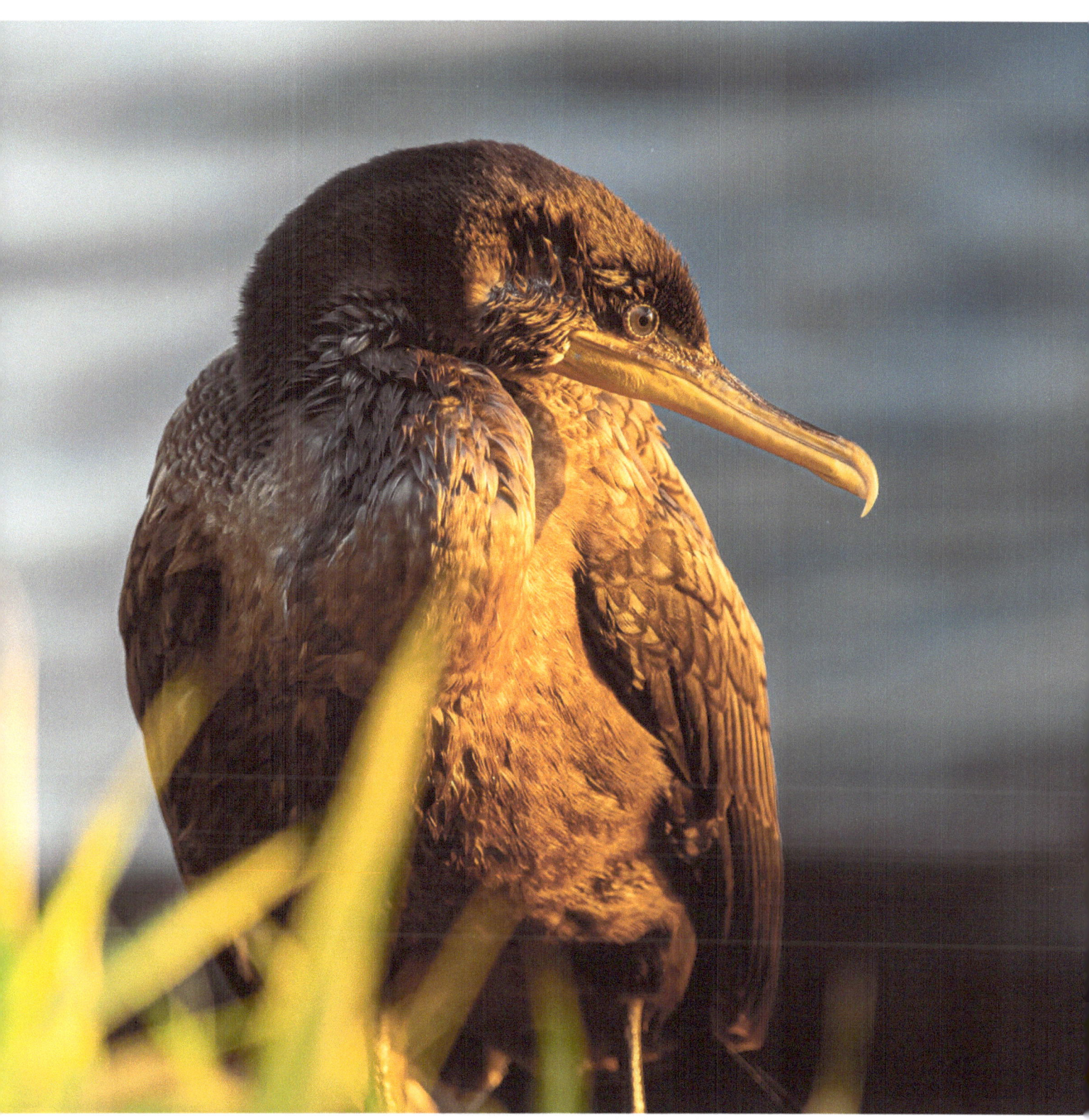

Cormorant gets a close-up in the setting sun.

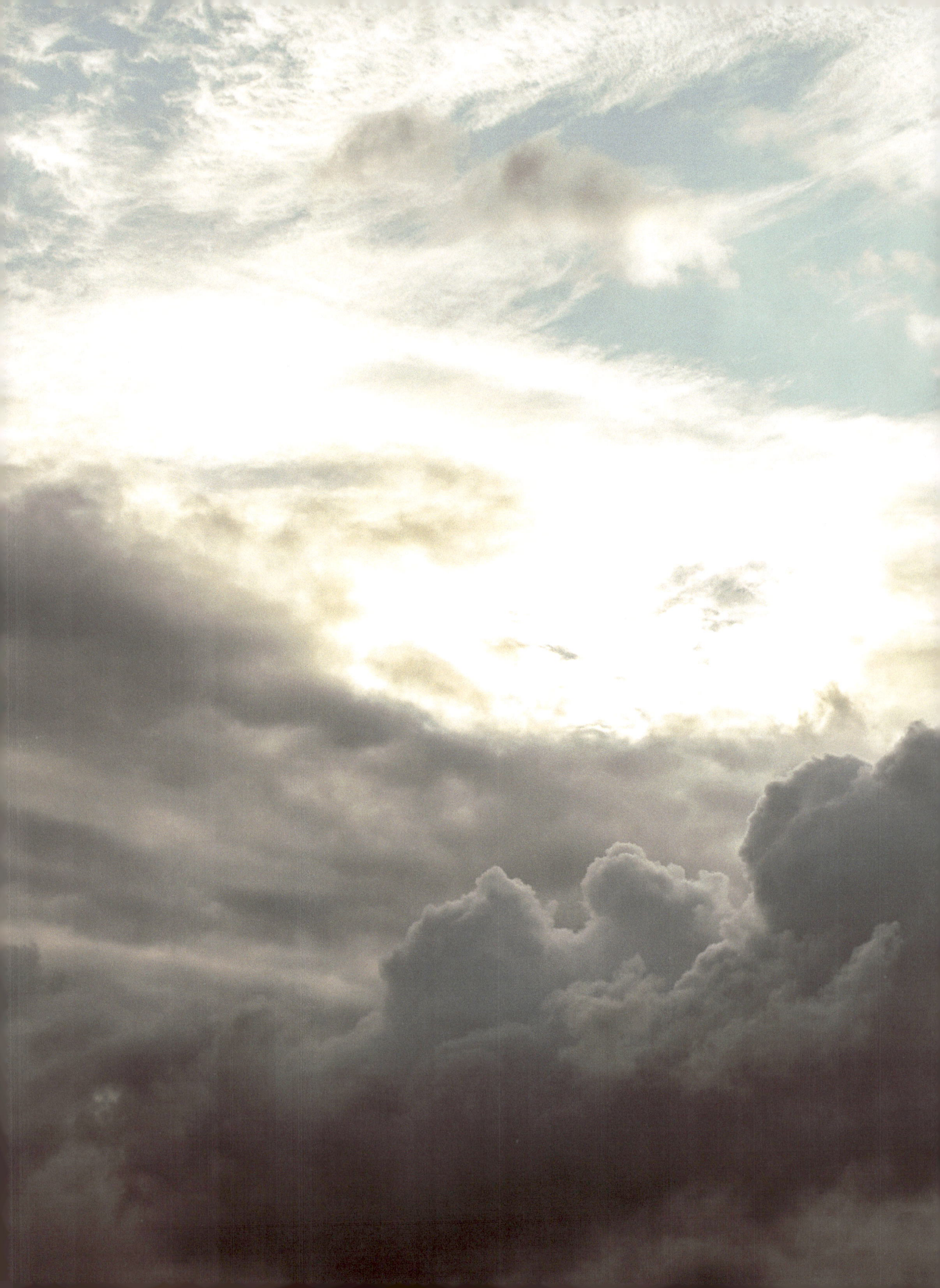

ABOUT THE END

As of this writing, I have safely relocated to the urban jungles of Detroit, Michigan. My opportunity to have this experience has brought a true appreciation for the solitude and peace that the great outdoors and wilderness offers. It also reminds me of just how good it is to leave society, technology, and the negativity of our urban reality behind. I look forward to the next adventure, and plan to share it as well. Stay tuned… stay safe!

Best,

J.A. Dunbar

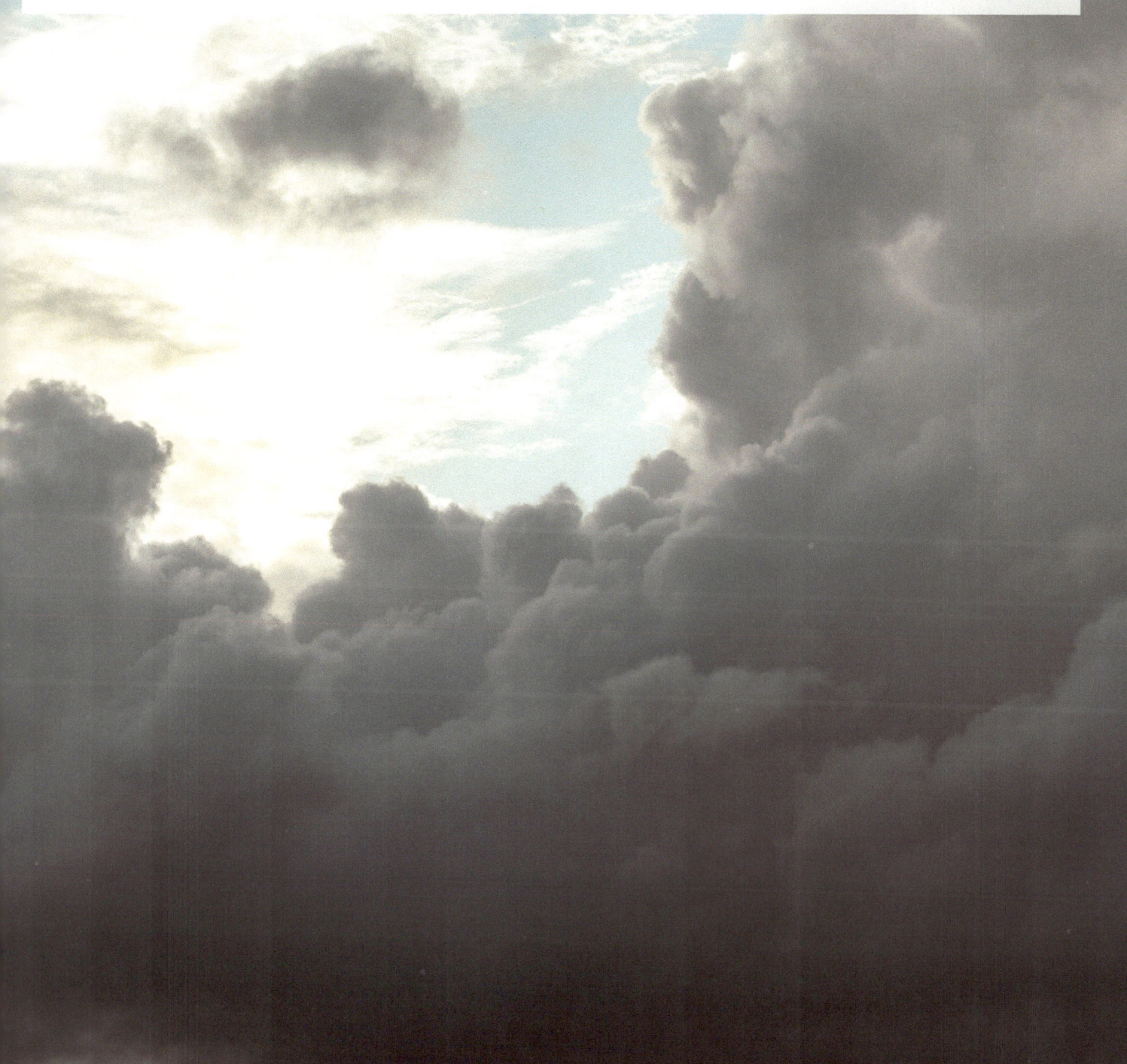

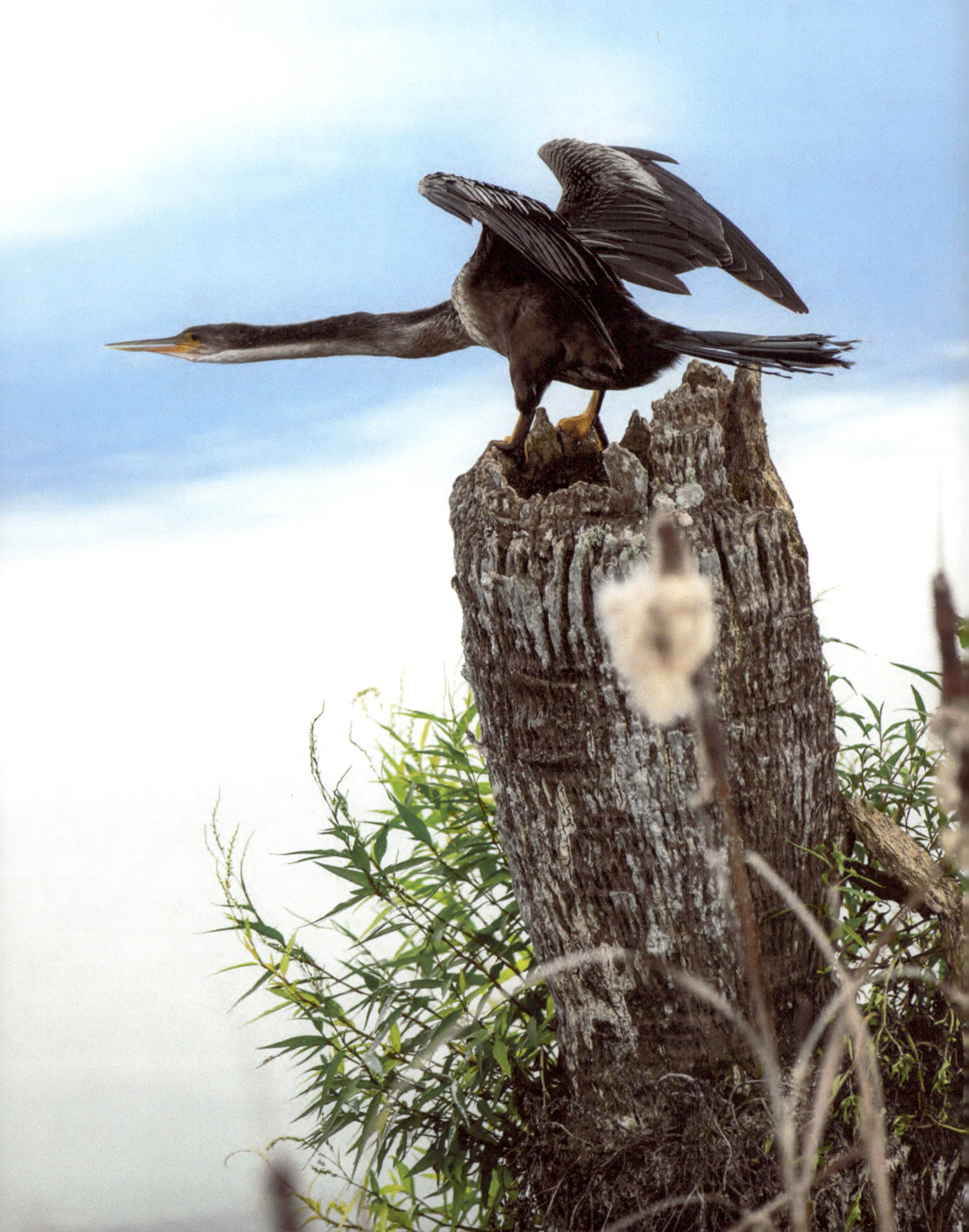